OUT OF TH... MEN'S ROOM?

Gordon Johnston

SOUTH BRUNSWICK AND NEW YORK: A. S. BARNES AND COMPANY
LONDON: THE TANTIVY PRESS

A. S. Barnes and Co., Inc.
Cranbury, New Jersey 08512

Thomas Yoseloff Ltd
Magdalen House
136-148 Tooley Street
London SE1 2TT, England

Library of Congress Cataloging in Publication Data

Johnston, Gordon, 1941-
    Which way out of the men's room?

    Bibliography: p.
    1. Homosexuality, Male—United States. I. Title.
HQ76.2.U5J63   301.41'57   79-63542
ISBN 0-498-02409-1

Printed in the United States of America

For my mother, father and sister,
who remain faithfully with me
in encouragement, and understanding.
For Stanley, at last, who lifted me
from earth into air.

Contents

Preface: Advance Payments for Single-Room Occupancy

> I was at the door with my suitcase. With my hand on the knob, I looked at him. Then I wanted to beg him to forgive me. But this would have been too great a confession; any yielding at that moment would have locked me forever in that room with him. And in a way this was exactly what I wanted. . . . It had not occurred to me until that instant that, in fleeing from his body, I confirmed and perpetuated his body's power over me.[1]
> —James Baldwin, *Giovanni's Room*

Baldwin, the novelist, creates a masculine character conflict between two men who have had sexual experiences with women. They discover they are also capable of emotional and sexual involvement with each other. The narrator denies the possibility of a life which includes his sexual love of another man. The social expectations which define his understanding of manhood urge him to leave his male lover's room.

He pays an emotional price for lying to himself about his capacities. Marriage to a woman, the production of children, the competition with other men in career pursuits, all help define the parameters of the heterosexual's sense of manhood.

The narrator doubts his normality. If he remains in this man's room, he labels himself deviant. Illegal. Immoral. A social pariah. The truth of his life forbids him the convenient label of heterosexual. If he vacillates between the extremes of sexual definitions, such bisexuality speaks more to his activity than to his state of being. He is much more than what he does.

9

His anxiety over definitions is shared by all American men. Social definitions of sexual behavior create boundaries for "masculine" behavior. These boundaries help predict and control those attitudes, images and activities expected from men. Their emotional content is shaped by two ideas: woman is the complement of masculinity; man is a competitor to other men. Despite asceticism, the philosophical and religious concepts of brotherly love, or variations of essential masculine modes—each man's mind, emotions, and actions are shaped to respond to women and men differently.

Within most men, social opinion outweighs personal opinion or belief. We do not ask ourselves, "How should *I* live?" We allow others to tell us. Yet, the artist Ben Shahn describes an artistic phenomenon which often occurs in the process of living. He writes of the art student who lacks strong motives or opinions. The student simply paints copies of others' works of art. During this process, "a kind of self-recognition" takes place. "Gradually his own personality emerges; he develops beliefs and opinions."[2] So men work upon the shape of their lives, formed by the emerging self-concept they practice.

The narrator of *Giovanni's Room* emerges from his relationship with a man, recognizing that he is not what others tell him he should be. He has crossed the sexual boundary of prescribed masculinity. He senses he is alone within himself. He has forfeited his claim to the male space. He has become an alien within the boundary of social masculinity. He must paint his own life as a homosexual, with few positive social patterns to imitate.

His life now becomes patterned by minority behaviors. The heterosexual majority views these behaviors from the perspective of moral and social value. The homosexual concept has negative value to heterosexual males. Homosexuality seems to deny the necessity for women or competition in normal male-to-male exchange. Social values often assume categories which are arranged by hierarchy. Vertical values usually omit the horizontal nature of personal behaviors: *I* behave in continuum; *we* behave in vertical categories.

If I love a man, I have negative value to heterosexual men. I am told by law, by religion, by medicine and tradition that I must pay in advance for the negative space allowed me by the majority of men. Such payments emotionally bankrupt many homosexual males.

Some homosexuals pay with silence and disguise, and thus

diminish the full range of their personality growth. Others pay with social sanction, economic deprivation or alienation from families and friends. All experience a sense of confinement. Homosexual males live within the confines of definitions for manufactured masculinity exalted by the heterosexual American male. In a sense, heterosexual males also suffer the rigidities of such masculine requirements. They compete on the basis of style, deportment, attainment and accomplishment of social roles valued by a patriarchal society. Heterosexuals "win" their masculinity with these emblems of heterosexual success. The absurdity within the heterosexual-homosexual tension resides in the degree to which maleness is championed.

Homosexuals tend to value the male mystique by eroticizing other men. Heterosexuals confirm their love of men through worship of machismo. Male heterosexuals' use of women betrays their implicit preference for men. "The image of women . . . is an image created by men and fashioned to suit their needs."[3] That image is subordinate to the male image. Thus, heterosexual males become adept at using women to confirm masculinity. They become adept in "loving" maleness through intricate subliminal behaviors which do not seemingly threaten the male-female social structure.

The question of why heterosexual American males concern themselves so negatively with homosexuality can be answered simply. Homosexuality contradicts the image of masculinity which is validated by the use of women-made-subordinate. All men—and women—in America are socialized by images of sexual inequity. Such images defined by sexual polarity are offered to all children. Society demands that they then be confirmed within accepted rituals of passage into adulthood.

Multiple sexual definitions subsequently create masculine arenas. Within these spaces, boys and men must traditionally act out their sense of obligation and contingency to masculine norms. The school, gymnasium, office, household or those fraternal organizations dedicated to recreation, philanthropy or war—all contain prescriptions for degrees of masculine behavior. All contain rewards and punishments attached to masculinity, earned or lost. Such arenas all contain atmospheres and requirements which psychologically (or socially) exclude the homosexual.

The homosexual usually functions within these masculine arenas secretly. Or else, homosexuals create a simulation of heterosexual environments. Homosexuals found businesses and hire or serve other homosexuals. Homosexuals form hiking clubs, bowling teams, Bible study groups, social welfare services, or various work and leisure outlets for themselves. Male couples attempt to foster or adopt children; occasionally they raise their own natural children. Homosexuals frequent predominantly "gay" beaches, resorts, bars, churches, steambaths, theaters, restaurants or travel excursions. These separatist alternatives momentarily release the homosexual from his sense of psychological confinement. They parody those fraternal activities and social institutions enjoyed by heterosexual men—and women.

Within the so-called homosexual milieu, the individual male congregates with his own kind. He receives positive reinforcement by realizing he is not alone in his alienation from the heterosexual world. And yet a more subtle form of alienation often occurs within the homosexual milieu. The individual enters it with defense mechanisms practiced in order to pass undetected through the heterosexual world. The homosexual male carries with him an ego concept more fragile than even the heterosexual male. He is hated by heterosexuals. He learns to hate himself. In other homosexuals, the homosexual male views subjects of violent social prejudice and disdain. The homosexual often withholds himself from full acceptance of other homosexuals who are termed inferior, or immoral or psychologically aberrant. To accept is to acknowledge his own unworthiness. To accept is to risk absorbing such hatred as his own. To deny is to confirm his own hatred of himself.

This double jeopardy experienced by the homosexual male is the subject of this book. What happens to the homosexual male living in social arenas which select him to be hated? How does such hatred become internalized and often turned against other homosexuals to defeat the positive potential of the individual and his minority group?

To understand the homosexual male, and help him to understand himself, I choose to examine him in relation to his counterpart—the heterosexual American male. Because of the current nature of dominant masculine politics in America, I limit my focus to the white, middle class male. The relationship of the homosexual male to other homosexual males is first defined by the heterosexual male. My limited references to women and racial minority groups serve to clarify the tension between heterosexual and homosexual males. I do not mean to imply any lack of importance of heterosexual women, lesbians or non-white male homosexuals. Indeed„I hope that my perspective will underscore the complexities of their relationships to white heterosexual males.

The interplay of male and female is made more complex through race; and competition, self-concept and aging also render American society as sexually ambiguous. Men are particularly anxious because of ambiguity. They seek to reduce their anxiety by clarifying any ambiguity. The chief mode of reducing anxiety used by American men is to view everything outside of themselves with a penile attitude. The homosexual male also shares this perspective. How and when the heterosexual male uses his penis defines and clarifies most of the behavioral taboo in morality, law and social tradition. Such institutionalized thought and practice, in turn, then ratify male behaviors.

When the homosexual extends his penile responses into his environment, he commits trespass upon the social definitions of masculinity. The homosexual male is an anomaly. He is an ambiguity to the established order of American sexuality. His penis object is men rather than women. Thus, the heterosexual male becomes anxious.

Relief for heterosexual anxiety is achieved by establishing social and psychological distance from what these men fear. What is feared is often hated. Prejudice creates various structures of fear and hatred to militate against the selected subjects for attack. White heterosexual males fear women, black males and homosexuals. Each represents a sexual power imagined to be potentially stronger than the white male's. Each "opponent" must then be coercively persuaded to accept a psychosocial position inferior to that of the white heterosexual male.

Once the majority assignment of negative value is accepted, a minority psychology occurs. Majority fears become attached to expectations, which are conveyed as assignments of behavior. Minority members internalize these prescriptive "monologues" and then act them out—consciously and unconsciously—thus confirming their minority status and ethos. Each minority group member responds by degree to those fictions imposed by white heterosexual males. Minority members inadvertently help majority white males to maintain their own social fictions about themselves.

Contemporary women and racial minority groups now realize the fictions which were given them. They know why they were given and recognize certain attitudes and behaviors offered as training for subordination. Yet, habits are difficult to break. Attitudes are difficult to reconstruct. Women and racial minority members have won some personal and civil concessions from the dominant white heterosexual males. Homosexual males have gained little by comparison. Homosexuals still tend to perpetuate negative fictions created for them by heterosexual male monologues.

This book provides moments for re-evaluation of the fictitious social and psychological spaces reserved for homosexual males' concepts of masculinity. Within these narrow and narrowing spaces, the homosexual male must define himself and his life. He often lives in socially ascribed "rooms" as a person less than he could be, less than he should be. Others convince him of his own fictions. The homosexual then becomes an imitation of the heterosexual male's own frightened self-distortions.

This book offers a series of comparative "monologues" and "dialogues." The monologues are designed to isolate and examine certain heterosexual fictions imposed on homosexuals. The dialogues attempt to create a structure of exchange for these ideas and opinions. Hopefully, they will engage the homosexual male in a rephrasing of fiction to create internal and external realities.

Rephrasing does not encourage a belief in word-magic. The wished for does not necessarily become actual. Yet, a changing state of mind converts into statements of renewed conduct. Homosexuals have listened to the monologues of heterosexuality much too long. Such monologues speak of a monopoly of behavior, attitudes, values and rewards which exclude the homosexual. Dialogue implies the freedom of exchange . . . the validity of the self.

The following comparison of monologues and dialogues is offered to redefine options for the homosexual to achieve his creative potential for a positive life. Strategies for actualization of the whole person will lead the homosexual towards an emergence from men's rooms. To remain in the confinement of any masculine space argues the homosexual towards confusing human freedom with personal patience. Self-actualization can even be thwarted by the strategy of civic appeal. Patient appeals by homosexuals to be allowed access to their full humanity have gained little redress. We are human now, not tomorrow.

To be a homosexual male in America is to be contained within monologues of ascription and description. The content of these monologues contain imagery of the ideal. The structure of these images supports every institution within American society. Challenge to these monologues, failure to act out these monologues—alters the essence of male space. Such space then becomes ambiguous to both heterosexual and homosexual males. Fear of forfeiting their claim to male space is shared by all men in America. Maleness is only one's place of birth; symbols of masculinity psychologically enlarge the territories of men. Our social imagination demands that such symbolic ideals become real. The motive is political.

Thus, male space is both symbolic and real. It is internal, as well as social. Social space is defined by boundaries of behavior. Suspected trespass across sanctioning boundaries then argues for aggression and defense. The "enemy" must be contained or defeated. This describes the current border war mentality of heterosexual with homosexual males.

Social reality presently indicates that the homosexual male lives in a state of real and symbolic siege. He also affects an uneasy and false truce with the heterosexual majority. Yet, the homosexual need not live in defeat.

The homosexual male can choose his own space and contradict those narrowing monologues dictated by the heterosexual. Rephrasing those myths of masculinity begins with a reassessment of one's inner self in relation to the social environment. The following dialogues select aspects of the homosexual's external world, and rephrase them to suggest positive reconstruction of social and psychological components. Hopefully, such rephrasing will suggest enlargement of the homosexual male's potential life space.

Each homosexual male in America must face the meaning of himself. He must learn why the difference of his sexuality troubles others more than himself. He must also recognize that when the heterosexual male flees from the meaning of the homosexual's body, such flight confirms the power the homosexual has over his "straight" counterpart. Any man could paraphrase the concern of Baldwin's narrator in *Giovanni's Room:*

> I look at my sex, my troubling sex, and wonder how it can be redeemed, how can I save it from the knife. . . . Yet, the key to my salvation, which cannot save my body, is hidden in my flesh.[4]

The territories of masculinity are men's rooms used as arenas of success, of defeat for homosexuals. They exist primarily in the mind and heart. To such areas are addressed the following reconstructions. How did we get in? What happens to us there? How may we get out?

Acknowledgments

Grateful acknowledgment is made to the following publishers for permission to quote throughout this book:

The Adjusted American by Gail J. Putney and Snell Putney (Harper & Row, Publishers Harper Colophon Books). Copyright © 1964 by G. J. Putney and Snell Putney. Reprinted by permission of Harper & Row, Publishers, Inc.

The American Male by Myron Brenton. Copyright © 1975 by Fawcett Publications, Inc. Reprinted by permission of Coward, McCann & Geoghegan, Inc.

The Best Little Boy in the World by John Reid. Copyright © 1973, 1976 by John Reid. Reprinted by permission of the publisher, Ballantine Books, a Division of Random House, Inc., and The Sterling Lord Agency, Inc., New York.

The Boys in the Band by Mart Crowley. Copyright © 1968, 1969 by Dell Publishing Company. Reprinted by permission of Farrar, Straus & Giroux.

"The Boys on the Bandwagon" by Gene D. Phillips. From *Sexuality in the Movies,* edited by Thomas R. Atkins. Copyright © 1975 by Indiana University Press. Reprinted by permission of *Take One,* Montreal.

"Dispatch," *The Advocate,* December, 1977. Reprinted by permission of *The Advocate,* Los Angeles.

Familiar Faces, Hidden Lives by Howard Brown. Copyright © 1976 by Harcourt Brace Jovanovich. Reprinted by permission of the publisher.

"The Heterosexual Solution: A Dilemma for Gay Mormons," author Anonymous. Reprinted by permission of *The Advocate,* February, 1978, Los Angeles.

The Homosexual Matrix by C. A. Tripp. Copyright © 1975 by

Which Way Out
of the Men's Room?

PART I/The World as Vagina

1/Homo Erectus Awakens to Vaginal Consciousness

... In the United States we use space as a way of classifying people and activities. ...[1]
—Edward T. Hall,
The Hidden Dimension

The men's room mentality views the world as the natural setting for man's erotic domination. The masculine concern is to extend man into the social divisions of space, identify with such divisions of territory and then occupy them to his unique advantage. Territories are assigned in a hierarchy of values. Each value is attached to current agreement of what is masculine. Masculinity factors are derived from any definition or expression which supports the social mythologies of male sexual superiority.

In early societies, men attempted to explain their sense of male place within the universe. The earth represented the female principle and the maternal force. The sun defined the male principle and patriarchal power. Cosmically, woman was thought to be beneath man. The position for most sexual intercourse within world art and myth represented the domination of earth-woman by solar-man. Such domination assured the male position as psychologically and socially superior to women. It implied a sexual-political competition based on role division. Men penetrated their environment as they did their women.

In their competitive dealings with other men, the same sexual ethic was held. Penetrate, render impotent and feminize others into submission. This ethic permeated war, commerce and the erection of empire. Eunuchism, vassalage and servitude all spoke of sexual domination by reducing male opposition to the status of

23

women. For men seeking to find a logical position in the cosmic order, everything external to themselves was converted to a vaginal position. Historical man thus used his penis to define himself.

Geza Roheim writes of a primitive initiation myth in *The Gates of the Dream*. It is one of many cross-cultural views of the earth as vagina—or, women as threats to masculinity:

> . . . At Kuna-tari (with the vagina) an old man sat with erected penis. A woman had been urinating there, and the urine made a hole in the sand. . . . The penis went into the hole; it got bigger and bigger, and it coiled around. Then he pulled it out again. . . .[2]

The remainder of the myth includes the ascription of demonhood to women and Roheim's interpretation of the myth as a charm to alleviate man's castration anxiety. Although this demon woman chops the old man's penis with a tomahawk, pieces of it convert into stone monuments. The man preserves himself. Moreover, by smelling his penis, the man evidences a narcissism with his bodily part. He confirms himself.

Samples from more contemporary literature reveal an updating of this idea of earth as woman—beneath the dominion of man. John Steinbeck writes of the tractor driver sent to plow together the small, separate farms of evicted landholders. The corporation's impact on the land is sexual:

> Behind the tractor rolled the shining disks, cutting the earth with blades—not plowing but surgery. . . . Behind the harrows, the long seeders—twelve curved iron penes erected in the foundary, orgasms set by gears, raping methodically, raping without passion.[3]

Steinbeck notes that man's sexual power is detached, mechanical, yet germinal. Dominant men have removed weaker men from a land area. The source of the dispossessed men's identity, stimulation and security has been taken. Their masculinity has been trespassed upon. They are forced to watch the rape of their vaginal possession. Their manhood is thus diminished by their own helpless conversion into vaginal subordinates.

Another contemporary rendition of males more directly raping males, and reducing them to the status of women, occurs in James Dickey's *Deliverance*. Four urban Southerners plan a canoe trip into "virgin" territory. Two of them are separated from their companions and are captured by mountain men. One mountain man anally rapes the urban vacationer as an act of domination and punishment for trespass. The other urbanite is rescued by his friends before he is forced to commit fellation on the second mountain man. The rapist is killed with an arrow. The other attacker escapes. The story's narrator is later forced to climb a cliff from the river bed to kill the remaining mountain man and save his friends. At the height of his climbing ordeal, he eroticizes the earth:

> Then I would begin to try to inch upward again, moving with the most intimate motions of my body, motions I had never dared use with Martha, or with any other human woman. Fear and a kind of enormous moon-blazing sexuality lifted me, millimeter by millimeter.
> . . . I was crawling, but it was no longer necessary to make love to the cliff, to fuck it for an extra inch or two in the moonlight. . . . [4]

The narrator achieves his objective of revenge by symbolically raping his quarry with an arrow. He withdraws with his friends from the wilderness ordeal still erect. His masculinity is confirmed.

Both the historical and the more contemporary male myths view the wandering hero as phallic hero. Norman O. Brown writes of these male figures as being "in a permanent state of erection. . . . "[5] They wander in space which serves as their receptacle—or earth mother. For the heterosexual male, all space in which he lives or thinks, serves as an envelope for his sexual identity. Sexual identity is primordial identity. From that aspect, all other things are defined as relative to his penile orientation. His virility—or degree of sexual energy—is confirmed by his owner-ship and manipulation of things in space. His subsequent control of others is given impetus by his dreams of self-enlargement.

The heterosexual male's life is an effort to achieve and maintain a posture of tumescence. The self is conceived as a penis in varying states of erection. The "other" is always designated as space in which to enter, explore, enjoy or subdue according to each man's personal passion or will to power. Tradition teaches that the paradigm for masculine space is the earth-vagina. From this proceeds the heterosexual male's construction of vaginal attitudes towards everything and everyone separate from himself.

The vaginal attitude views the world as territory in which to exercise masculine prerogatives. Male rights dominate thought, feeling and social constructions. Domination implies politics. Sexuality is visualized symbolically within myth, to shape each man's psychology. Myths enter social tradition through ritualized behavior. Divisions between dominance and submission are conveniently marked by sexual stereotype. Sexual myths serve the male in his role as competitor with everyone beyond himself. Myth and tradition thus view women as secondary, evil or of little value. Men convince women to internalize this stereotype through psychological and physical force.

With the early growth of private property, each man became competitor to all other men. Economics created degrees of wealth. Wealth equated with power. Less capable men became the slaves of more economically capable men. Power through economic manipulation of world space became attached to sexual vigor. The male vaginal attitude viewed everyone and everything as potential territory for occupation. Each man erected himself within his chosen territory. The burden on each man was to maintain his erect stance, while avoiding any possible detumescence in self-concept.

As physical detumescence follows completion of sexual intercourse with a woman, it follows that a man would associate his dwindling erection with a feeling of psychological weakness or loss. He feels anger that a woman's sexual vigor is not dependent on maintenance of an erection. He feels threatened by her limitless ability to perform sexually.[6] He projects his weakness onto her and then calls it passivity. He fears contamination by those very personal qualities he projects onto her. From this, the man turns to the competitive comfort of male company. Each man knows the other has a predictable limitation of vigor. The challenge of male competition is to reduce the other man to a flaccid state. This weakness or sense of loss is then associated with the feminine stereotype of inferiority, i.e., it is called unmanly. The weaker man thus becomes vaginal to the more vigorous man. The "vaginated" man occurs in politics, economics, athletics, or any space in which men interact.

The historical traditions and imaginations of men allow them vehicles of social approval for their male capacities. The vehicles of family, business, religion, the armed forces and other institutionalized male endeavors, all contain elements of masculine mythology. Personal power and skill give *shape* to this masculine mythology. Achievement by control forms the mythical *content*. Competition supplies the *psychic energy* within the shape and content of any masculine space.

Male rights historically dominate thought, feeling and social constructions. Myths within religion and law, as well as social custom, ratify the male's sense of property rights. Theories within biological comparative studies also reinforce power claims of heterosexual males. Such quasi-scientific myths maintain women and children as property. Men whose power has diminished become the psychological, economic or political slave class. Slavery implies impotence; it argues for reduction of males to the subordinate status of women.

In ancient times, the law codes of Sumerian and Assyrian cultures schematized the rights of men and the limitations of women. These codes pre-dated our current laws and social attitudes which view citizenship concomitantly with sexuality. Early Hebrews equated sex with nationalism. To fulfill their destiny as uniquely separate from their ungodly neighbors, they declared women as property. The vagina was viewed as a territorial claim through divine right. Hebrews constructed a series of social and psychological barriers concerning sexual conduct. Hebrew men defended their territory from trespass, regulated internal male agreements relating to sexual conduct, and confined the suspected sexual wantonness of women. Hebrew concepts of vaginal control also hold currency in contemporary religious attitudes in America, and help shape our nationalistic world-view.

The early Greek culture did not share the extreme Hebrew patriarchy as justification for male sexual power. The Greeks viewed women as wife-mother-housekeeper. However, Greek legends and literature also reflected a strong misogynous content. Such writings lionized male rights and achievements. Renowned philosophers of that period continue to penetrate our contemporary society's ethics and traditions with their phallic tone and content. Plato's ideal love object was a male, rather than a female. Aristotle's conceptions permeate contemporary thought concerning our sexual nature:

A belief in female inferiority entered into his physiology and biology, as well as his political, ethical and aesthetic theories. Quite simply to Aristotle women were intellectually and morally inferior to men.[7]

The Romans' laws, literature and social stereotypes were clearly defined by men to create a hierarchy of use and value attached to vaginal attitudes:

> Romantic love was considered degrading since it brought men into the irresistible power of women—something to be avoided at all costs. . . . The Romans were too much male-centered to allow themselves to fall under the sway of any woman. . . .[8]

The chronic message entering our own society from history is male hostility towards women. The other message is that men value each other more highly than woman. They institutionalize male ideals and venerate them.

Christianity incorporated many of the earlier sexual beliefs of Israel, Rome and Greece. Christianity was (and is) a male institution which competed with neighboring cults and philosophies for supremacy of thought and practice. Christianity was a male-centered, sex-negative religion which placed women in the role of sexual property to be controlled, protected, and husbanded by males. Its moral systems provided the already familiar barriers to property—trespass or loss. Morality became internalized politics—for male convenience.

While the most complete references to sexual codes within the Hebrew, Roman and Greek cultures concern heterosexual conduct, references to homosexuality also occur for several purposes. These were to clarify ambiguities within the heterosexual male's self-definition, or to clarify ambivalent sexual attitudes and practice.

Tolerance or intolerance by male power groups of sexual or emotional involvement of same sex partners, shifts with time to suit heterosexual males' needs. Homosexuality thus becomes affected by those necessary social interpretations of masculinity which are always related to the contemporary imagined—or real—status of women. Heterosexual attitudes towards homosexuality also fluctuate according to the complexities of the heterosexual male's sense of security or insecurity over his control of space. Confirmations of control over space are viewed through the conversion of "other" into vagina. Homosexuality also serves these heterosexual conversions.

The vaginal attitudes of heterosexual males require that they achieve necessary psychological distance from women. This is often fulfilled through a strong idealization of masculinity. Homosexuality could then be periodically tolerated or elevated as a psycho-emotional relief from a prevalent fear or loathing of women.

Role differentiation—and thus necessary psychic distance—

between heterosexual men and women sometimes blurs despite legal, religious or social tradition. Homosexuality could then ideologically replace or serve to deny women. This does not mean that heterosexual males practice homosexual activity as a sexual substitute for heterosexual modes. Incipient homosexuality can provide enough relief through various forms of male-to-male contact so as not to upset the heterosexual vaginal viewpoint. Exaggeration of the masculine principle through degrees of homosexuality, paradoxically bolsters and reclarifies those necessary male-female differences.

However, when vaginal attitudes of males are clearly intact, then homosexuality could conversely threaten the imaginary relation of male to female by altering the arena of male competition. On the one hand, women challenge the masculine definition. Recourse to other men offers each male psychological—even physical reaffirmation. On the other hand, homosexual males viewed as equals also challenge the vaginal perspective of heterosexuals.

If the heterosexual male's real relationship with women approximates his vaginal conception of women, then homosexuality is not needed to achieve distance from women. Homosexuals then become secondary, subordinate—vaginal. The vaginal still threatens the heterosexual male. As usual, the vaginal must then be isolated or controlled.

Homosexuality accompanies heterosexuality in almost all societies—both historical and contemporary. It often had socially legitimate purposes beyond being a mere perversion, an aberration of social averages, or a psychopathology. Homosexuality either ratified or denied the heterosexual male's vaginal concept within the masculine description. Inevitably, homosexuality paralleled each unique social prescription for the status of women.

Westermarck's study of anthropology is summarized by sexologist Donald Webster Cory who notices "he returns again and again to the thought that indulgence in pederasty 'goes hand in hand with great isolation of the women. . . .' "[9]

> It probably occurs, at least sporadically, among every race of mankind. And among some peoples it has assumed such proportions as to form a true national habit.[10]

In world survey, Westermarck notes that homosexuality

existed in American Indian tribes, and diverse areas such as Sumatra, Malay, New Guinea, the Marshall Islands, Tahiti and Hawaii, and Australia. In Madagascar, the urban areas of Africa, the peasantry of Egypt and in Morocco, homosexual love spread to varying degrees. Asia Minor and Mesopotamia contained the practice. Among the Persians, Sikhs, Afghans, the Mohammedans of India and the Chinese, homosexuality was especially frequent. In Japan, homosexuality claimed introduction concomitant with the rise of Buddhism. It was wide-spread among Greek city-states and rose to prominence in Rome and among the Celts and Scandinavians. In modern Europe, "No country and no class of society is free from it."[11]

Such widespread homosexual activity was not exclusively male-to-male. Women practiced the same throughout the territories mentioned. Anthropological studies and psychological speculations have examined cross-cultural sexual practices to determine reasons or origins for homosexual behavior. Freud, Krafft-Ebing and Ellis have suggested reasons which range from congenital inversion to overly close and frequent association with same sex members. Hormonal deficiencies or the existence of a national psychosis have been offered as precipitating factors by analysts of homosexuality. Enforced celibacy or the low esteem of women are also cited.

Selection of such origins or motives for male homosexuality does not account for the existence of lesbianism, nor for the often high social standing of women in a society which has high incidence of homosexuality. To date, there is no conclusive evidence that homosexual behavior is necessarily socially acquired, genetically transmitted or exists as a combination of both. There also exists no firm evidence that homosexuality is not a *normal minority behavior on a continuum of sexual capacity*. Its "normality" appears to hinge on the directional swing of heterosexual security in aspects of current masculine identity factors.

Concern over homosexual practices historically has taken various forms. Disregard, assimilation into generalized sexual practices, outright public censure or punishment have served heterosexual definition, control or dismissal of homosexual phenomena. Again, such treatment occurs relative to heterosexual male attitudes towards women, and the competitive intensity between males.

At various periods in many societies' historical development, homosexuality has been accorded varying degrees of negative status and censure. When men behaved like women, many societies hated that behavior in men and punished it. In some cultures, homosexuality was associated with shamanism or spiritual power. It enjoyed a degree of status and respect. In other cultures, it was associated with witchcraft and was worthy of death.

The Greek and Roman cultures viewed pederasty as a form of youth worship. A refinement of the heroic ideal of masculinity was elevated in social consciousness through the form of young boys. They embodied artistic perfection and the tragic transitory nature of perfection in human pursuits. Such intellectual and emotional focus on perfected masculinity lionized the male attributes for each man. Such pederasty deteriorated in time to later include a bastardization of ideals in both Greece and Rome. Idealization of the erotic in masculinity shifted to focus on mere sexuality. Boys were often lured into prostitution. Pederasty lost its romance of masculinity and fell out of national favor.

When Greece introduced homosexuality into Persia, the Zoroastrian religious books strongly prohibited the practice. Judaism and Christianity subsequently attached moral sinfulness and ultimate damnation for its practice. The roots of such negative attitudes appear to be founded in the religious problems of idolatry, unbelief and potential heresy. "Zoroastrianism stigmatized unnatural intercourse as a practice of infidels, as a sign of unbelief."[12] The Hebrews also competed with foreign cults and required strict separation from religious and sexual practices which might link them to Canaanite groups. Kedeshim were male prostitutes dedicated to various deities other than Jehovah. The Kedeshim were known as sodomites. Old Testament appeals for death to sodomites were not necessarily prompted by the curious sexual practices of Kedeshim, but rather because their sexual practices lauded false gods. The religious competition among men assumed sexual overtones.

The Hebrew connection of homosexuality with the practice of false religions affected Mohammedanism and later Christianity. St. Paul assailed those who turned the truth of God into lies and worshiped and served the creature more than the creator, thus viewing idolatry in sexual terms. Paul's problem with sex appears prejudicial in tone, and separatist in intent. Sexual restrictions were designed to avoid foreign idolatry; same sex intercourse implied self idolatry. Sex became integral to religious fidelity.

Subsequently, "Heretics were accused of unnatural vice as a matter of course."[13]

The above religions mentioned are, of course, conceived and perpetuated by males. The strong misogynist restrictions in all major religions argues that religion attaches moral principles to male power ethics. It seems likely, then, that homosexuality is condoned, tolerated or condemned on the basis of how it either reinforces or threatens masculinity and the male construction of a vaginal world.

Cross-cultural comparisons of homosexuality do little to solve the puzzle of the origin of homosexuality, either in time or location. They do little to answer why homosexuality is widespread in certain cultures and extinct in others. Cultural comparisons do serve to give an intellectual and emotional framework for a contemporary homosexual living in our culturally and sexually ambiguous American society.

Current American males' attitudes towards homosexuality have specific historical, religious, legal and philosophical connections with the past. As Westermarck comments:

> . . . In a society where the large majority of people are endowed with normal sexual desires their aversion to homosexuality easily develops into moral censure and finds lasting expression in custom, law, or religious tenets.[14]

Hopefully, Westermarck's use of the word "normal" implies reference to majority behavior.

Implications of male "norms" are part of the focus in C. A. Tripp's *The Homosexual Matrix*. He speaks of male bonding as potentially threatening to male camaraderie through the specifics of their sex. Barriers are constructed which regulate or prevent male-to-male contact from erupting into those overt homosexual forms which conflict with other male norms:

> Beyond all "distancing" arrangements, there is much evidence to suggest that a society's concept of maleness and the values it attaches to it are what most control the amount of homosexuality. It is not quite possible to say that the degree of male emphasis or the height of male ideals are what count; in one version or another male values are upheld in every society. . . . Where male aspirations are cast in a non-competitive mold, homosexuality tends to be low, but where perhaps the very same aspirations are rated individually with a consequent emphasis on such concepts as the winner and the hero, the homosexual potential is readily activated.[15]

If homosexuality is aroused or inspired within a context of male competition, it seems uniquely attached to the heterosexual male's image.

Our law codes, religious writings and social custom come to us from different periods of time, through differing interpretations and from varying locations and degrees of male "space." Written records passing through these time-space factors can coincide with contemporary American needs and attitudes of maleness. Values currently acted out, may either contradict or reinforce earlier historical male values. The implications of "competition," "winner" and "hero" from Tripp's comments, seem directly to bear on masculinity as now defined or earned in America. Apparently the homosexual potential is needed for such exaggerated masculine concepts and forms. The contemporary American hero is obsessed with winning in many arenas of endeavor. He can also lose.

With the rise of the feminist movement and the demands of racial minorities, stock definitions of the white heterosexual male are now besieged. He is anxious to achieve psychic distance from these basically sexual threats. The homosexual potential now serves its part to redefine heterosexual masculinity. At the same time it adds ambiguity to any definitions. The heterosexual male remains wary on all fronts.

Those arenas designated as men's space contain the necessary apparatus associated with skill, power or status. Apparatus can be physical or symbolic, and thus the men's rooms can be real or imaginary. Male space exists wherever masculinity claims a need for dominion or extension. Such masculine activity is erotic in origin and vaginal in attitude. Historically, the male space has been the geographical division of kingdoms, hunting and grazing preserves or domination of oceanic regions. Temples, throne rooms, initiation huts, weaponry, rituals and ceremonies existed primarily for the use of men. As the man's world is supported upon the shoulders of Atlas, so is every man's home his castle—a claim for masculine sovereignty.

The contemporary American masculine space has dwindled on the individual level—emotionally, imaginatively and physically. The backyard patio or one's office desk with three drawer filing cabinet, too often describes the American male's work and leisure space.

The American male's imaginative self-definition, once achieved through confrontation with a physical or psychic frontier, is now simulated by other-given definitions, such as television. As spectator, the American male vicariously and anonymously claims entrance to location and power. He retains his security, is somewhat stimulated and avoids challenge to his sense of identity through the absence of risk.

In 1972, it was estimated in *The New York Times* that sixty-five million people watched the annual Super Bowl. Warren Farrell wrote about the televised event, beginning with a pregame display of regimented power by the U. S. Air Force in Phantom jet maneuvers:

> *No deviance is tolerated* in this display. . . . Football, like war, is a scientific and brutal game; even the vocabulary of football is similar to that of war. . . . (When the vocabulary is not interchangeable with that of war, it is with that of sex: "getting into the hole," "thrusting," and the announcer's admiration for each man successful at "deep penetration."[16] [emphasis in original]

One message given to men, is that deviation from execution of male power patterns is not allowed. The structure of such games, viewed as male territory, also assume a vaginal structure—given sexual terminology for strategies of success. Such vaginal structures confirm aspects of masculinity necessary for contemporary heroics. Players achieve psychological domination of the opponents viewed as inferior . . . or women. Male spectators identify by the millions.

As the contemporary American masculine space diminishes both physically and experientially, its personal character also alters. Space becomes incorporated into each man's efforts and identities by cooperation with other men.

David Riesman describes the contemporary middle class man in *The Lonely Crowd,* as being "other-directed." The bureaucrat and the salaried business employee develop needs to be popular and to receive approval and direction from others. Males who welcome routine in daily living also tend to remain alert to qualitative potentials within their emotional associations. The stimulation and identity gathered from accomplishments of national and international corporate business ventures, give such men vicarious gratification. Profit and success increase their sense of security. The highs and lows of Dow Jones averages measure the extent of the phallic state. Yet, such mass ventures often produce feelings of anonymity and short-lived stimulation for men, which then dissipate into boredom. According to Riesman:

Sex, therefore, provides a kind of defense against the threat of total apathy. This is one of the reasons why so much excitement is channeled into sex by the other-directed person. He looks to it for reassurance that he is alive.[17]

In contrast to Riesman's "cooperative" man, Robert Ardrey sees man's *aggression* as sex-related.

In *The Territorial Imperative,* Ardrey notes that our identity, security and stimulation achieve their behavioral outlets through war, love and territory.[18] These phenomena offer the individual man the most intense opportunities to confirm his masculinity.

In war, the individual can achieve glory and attainment— leaving behind the boredom of peaceful routine. Ideological quarrels convert into border disputes. The test of nationalism in war then turns the attention of citizens from prejudicial concerns with their neighbors, to prejudice against their enemy. The enemy other is one who does not share the territory, but rather threatens it. Security is disrupted. The disruption is nevertheless stimulating, because a man may achieve heroism and confirmation of masculine virtues in this arena. Identity is clearly confirmed. War, as paradigmatic for the homosexual-heterosexual tension of enemy-other, is obvious.

As in war, love also offers a man his unique sense of identity— achieved through the one he selects to love. Love contains opportunity to stimulate the emotions, imagination and body. The security of love can be threatened by intruders, or by failing to maintain the interest (loyalty) of one or both partners:

> As the history of war is in large part the story of peoples who will risk all for the release from boredom, so the history of adultery is in large part the story of individuals who will risk everything of apparent worth for a brief exploration of distant coasts. . . .[19]

Ardrey notices that contemporary American society offers little opportunity for satisfaction of our needs for stimulation and thus an attendant confirmation of identity. Men tend to compete in order to achieve such stimulation. For men, this competition achieves the necessary confirmation of their masculine social rank. Ardrey states that when "ingenious man turns to . . . sexual experiments. He is achieving identity otherwise denied him. . . ."[20] That the identity in question is basically masculine, i.e., sexual, indicates the traditional tendency for men to see themselves as phallic identities. Since everything beyond the penile self is imagined as vaginal other, men's social environments contain imaginary and real phallic threat factors. Tumescence can be lost.

Phallic threat factors include people, events, processes or internal states of mind which carry potentials to weaken or nullify the will to masculinity. Masculinity is an artificial and arbitrary system of behaviors which varies from culture to culture. Aggressiveness may serve masculinity in one society, while passivity serves masculinity in another. Masculinity definitions may be altered by time or circumstance, but only so far as they do not damage male space concepts necessary for security.

Ameliorating (and deceiving) changes in American legislation currently provide benefits to various secondary classes—women, racial minorities, the very young and the elderly. They are given semblances of equality to majority males, by male concessions. Yet, American definitions of masculinity continue, at present, to insure the preservation of male power for and by males. Such preservation is founded on male sexual components transmitted into social institution. Threat factors to majority defined masculinity, which appear to encroach into masculine space, are warded off with emotional and physical barriers erected by men. Encroachment requires resistance, denial and punishment by the male power majority. Civil rights for all may be legislated. Token gestures in employment parity may be judicially mandated. Yet, male concessions seem to fulfill only the letter of the law.

The spirit of the law rests on the acceptable emotional homeostasis of majority masculinity. Such spirit assumes interesting and diverse attempts to acknowledge and alter majority male power ethics. Men enter private or group therapy; they join male consciousness-raising seminars; they seek out religious or philosophical renewal; they pursue emotional outlets through sports, pack trips and experimentation with various philanthropic outlets. Such meek machoism replaces the babbitry and good-guy jingoism of the past. The meek macho still guards against the suspected feminine components within him. The male majority never concedes more in image and practice than is comfortable to its continued enjoyment of male privileges.

To prevent assaults on masculinity from without, prejudice is employed as a complex psychological barrier to redefine and regulate the male majority's social environment. Gordon Allport writes of the relationship between sex, aggression and prejudice in his comprehensive study, *The Nature of Prejudice*. Because

young men carry an inner impact from early and strong identification with their mothers (women), they must reject internalized
femininity because they also learn misogynous traits from fathers
and other males.[21]

Boys' reaction against women then seems likely to turn them
towards men. "Therefore, it would seem that men would be
considerably more likely to act out homosexuality than women."[22]
That they don't more often than they do is dependent on complex
factors in image conversion. Male images are enlarged internally
to overwhelm inner female images. Those emotional attachments
to images of masculinity become internally integrated; female
images with their emotional attachments become disintegrated.

However, social sanctions prevent heterosexual males from
externalizing emotional attachment to masculine images in other
males. Desire or need for such emotional attachments are
ritualized for their control. Various types of male to male contact
are permitted to relieve the sexual isolation of males from other
males, and to compensate for intrinsic hatred for women. At best,
*the white heterosexual male is fraught with anxiety due to
emotional attachments to images, which form the core of prejudice.*

It is difficult to distinguish masculinity traits which are a male's
own from those imposed or expected by valued others. It seems
reasonable to assume there exists combinations of masculinity
and pseudo-masculinity within each man. *Pseudo-masculinity* is a
combination of *idealized* traits, behaviors and symbols which are
given to males as admission requirements into any immediate
male in-group.

Mannerisms, skills, leisure pursuits or ownership of things
valued by one's in-group, encompass the male with an aura of
specialized masculinity which peers define and reinforce.
Coupled with general aspects of masculine expectations for the
general male population, such pseudo-masculine postures
enhance motives for aggression against one's out-group. Such
aggression solidifies in-group membership by confirming shared
pseudo-masculine values. Prejudice provides expression for the
dynamic quality of making masculine images one's own.

Both heterosexual and homosexual images of masculine sexual
behavior contain variations which are interesting and exotic.
Sexual taboos often serve as stimulants to a man's curiosity. The
illicit is fascinating. Allport relates sex and prejudice to the
attractiveness of the forbidden. Allport argues that the technique

of psychological projection stimulates prejudice. "What is an inner temptation is perceived as an outer threat."[23] Psychological barriers to protect definitions of masculine space are then erected:

> Suppose he [the white male] is anxious concerning his own sexual adequacy and attractiveness. One study of adult prisoners discovered a close relationship between this condition and high prejudice. Men who were antagonistic toward minority groups, on the whole, showed more fierce protest against their own sexual passivity, semi-impotence, or homosexual trends. The protest took the form of exaggerated toughness and hostility. These individuals committed more crimes of a sexual nature than did those who were sexually more secure. And the pseudo masculinity of the former group made them more hostile toward minorities.[24]

Psychological projection of fears or forbidden desires forms one masculine defense mechanism. Social reward for personal masculine expressions and activities forms another. Inner erosion of male virtues is prevented through presentation of approval by the male (often the female) majority group. Such approvals could be oral or symbolic: cheers, commendations, awards, promotions or other forms of acceptance comprise insignia of approval.

Additional defense mechanisms based on prejudice can also provide punishment for deviation from masculinity. Punishment maximizes predictable majority behavior. It minimizes deviation from recognized and approved norms. Sex grouping thus offers the strongest and most primary identification for a man's membership in an in-group:

> For some people—misogynists among them—the sex grouping remains important throughout their lives. Women are viewed as a wholly different species from men, usually an inferior species. . . . With half of mankind (his own sex) the male may feel an in-group solidarity, with the other half, an irreconcilable conflict.[25]

Such prejudice of men in favor of their in-group interests allows them varying degrees and kinds of selective prejudice against some or all out-groups. Prejudice can define a men's group enemy; women, racial minorities, political or religious categories or homosexuals become the imaginary foes of white heterosexual males. From definition of the opposition, prejudice provides cohesion within a men's group. It activates participation and attitudes of loyalty to one's own. Prejudice can then reduce the individual male member's alienation, relieve his self doubt and assuage anxiety concerning his claim to masculinity. Such prejudicial exaggerations are justified by the heterosexual male's concept of sex. The enemy is vaginal.

Ratification of a man's masculinity requires prejudice as an internal stimulation. The imaginary existence of phallic threat factors also demands more concrete external ratifications of phallic supremacy. Rationales for masculinity are acquired chiefly through biology, law and religion. Strategies for phallic threat reduction are then codified from these sources. Such codes, beliefs and "facts" of reality chronically serve to legitimize male behaviors and ideals.

Phallic threat reductions range from invocation of God's commandments and the sanctity of the nuclear family, to such folk beliefs as "anatomy is destiny." They become propaganda instruments to operate continual institutionalization of the status quo for heterosexual males. The phallic state remains intact.

Such instruments also become avenues of logical attack against those who threaten traditional definitions of male space. Such semantical propaganda techniques were called *doublethink* in Orwell's *1984*. Male in-groups could be likened to the Party. Winston Smith, the rebellious believer in truth and humanity over the deceitful power of the Party, is mocked by his captor, O'Brien:

> . . . I tell you, Winston, that reality is not external. Reality exists in the human mind, and nowhere else. . . . Whatever the Party holds to be truth *is* truth. It is impossible to see reality except by looking through the eyes of the Party.[26] [emphasis in original]

The dominant attitudes and practices assume an ethical atmosphere of moral rightness. Deviations from these then assume the category of moral wrongness. Right and wrong proceed from description of an attitude or practice, to evaluation. As John Hartland-Swann implies in *An Analysis of Morals,* social utility is the matrix of morality. Men can make whatever they need to believe as moral or immoral, by definition.[27]

In American society, we are well trained to divide seeming opposites into good and bad, moral and immoral—us and them. Behaviors are sweepingly defined as normal or abnormal. Americans rush to differentiate and decide for or against. They avoid reasoning on the basis of finer and more complex discriminations.

There are many conflicts within the vast storehouse of information available to us. Knowledge can be ambiguous and anxiety producing. S. I. Hayakawa notices that "... in the gathering of information, the making of judgments is often conditioned by prejudice toward those judgments which it will benefit us personally to make."[28] So, dichotomized thinking becomes convenient. It reduces our need to deal with ambiguities in people or events.

Dichotomies simplify the assignment of labels to groups and individuals. Classification becomes a mode for giving moral order to thought and behavior. Classification ultimately gives rise to stereotypes which contain overly-simplified positive and negative images. These are then transmitted and perpetuated through a culture, as they are needed or tolerated by the majority male group. Such images provide emotional reaction and intellectual relaxation.

The majority behavior pattern in America is relative to white heterosexual males. This grouping crosses most religious and social divisions. It incorporates differences in economic achievement or employment categories. It exists despite differing educational attainment or political affiliation. Always, the male who is not white and heterosexual is less than male. He is subordinate. He is vaginal. Patricia N. Dutcher writing "The Meaning of Whiteness," in *Straight/White/Male* notes:

> Not only in the attempts to convert others to the "white is right" way of life, but also in the daily workings of our system, we are oppressive. . . . We must recognize that our lifestyle, our culture, our institutions require in their normal operations the perpetuation of exploitable and exploited groups both at home and abroad.[29]

Such oppression requires a shared ideology which protects heterosexual males. An obvious ideological basis is race. The most common ideology is sex.

However, sexuality qualified by race also contains a phallic threat factor to white males. Initially, skin color provides the white male enough emotional distance to diminish social insecurity. The sexual mythology of nonwhite males contains a foreign and exotic mystique to provide out-group protections for whites. This mythology is permeated with subhuman or primitive sexual judgments by whites, which are then internalized by nonwhites. If a nonwhite male happens also to be homosexual, the white heterosexual male can continue to group this sexual behavior within a category different from his own. The white male attributes exaggerated sexual prowess to the nonwhite male, not from admiration, but rather from fear.

Beyond preoccupation with nonwhite male genitalia size and ability, the white man achieves a psychological castration of this threatening sexual potency. Racism is the technique. Yet, the white male fears that what he exaggerates will be used as a weapon against him. Racism is used to humiliate, castrate and subordinate nonwhite males. They, too, become vaginated males.

Dehumanization is a process of subordinating people to a vaginal level. The prejudicial forms of misogyny carry the same intention and content as racism. To view the outsider as inferior, i.e., vaginal, keeps the dominant white male group separate and intact from the potential threat factors of vaginal contamination. Concern for maleness turns such men towards each other.

A pertinent analogy for such male concern is Ardrey's summary of the Irish ornithologist, C. B. Moffat's study of birds. Moffat noticed that male bird song was an assertive display of power directed towards other male birds. Ardrey concludes that Moffat's studies contradict Darwin's overly exclusive theory of sexual selection in which Darwin believed that masculine life focused on the female:

> What the male has on his mind is the male. . . . What is eternally bothering the male is not female estimate, but how he is doing in the eyes of his fellows.[30]

Thus, women—or anyone else conceived as vaginal—represent the antithesis to "real" male characteristics and concerns. From alleged biological differences, men handily construct gender differences to polarize phallic conceptions from vaginal ones. Gender traits are really *monologues* which describe and then validate social roles. Such monologues are sexual in origin and political in intention. Gender traits are reality distortions which restrict, depersonalize and thus create people as multiple abstractions.

Millett notices the novelist Henry Miller's unique ability to depersonalize through vaginal ascription. He represents the typical heterosexual male ethic:

> Miller's scheme of sexual polarity relegates the female to "cunt," an exclusively sexual being, crudely biological. Though he shares this lower nature, the male is also capable of culture and intellect.[31]

Heterosexual males abstract and depersonalize women, vulnerable men, events and territories into vaginal space. They also depersonalize themselves with their restrictive phallic consciousness. Independence, strength, resourcefulness and daring help define the phallic thrust into vaginal space. Dependence, tenderness, passivity and timidity become feminine qualities. These latter traits also serve male needs, but only when they are attached to the non-masculine other. Many contemporary men are aware that such feminine capacities reside in them also. Yet, awareness and experimentation with a man's more vulnerable aspects are primarily intellectual exercises in masculinity enlargement.

So-called male consciousness-raising groups attempt to emotionally ameliorate gender differences, first among men, and then between men and women. Such groups' success rests on the dynamic within each encounter group. Their value occurs only at the individual level. *The larger male heterosexual power group continues to remain inflexibly dichotomized from anyone vaginal, as well as their own full range of human capacities.* This larger male group dominates the social structures and images for any single American male.

Yet, the individual man who wishes to achieve greater authenticity through self-vagination, may do so. Personal rewards may accrue. However, if self-feminizing is too extreme, such a man will be ridiculed and ostracized from his majority in-group. Often, such a man's identity spectrum shrinks to conform again to male majority distinctions. Consciousness-raising participation gives benefit as long as the male discussion group remains intact. The man on his own must be exceptionally strong, both intellectually and emotionally, to continue to act out both his male and female components. His only model is the socially dichotomized extreme of either one role or the other.

Self-vaginated males require an already high masculinity "quotient." Gender characteristics of masculinity occur on a socially constructed, yet inexact scale. By appearance, accomplishment and development of style, a man may rank high in some or all masculine gender traits. A relatively high masculinity quotient could allow a man frequent or publicly displayed borrowing of feminine characteristics. He may cry at funerals, hug men if his team wins, or crochet pillowcases as therapy for the ulcer-forming rigors of the office.

A low masculinity quotient makes borrowing of feminine

characteristics more dangerous to a man's self concept, or his esteem by others. The other-directed man risks the censure of his sex group according to the type, degree or occasion of borrowing. The man who cooks must pursue gourmet meals or fry his steaks outdoors. The demonstrative man who consistently touches other men or effusively expresses his feelings makes his peers uncomfortable. The man who cross-dresses and wears makeup may do so only on Halloween or at costume parties; he arouses humorous toleration if he is a hairy linebacker type who burlesques women through comparative comedy. He is deliciously queer. Social toleration of a man's fluctuating masculinity quotient rests on his reasonable proximity to general masculinity norms. The toleration proximity scale fluctuates according to a man's geographical location, educational level and employment description. Marital status, age, physical appearance, mannerisms and occasion also affect a man's masculinity quotient.

The individual man who is anxious about his masculinity quotient, often bands with other men to reinforce similar masculine needs and desires. The masculinity quotient contains a social sense of power, emotional influence and various badges of accomplishment which attach him to other males. Together, men reinforce each other psychosexually by establishing common goals. They participate together in strategies and rituals for goal achievement. Chosen goals then metamorphose into enemy-conceptions. These become vaginal space or territory to conquer and occupy. The bonds men experience are circumstantial and psychological. They are sometimes physical. They are always masculine.

Male bonding occurs within the context of simulated war. Athletics, business, love or a simple game of poker all provide imaginary images of an enemy. Endurance, skill, accomplishment, style and wit all unite men in competitive ratification of their sexual identity. There is an integrating dynamic between the male territory, phallic threat factors and masculinity quotient. The dynamic of anxiety accompanies phallic threats to any momentary or permanent declaration of male space. Anxiety is reduced by a successful extension of the phallic mentality into any space defined as vaginal receptacle.

Such vaginal attitudes inspire men to subordinate their environment for the service of the man who dares, the man who wills and the man who believes the body politic is his for the taking. The dynamic of anxiety argues for success. A winner is more masculine than a loser. Manhood can be lost on the basis of incompetent performance:

> . . . Personal achievement . . . is a thrilling test of self, played according to a demanding performance ethic which steers the athletic "hunter-fighter-fucker" past the land mines of homosexuality, onanism, impotence, and capitulation to women. . . . As the formula of "fucking as conquest" holds true, the conquest is not only over the female, but over the male's own fears for his masculinity, his courage, his dominance, the test of erection.[32]

Anxiety is somewhat diminished if the male loser played well. Again, recourse to style or endurance allows this man to save face, to retain some degree of male standing. Obviously, severe loss insinuates a radical reduction in masculinity quotient. The vaginal implication is apparent. In marriage, the "battle of the sexes" is continually won as the male assumes responsibility for major decisions, produces and controls his children (especially sons) and successfully resists a wife who nags, demands indulgence or earns more money at her job than he does.

Phallic props thus serve to keep the heterosexual pseudo-male erect. His threatened impotence is shielded by the prophylactic of manufactured masculinity. He is free to enter his vaginal space.

The white homosexual male also shares this larger social conditioning of men who view the other as vagina. He also subscribes to power strategies in competition with other males. The white homosexual male is conscious of masculinity quotients and shares similar threat factors which elevate anxiety concerning his sexual potency.

Both white heterosexual and homosexual males are members of the power elite in American society. Race and anatomy link them. Their sexual practices seemingly alienate them. The homosexual and heterosexual male appear to be locked into a mutual effort to make each other vaginal. Because the homosexual and heterosexual male are so close in spirit and practice, the heterosexual majority is most threatened by the existence of homosexuality. American heterosexual males are particularly vulnerable because their interest in all things masculine is as intense as that of most homosexual males. Heterosexuals shield their vulnerability with myth, stereotype and tradition. Annihilation or containment of homosexuals is paramount to keeping their male power structure intact. Homosexuality in males defeats the precarious logic heterosexuals erect for themselves within vaginal fiction.

Both heterosexual and homosexual males share these fictions. Yet, the implications of the homosexual as vaginated male create unique self-concepts and shared behaviors within the homosexual minority. Because masculine fictions are believed and acted out, the vaginated male then enters the psychological space uniquely designed for him. He tends to constrict and confine himself. He accommodates to survive. He repeats the white heterosexual monologue for himself. We now will observe how such fictions become true.

PART II/The Vaginal Male

2/Homo Chronic Slips Deeper into Vaginal Confinement

> It is characteristic of the illusion that it is derived
> from men's wishes. . . [1]
> —Sigmund Freud,
> *The Future of an Illusion*

> . . . You often doubt if you really exist. You
> wonder whether you aren't simply a phantom in
> other people's minds. Say, a figure in a nightmare
> which the sleeper tries with all his strength to
> destroy.[2]
> —Ralph Ellison, *The Invisible Man*

In the previous chapter we observed some of the available
monologues which construct male space. They sexually define
the requirements and privileges of masculinity. They contain
social images which describe and reinforce an authoritarian
power base for white heterosexual males.

These sexual monologues convert all others into vaginal units
which are used and abused at the pleasure of the heterosexual
male. The homosexual male suffers such conversion too. He is
humiliated, attacked or contained because he admits the sexual
preference he has for men. Heterosexuals must chronically hide,
deny or sublimate this similar male preference. The homosexual
male thus exposes the heterosexual's dichotomized sexual politics as fraudulent. The heterosexual reacts by claiming homosexuality is fraudulent masculinity. Heterosexuals create multiple
illusions which claim that homosexual males are a deviant threat
to society. They erase homosexuals as real men. They make them
vaginal. The effort is political and personal. Fear is the motive. If

heterosexuals were to allow homosexuals validity, the conceptual structure of their internally and externally vaginated world would collapse.

The conflict occurs because all men fuck each other, one way or another. Homosexuals merely actualize what heterosexuals rationalize. Heterosexuals defend themselves against the threatening homosexual spectre haunting their political-sexual nightmare. They create strategies to exorcise any claims to masculinity the homosexual might make. They speak monologues of illusion as belief. These beliefs assume alleged reality as normative behaviors. Such illusions then become in-stitutionalized. It doesn't matter whether the homosexual be-lieves the monologues or not. He remains the spectre-victim. He must share the heterosexual nightmare. The heterosexual con-tinues to dream illusion into reality. The homosexual must be destroyed.

Techniques of destruction must carry social approval. They emerge into social consciousness through various sources of masculine monologues. Contradictions to male monologues are neatly nullified by appeal back to those very institutions neces-sary to any society. Religious, legal, scientific and social-traditional behaviors are used to politically oppress those who do not match white heterosexual male concepts, values and be-haviors. These images of male virtue assume a "moral" structure for all. The structure's foundation is guilt and fear. Lawrence K. Frank writes in *The Conduct of Sex* on masculine definitions of morality:

> Traditional morality is primarily an attempt to maintain social order with little concern for what that morality does to and for human personalities. . . .
> If we reflect upon morality, we will realize that, moral codes are rules which have been proclaimed usually by some authority, a leader or prophet, who invokes whatever sanctions his people believe in to call for unquestioned acceptance of these moral codes.[3]

One contemporary source of male monologue which has great vogue, combines the authority of prophet-shaman with patriar-chal invocation to obedience. The *monologue of psychiatry* does more psychological damage to white homosexual males than is achieved within any other social institution. Psychiatry unites the mythology of religion with the judgment of law to define normal human behaviors. Psychiatry's norm is the dominant white heterosexual male power group it represents. The psychoanalyst Irving Bieber, speaking in the book, *Homosexuality,* collaborates with other psychiatrists who form the white heterosexual male's monologue of judgment against his homosexual counterpart:

> . . . Homosexuality is an adaptation to fear of heterosexuality, and we extend this proposition to account for all homosexual behavior.[4]

Such smug dismissal of homosexuality as fear adaptation hides the more pertinent issue. Heterosexual males fear everything external to themselves which threathens their phallic image and authority. They fear symbolic castration based on losing their dominance over others. To be castrated is to become vaginal. Any qualification of homosexuality as fear adaptation primarily serves to screen the heterosexual's own fear of sexual domination by others.

The white homosexual male increases the anxiety level of his heterosexual associate more than women or racial minorities. Heterosexuals can tolerate the challenge of opposing political groups, differing social customs or disparities in heterosexual competitive achievements, far more comfortably than their fear of homosexuals. The white homosexual male reveals to the heterosexual that his sense of justice is a lie. His religion of love is a sham. His system of value hierarchies is based on sexual oppression. His majority male virtues overwhelmingly contain principles which maintain white heterosexual supremacy over those considered less than men. This includes everyone outside of his own classification.

Not all white heterosexual males feel comfortable with such sexual-political hypocrisy. They wish to soften masculine rigidities for their own welfare, as well as to be fair to the imaginary opposition. Fear becomes rationalized into caution. The excuse is heterosexual conditioning.

Marc Fasteau thus softens Bieber's position on fear of heterosexuality as the cause for homosexuality. In his chapter, "Androgyny," from *The Male Machine,* Fasteau speculates about the impact of androgynous behaviors and attitudes on rigid sex role expectations:

> It is possible to be less phobic about homosexuality and freer emotionally and physically with friends of the same sex without

engaging in overtly sexual acts—this is probably as far as most exclusively heterosexual men now past puberty will move.[5]

While Fasteau writes within a contemporary male consciousness-raising framework, and acknowledges homosexuality up to the point of sexual intercourse, conditioning makes him hesitate to act out the truce within androgyny. He begs the question within the heterosexual-homosexual debate by retreating into generalities about the issue of sexual fear. So, Fasteau struggles for a balanced solution to polarized male sexuality:

. . . Some homosexual behavior, like some heterosexual behavior, is prompted by fear. The image of masculinity as requiring constant toughness, competitiveness, and dominance, especially over women, leads some men, in attempts to prove their masculinity, to hyper-aggressive, exploitative, and humiliating behavior in their sexual relationships with women. Another reaction to the same extreme version of the male stereotype is to shun entirely the role it implies, giving up full masculine status and taking refuge in the alternative of homosexuality. An androgynous society, which would not teach the association of maleness, constant dominance, and aggressive sex, would make both compulsions less likely.[6]

The implication here is loaded against the homosexual. Fasteau cites the homosexual as "giving up full masculine status" (always defined as heterosexual). One negative male stereotype is exchanged for an even more negative—and compulsive—stereotype. While Fasteau implies that androgyny offers neutrality, he only offers a less strident return to Bieber's one-sided argument against homosexuality as a fear reaction to heterosexuality.

The origin of sexual fear begins within the white heterosexual male. The homosexual provokes masculine anxiety because he shares the heterosexual's ethic and point of view; he competes with heterosexuals in the same manner. All American men view themselves as phallic. All men seek to control and use their environment-as-vagina. Desmond Morris clarifies how homosexuals confuse the competition for this penis ratification by heterosexuals in *The Human Zoo:*

It is relevant here to mention the special attitude of heterosexual Status Sex devotees towards homosexual males. It is an attitude of increased hostility and contempt, caused by the unconscious realization that "if they won't join the game, they can't be beaten." In other words, the homosexual male's lack of sexual interest in females gives him an unfair advantage in the Status Sex battle, for no matter how many females the heterosexual expert subdues, the homosexual will fail to be impressed. It then becomes necessary to defeat him by ridicule.[7]

Heterosexual conceptions of other as vagina complicates the issue further. Homosexuals are taken to view all men as objects to ratify their brand of masculinity. Such logic requires that heterosexual males then become what they have traditionally created apart from themselves—vaginas.

Heterosexual males cannot tolerate their logic turned against them. Thus, they suspect homosexuals hate them because homosexuals view them as vaginal territory. They also know that vaginal subordinates (women, blacks, Jews. . . .) develop self-hatred as a result of their treatment by majority power groups. To allow homosexuals to view heterosexuals as vaginal becomes psychically impossible; heterosexuals will not hate themselves because they will not be subordinated. Heterosexuals must convince homosexuals to accept vaginal logic in order to maintain their own illogical definitions of masculine superiority.

Homosexuals may champion the male attributes to a greater extreme than heterosexuals—in only one way. Homosexuals break the taboo of same-sex intercourse which heterosexuals maintain to define and defend their masculine power balance. When a man engages in sexual intercourse with another man, that act implies a personal and political rejection of traditional sex roles based on dominance and submission. The male-to-male sex act blatantly challenges traditional sex roles that are created and maintained for the sexual hegemony of heterosexual males. It also implies an inversion of hopefully foolproof strategies, attitudes and behaviors which heterosexuals employ against those without a white phallus, used heterosexually, to insure that destiny is controlled by this masculine power tool.

The white heterosexual male must refuse to view himself as vaginal. Suspecting that his homosexual counterpart ignores such refusal creates an anxiety threat to the heterosexual's power symbols (phallic), institutions and self concept. Warren Farrell focuses on the essence of heterosexual anxiety, even among more open and tolerant men. In *The Liberated Man,* Farrell speaks of a homosexual member of a male consciousness-raising group:

. . . When he had expressed an interest in a few members of the group who were heterosexual, we experienced the uneasiness of being treated as a sex object.[8]

The homosexual looms as arch enemy to the space which the heterosexual claims as his. The homosexual is then beaten back into an inferior role conception. Whatever religious convictions homosexuals embrace, whatever political activity they engage in, whatever level of employment they reach—wherever they might be—homosexuals threaten. Should homosexuals become visible, they may be jailed, fired, declared mentally ill, evicted, disenfranchised, ignored, tolerated, pitied, hated or killed. Whatever form of attack the heterosexual male chooses, it serves as a containment of homosexuality and a concomitant relief for heterosexual anxiety and fear.

The visible or invisible homosexual may be contained by law, religion, medicine, social tradition and psychological conspiracies designed to keep them less than equal—less than human. Containment becomes expulsion from the heterosexual male territory. Containment also becomes a uniquely vaginal space which *defines* the homosexual's role in society. Such space exists only in the imagination—yet other minorities share it with the homosexual, and suffer from it in their special manner.

Subordinated males have labels attached to them by the masculine majority. These labels are vaginal attachments which categorize men into their assigned area. They are related to behaviors which are low in masculinity quotient. They imply a deviance from the preferred masculine norm. Negative labels offer functional significance to those who use them, as well as those on whom they are placed. Functional significance for the user is based on emotional and behaviorial distance achieved from the rejected male. Functional significance in negative labels for the bearer of them broadens to include a sense of isolation, a denigration of self-regard, belief in one's own deviance and a tendency to act out expected behaviors attached to vaginal labels.

The heterosexual male who allows latitude to his wife is "pussy-whipped." The intellectual male is "prissy." The sensitive artist is a "long-hair." The nonassertive male is a "milquetoast." The homosexual male is labeled "queer," "pansy," "fairy," or "flit." Associations with feminine, i.e., "bad" behavior, are attached to men who appear or act soft, tender, emotional, passive or effusively demonstrative.

The heterosexual male drives deeper into vaginal fantasy. *Webster's Seventh New Collegiate Dictionary* backs him up by defining effeminate as ". . . Having unsuitable feminine qualities: UNMANLY. . . ."[9] Manliness demands virility. The "real" man must show the hardness, thrust and power of a perpetually erect penis. The heterosexual's problem is, the homosexual male can achieve one too.

Labeling, or feminine name-calling, is one method the heterosexual uses to reduce this problem—by reducing the homosexual to a flaccid state. The heterosexual believes that homosexuals are, at best, women in disguise. At worst, they are renegade men who upset the orderly control of a patriarchal society. From beliefs, the heterosexual creates socio-psychological strategies to subdue minority males. These strategies delineate and confine homosexuals within a vaginal description. Their purpose is to convince homosexual males to believe what the male majority says about them. An additional purpose is to help heterosexuals deny their own interest in males.

Once the homosexual assimilates heterosexual male beliefs and expectations, the homosexual becomes a vaginated male. His sense of identity becomes submerged in the hostile and fictitious illusions of the heterosexual. He has no other socially approved model for himself. He thus has little resistance to transforming himself into the spectre within the heterosexual male's sexual nightmare.

Acceptance of self-as-vagina can be avoided. Socio-sexual subordination can be refused. However, the homosexual male must first be aware of the process by which beliefs merge into behaviors, and how behaviors become patterned into rigid symbol and ritual.

The remaining discussion then deals with an overview of beliefs and behaviors which homosexuals act out because these are expected from them. Vaginal symbols and rituals affect each homosexual male uniquely; however, each shares his vaginated masculinity in multiple forms which always maintain degrees of confinement in his group. Learned self-hatred can project as techniques of hatred for the homosexual's own kind. Hopefully, a closer examination of homosexual strategies of coping with learned hatred will help prevent such typical minority membership reactions. The homosexual can then resist a habitual fulfillment of the heterosexual expectation for him.

Negative behavioral labels for the homosexual originate or gain credence from often conflicting, but usually condemning theoretical speculation by psychiatry about why homosexuality occurs. Reasons offered frequently depend on the vivid imagination of researcher-psychologist or writer-psychiatrist. Such speculation creates and then maintains a class of "sick" people which is lucrative for analysts to maintain as deviant, so that their books sell and homosexuals "turn themselves in" for psychosexual remodeling. Remodeling becomes a euphemism for conformity to heterosexual male standards for sexual behavior. Peter Fisher offers pertinent remarks on an essential problem for homosexuals who respond to such sexually scientific mythologies, in *The Gay Mystique:*

> Sadly, not a few homosexuals accept one or another of these theories and spend years in self-mutilating introspection and self-criticism, striving to suppress and erase major portions of their personality in order to conform to "expert" diagnoses.[10]

The psychiatrist Edmund Bergler perhaps surpasses many of his fellow analysts of homosexuality as an adroit manipulator of scientific terminology and logic to achieve a neat cause-effect relationship for homosexuality. He summarizes his repugnance for homosexuals in *Homosexuality: Disease or Way of Life?:*

> The homosexual's infantile fears, centered on the mother image, are greater than those of other neurotics. . . . Having elevated himself to the "breast-barony", the new aristocrat is not certain of the permanency of his rank. . . . This also explains the fantastically exaggerated narcissism (self-love, self-concentration) of the homosexual. His megalomania was wounded at a very early age and he could not "take it." . . . This explains, too, why nearly every homosexual recites a story of early feminine identifications, telling how he loved to play with dolls, wear girl's clothes. . . . This identification is a classic example of one of the tricks in the inner lawyer's bag: "admission of the lesser crime." The inner conscience accuses the homosexual of the felony of psychic masochism; the inner lawyer instructs his client to admit to a misdemeanor: Oedipal femininity.[11]

Within Bergler's hysterical diagnosis exist many accoutrements of typical American male homophobia.

Homosexuality is infantile behavior; the mother (woman) is to blame. The homosexual takes pleasure in being dominated (masochism), a male assumption also applied to women. Bergler then reveals his politics with terms like "breast-barony," "aristocrat," and "rank." If breast-barony is neurotic, then the majority of American males are expeditiously educated into neuroticism. Breasts are a traditional heterosexual fetish.

Bergler accuses the homosexual of trickery—the "imitation" man is not to be trusted. Homosexuals cannot "take it," thus apparently missing another medical criterion for masculinity.

Bergler reveals his negative attitude towards women as inferior; no man would be attracted to dolls or feminine apparel.

Bergler shifts to legalese. "Lawyer," "felony," and "misdemeanor," invite the homosexual to indict himself; "Oedipal femininity" is the "crime." The crime originates in the imagination of heterosexuals; they provide *a priori* judgment to derank the homosexual male to vaginal neurosis.

Another psychiatrist, Thomas Szasz, has written of the tendency by psychiatrists to move from medicine to social prescription. The so-called average behavior, or "rules" for living, stem from biases of heterosexual white males. Their power group designates normality for all. In *The Manufacture of Madness,* Szasz notes:

> . . . Deviance is not, as it is often erroneously believed, a defect exhibited by, or contained in the personality of, an individual actor. . . . it is, instead, an inevitable consequence, and indeed an integral part, of the construction of social compacts or groups. . . . For example, Howard S. Becker writes that "*social groups create deviance by making rules whose infraction constitutes deviance,* and by applying those rules to particular people and labeling them as outsiders. From this point of view, deviance is *not* a quality of the act the person commits, but rather a consequence of the application by others of rules and sanctions to an 'offender.' The deviant is one to whom that label has been successfully applied."[12] [emphasis in original]

Thus, psychiatrists politically mix legal and moral judgment of homosexuals according to the heterosexual male power elite they represent. Their personal reward accrues from the mysticism attached to mental behaviors; American society is absorbed with techniques of behavioral conditioning, guided by their "expert" seers reading the auguries of homosexual aberrations.

Even the well-intentioned clinical studies of male homosexual phenomena move the homosexual towards normative behavioral conditioning, and a subsequent loss of his individualism within tentative group description. The focus of such studies is on the penis as seismograph for human thought, feeling, and motivation.

In *Homosexualities: A Study of Diversity Among Men and Women,* Alan Bell and Martin Weinberg border on a prostitutional profiling of their homosexual interviewees. Choosing park, steam bath, and bar habitues, their investigation focuses on cruising patterns, pick-up techniques, numbers of sexual partners, etc. Creating categories of "close-coupled," "open-coupled," "functionals," and "dysfunctionals," Bell and Weinberg argue that ". . . Using a typology of homosexual experience helps to clarify whatever differences there might be between homosexual and heterosexual adults."[13] Their summary ultimately reduces to a rather unastonishing acknowledgment that homosexuals are a diverse group, similar to heterosexuals except for their same-sex orientation. While softening the deviancy aspect of homosexuality, Bell and Weinberg create patterns of homosexual normalcy which blend into a doctrine of types. Such clinical typologies cast homosexuals in role expectations, especially when field studies are conducted in stereotypical arenas fraught with extreme sexual rituals and motives. Data may present a unique composite of homosexual behaviors not representative of the male homosexual majority.

A much more doctrinaire approach to the study of homosexual behavior is employed by William Masters and Virginia Johnson in *Homosexuality in Perspective.* Masters and Johnson label their study group as "conversion clients" and "reversion clients." The conversion client's fear of the unknown apparently worked against his successful abandonment of homosexuality in favor of heterosexuality. The reversion client was handicapped by negative heterosexual experiences because they were "unrewarding" and/or "repulsive."[14]

In the Masters and Johnson therapy program for sexual dissatisfaction and dysfunction, they noticed that one in three homosexuals treated for sexual dissatisfaction failed to convert or revert to heterosexuality. One in ten failed in therapy for sexual dysfunction.[15] Responding to the elevated failure rate, Masters and Johnson consider their own facts scientifically unacceptable. They believe failure rate should be no higher than twenty percent, although one wonders why such an arbitrary figure is expected.[16]

One weakness to the Masters and Johnson study is their acknowledged possible bias and prejudice of their sexual therapists, as well as evaluation criteria for admission to the Masters and Johnson Institute. Another, was their kindly call for "clinical cooperation." They believe that their results would improve if the gay community placed greater confidence in Masters' and Johnson's treatment modalities.[17] Apparently, homosexual submission to laboratory-monitored sexual performance must be accompanied by faith, in order for the heterosexual miracle to occur.

Perhaps Masters and Johnson's own tenet that solicited sex produces satiation, which then results in sexual dysfunction for homosexuals, also undercuts part of their study results. Laboratory sex does not represent the wider range of sexually connected motives, desires, feelings, ethics, or behaviors which randomly occur in the homosexual population. Laboratory sex does represent solicited sex under the guise of clinical study. Studies of prostitution have traditionally revealed that the bordello contains male clients who evidence varying degrees of sexual dissatisfaction and dysfunction.

However tenuous the Bell and Weinberg or Masters and Johnson findings appear, they generally carry a tone of clinical acceptance of homosexuality. Yet, the contents of both still depict the homosexual as possessed by his sexual performance. It appears as criterion for his whole personality. The ability of such studies to alleviate deviancy as a barrier between heterosexuality and homosexuality remains to be seen. The homosexual is still a curiosity, somewhat maladjusted, somehow sexually prodigious.

One cannot fault either study as directives of homosexual thought and behavior towards the normative. Norms remain the comfort station of most clinical studies which "clients," "patients," counselees or interviewees are encouraged to accept, even rely upon. Social engineering within the scope of medicine is a tempting placebo for personality distress, a regulation of sexual irregularities, and a pious concern of science to equate the penis with the human spirit. Often science is unable to touch either aspect, given the more complex social realities that the homosexual male must confront beyond the laboratory, the gay bar, or the toilet.

With the deviant label for homosexuality as popular currency, at whatever age the homosexual male first discovers his sexual-erotic interest in men, he breaks the first rule of manhood. He has little, if any, sexual interest in women—the proof of manhood. Therefore, he is different from majority males. If women clarify masculinity, the homosexual male has no model to help him understand who or what he is. Novels, films, family life, advertising, brand commodities and peer patterns all reinforce his sense of difference. He often does not conform to average sexual modalities which separate men from women. Logic argues that if women ratify their role through the male sexual subject, then homosexuals also share the same "feminine" ratification-association.

The homosexual male denies this socially ascribed definition of femininity, because he—like the heterosexual—has been socialized to consider women as secondary and threatening. They are objects for male domination and pleasure. Yet, the homosexual male tends to identify with women because he experiences a gradual internalization of the negative vaginal image given him by heterosexual males.

Techniques of homosexual denial of self-vagination range widely from disassociation through camouflage and projection, to distorted mimicry of femininity as a weapon against heterosexuals, to a final self-mocking retreat into total vagination. Variations of homosexual males' adaptation to socialized vagination are myriad. They originate from a minority sexual orientation defending itself against an obsessive heterosexual need to define a phallic identity with a vaginal role.

Most homosexual males consider their sexual identity to be male. Sexual *roles* can be a blend of masculine and feminine gender traits and atmospheres. Heterosexual males confuse sexual identity with role. It is this dominant confusion to which the minority homosexual male responds, to clarify himself as best he can.

Homosexuals sometimes marry women to hide themselves within a visibly normal and socially approved relationship. This personal and public strategy to deny one's homosexuality is frequently termed bisexuality. This subject will be covered in more detail in a later chapter; here, bisexuality becomes the homosexual's role-as-male in proximity to a woman. The appearance of sexual *activity* with a woman appeases society and assuages the homosexual's belief that he is really "that way."

In *Bisexual Living,* by Julius Fast and Hal Wells, the negative aspect of bisexuality is noted by a man who doesn't like to be identified as a bisexual. He believes society views bisexuality as worse than homosexuality:

"A bi is more hidden, harder to spot. A bi is more like a straight, therefore it's more threatening.

". . . Many men feel that homosexuality threatens them because they have homosexual elements in themselves. . . .
". . . Everyone has bisexual elements in them too. Men can love their fathers and brothers, and women their mothers and daughters and sisters. . . . But society says that love is a no-no, so we're afraid of it.
'. . . Since my marriage my homosexual experiences have fallen off. I still will occasionally have a sexual encounter with a man, but more important, my emotional relationships to men, relationships that can be called bisexual, still continue. . . . "I can appreciate him sexually, but I don't have to act out these feelings."[13]

The above quotation points to a difference between activity and desire—and perhaps role and identity as well. Heterosexual and homosexual men may both have sexual activity with women, and yet desire emotional-sexual closeness with men. They may both have sexual activity with men and desire closeness to women. *The crux of the bisexual issue is that role activity does not define identity.* Bisexuality tends to be a psychological accommodation to social role expectation. Psycho-emotional eroticizing of males by a man, whether acted upon or not, is a homosexual orientation, regardless of the bisexual euphemism.

Cory claims in *The Homosexual and His Society* ". . . that one's mode of sexual behavior is not always consistent with one's inner and conscious desire."[14]

Although a person's sexual desire may change from one choice of love object to another, nevertheless at all times within his life, from adolescence onward, a definite orientation toward one form must exist for the individual to be both psychologically and socially stable.[15]

For the "heterosexual" male, bisexuality seems to legitimize his occasional homosexual activity. It does the same for the "homosexual." The legitimizing factor is women. Perhaps bisexuality is a psychological term that describes a nonexistent bimodality. It serves the need to gratify social expectations for sex role dichotomies. It rationalizes same sex orientation and activity into an imaginary double identity. Despite the ambiguity in attempting to categorize behavior, claims to bisexuality, provide some social camouflage through women. The homosexual male can thus block total vagination by occasionally fulfilling his "masculine" role.

Another form of vaginal denial is the homosexual's search for anonymous sexual encounters. One night stands, where a man invites another man home after they find each other in a public restroom, park, movie balcony or steambath, can lead into friendship or at least a short term affair. The parallel of heterosexual "pick up" points and purposes to homosexual behavior is obvious. While I do not place a moral judgment on where homosexual men meet—since many homosexuals are socially forced to traditional cruising areas to maintain secrecy and freedom from harassment—often a denial of one's homosexuality simultaneously occurs in the secret location selected for anonymous sexual relief. Many homosexual writers tend to condone anonymous sex, providing logical rationale for anonymous sexual release. The alleged sexual permissiveness of the 1960s included allowing people to "do their own thing," "different strokes for different folks," and other cliched expressions which endorsed one's right to privacy and self-satisfaction; if "it" feels good, "it" should be done. We lately discover that the decade that sought human intimacy through hedonism, withdrew into the isolation of frustration. The sport of sex did not provide the need for intimacy with another's full range of human capacity.

Frustrated isolation is what the homosexual wants to alleviate within an anonymous sexual encounter. Yet, he cannot or will not integrate his sexual identity if he disassociates himself from what he does. In an effort to deny, he objectifies himself and the person he fellates. He isolates himself further. The repetitious search for anonymous sex often becomes a "comparison of alternatives."

If anonymous sex is a punishment reaction to denial of one's homosexuality, or even an unhappy exercise in futility, the homosexual remains at the level of anonymous sex until he can establish a viable (less punishing) alternative. If the homosexual cannot accomplish viable alternatives, he remains in the isolation of denial.

He often exchanges no conversation with his partner; he gives false information about himself; he remains anonymous through degrees of guilt, shame or fear. He becomes similar to heterosexual singles who reside in apartment complexes designed for unmarrieds. In the article, "Sex as Athletics in the Singles Complex," Cynthia Proulx viewed these people as having " '. . . different variations of a basic schizoid personality. I don't mean split; I mean cut off, afraid of closeness.' "[16]

Herbert A. Otto enlarges upon the American pursuit of sexual encounter which permits one to have sex with "anybody" rather than "somebody."

The myths that have so distorted sex have not helped to humanize man. They have only antagonized the difficulties which men have already known in trying to understand and appreciate the meaning of sex in the context of genuine human relationships. This is sex with a human purpose, not sex as an end in itself, as a self-justifying pleasure that needs no other human reference points. This is all part of the current myth that since 'sex is everything' then anything goes in experiencing or expressing it.[17]

Thus, anonymous sexual encounters achieve a variety of denials to the homosexual's whole identity. From this position, I criticize the practice. It habituates the homosexual to frustration, tends to depersonalize himself and others, and compartmentalizes him within an atmosphere of loneliness. He doesn't need people, he needs genitals. For the moment, he isn't a whole person—but rather a functional imitation of what sexuality could represent. He merely imitates what homosexuality often is for him . . . an illegitimate orientation which he must hide even as he seeks out (homo)sexual release.

From a functional imitation of what sexuality could represent, some homosexuals imitate what sexuality should represent. Some homosexuals dress and affect mannerisms of extreme machismo as compensation for masculinity they fear they lack. Sexually, they prefer males, but they also must appear to be as manly as heterosexual models. A common gibe cast at these men is that they are the real "lady" in bed. Butch men often are the first "to throw their legs up in the air"—it is speciously, but frequently assumed that macho men are imposters—they over-compensate for their fear and distaste of feminine associations. Sports clothing, leather jackets, boots and chains imply a fastidious attention to masculine surfaces and symbols. "Leather bars," complete with sadomasochist decor and entertainment, provide the extreme context for the macho homosexual.

Despite the cosmetic approach to masculinity, the homosexual who perfects degrees of exaggerated machismo attempts to deny the feminine in himself and in other homosexuals. The macho homosexual believes sexuality should be masculine; he grooms himself less from admiration for maleness, than he does to make his tough, remote and virile appearance contradictory to a vaginal identity given him by heterosexuals. Butch "drag" combines the cowboy, Hell's Angel, sportsman mystique into another role distortion based on masculinity defined as non-vaginal.

The pose, the bravado and the "cool" are similar in strategy to the black male's use of style to camouflage a sense of deficiency. "Playing cool" is a defense mechanism against admission that one is not making it, according to American standards of success. To "save face," the black male often exaggerates imitations of success through dress, verbal hipness and aggressive style. To avoid defeat he masters a surface of denial. Submergence into "cool" confines the black male to perpetual maintenance of visible fortifications against defeat.

So the homosexual male, resorting to exaggerated masculinity, attempts to "save face" by visibly denying the vaginal role he must resist to help his personality survive. Submergence into machismo denies the wider range of human emotions and behaviors available to him. His focus on the mono-dimensional definitions of heterosexual masculinity then creates a parody of his implicit critic. Retreat into machismo is still retreat; its rewards are as suspect as those the heterosexual male displays in chronic support against loss of psychic erection.

The homosexual's denial of his vaginated self-concept through imitation of heterosexual style, also affects the sexual act itself. Homosexuals sometimes perpetuate the active-passive sex role associated with male-female interaction. Certain homosexuals need to call the shots on what they will or won't do in bed, according to their concepts of appropriate masculine behavior. There is a fairly full range of physically and emotionally erotic activity available between two men. Not all sexual expressions fulfill, satisfy or interest everyone at any given time—or ever. People choose or avoid what they like or don't like, need or don't need—for a variety of reasons. However, the homosexual male who deals with hatred of himself as vaginal, or who wishes to make his sexual partner more vaginal than he is in order to claim "more" masculinity, consciously and unconsciously uses sexual behaviors as denial strategies.

There are extreme variations in sexual behaviors which do not necessarily entail denial of one's homosexuality. The heterosexual who has sex with his wife while wearing pieces of feminine attire; the heterosexual who simultaneously has sex with a woman and another man; the homosexual who plays the alleged active role with his male partner, and comfortably reciprocates by assuming the alleged passive role; the homosexuals who engage in anal and oral sex, mutual masturbation and are generally open to any sexual variation—all do so presumably because they like what they do and are not threatend by so-called masculine and feminine sex roles.

However, certain males interpret sexual behaviors as threatening to the internal image they have of themselves as men; they avoid sexual behaviors which seemingly challenge the sexual stereotype to which they cling in order to avoid being feminized. Some homosexuals thus attempt to heterosexualize themselves based on the model of "insertor-insertee." The Society of Medical Psychoanalysts explored such behaviors among homosexuals to determine components of sexual adaptation. They found difficulty defining "active" and "passive" in any sex role. One who sucks another's penis does so actively, even though the receiver is traditionally assumed passive. They then attempted to postulate psychological disturbance in homosexuals based on their insertor-insertee dichotomy:

> . . . We have adopted the terms "insertor" and "insertee." The insertor intromits his penis into an orifice. The insertee accepts the penis into his orifice. There can be no question in any particular act (other than in mutual fellatio—"69") who is the insertor and who the insertee. . . . The oral insertee therefore seems to show a greater potential than the anal insertee for becoming heterosexual.[18]

One suspects the hope expressed in the last sentence is due to the similarity to heterosexual male behavior; such an act stimulates the heterosexual's insertion of his penis into a woman's mouth, perhaps a more acceptable mode than anus penetration. The woman's vagina already exists for such a purpose.

Apart from fear or physical discomfort, homosexual males who rigidly define for their partners what they will or won't do sexually, often describe their need to parallel heterosexual male modes of penile domination, aggression and expression. They deny the vaginal in themselves through techniques of avoidance, and request or require a displacement of vaginal roles onto their sexual partner. Homosexual males who, in turn, require a sexually vaginal role—also respond through heterosexual role-as-activity definitions.

The issue is not that alleged passivity or "insertee" behavior is feminine, i.e., vaginal, behavior. The chief concern is compulsive role behavior can indicate a need to subordinate oneself deeper into a vaginal self-concept. Such subordination does not become personally satisfying, but ritualizes a surrender to the social expectation that homosexual males are feminized men. Such compulsively passive activity confirms this internalized belief; the homosexual eroticizes himself in a limited manner to satisfy his self-hatred, social role ascription or the vaginal-denial needs of his more active partner.

Heterosexual feminists urge the rejection of active-passive role requirements which ultimately depend on who has the penis, and what its mechanisms intellectually and physically require. Feminists reject penis tyranny and argue for sexual equality, both in attitude and behavior. The vaginated male could profit from a similar review of his sexual consciousness. Resignation to heterosexual role assignments, requires the homosexual to believe and practice narrowing and conflicting responses as complex charades.

The homosexual male thus deals with his denial of his vaginal status in subtle manners. All homosexuals are aware of the majority society's abuse and expectations for them. Ego defenses become necessary for psychological survival. These defenses are persecution-produced traits which are usually developed at the individual level. Homosexuals react to their minority group membership depending on their unique circumstances: childhood training; experiences with direct prejudice; quality and context of same-sex encounters; acceptance by family and friends; or their philosophical structuring of their lives, all affect ego defense traits. Subsequently, all homosexuals must deal with varying types and degrees of anxiety, conflict and strain.

I have cited denial of the vaginal role as varying in form. The homosexual can imitate the virile image of the heterosexual male role; he can withdraw into passivity to psychologically acquiesce to social expectations for him as "her."

The homosexual male can also accept his vaginal role in behavioral modes beyond the insertee-passive one in sexual activity. Such adjustments may be behavioral, visual or verbal. They ritualize and thus regulate the pain within prejudice. They can be aggressive forms which militate against heterosexuals, through apparent militancy towards fellow homosexuals. Adjustments by the vaginal male include: assimilation, clowning (or humor), *esprit de corps,* in-fighting, out-fighting back, and status fantasy. Such adjustments can be temporary or somewhat permanent. Acceptance forms are usually a homosexual male's attempt to achieve internal balance in a world which consistently works to render him imbalanced. Such active and reactive forms to vaginal expectation can be gradual or instantaneous. They are unapologetic challenges to acceptance of oneself as vaginated male. They say, "If this is what I am, it will be on my terms—with a vengeance."

The most gentle challenge, as well as acceptance, of vaginal confinement begins with assimilation, and thus a return to the ideological motif in androgyny.

Homosexuals who deny their sexual orientation to "pass" among heterosexuals, often reveal no observable characteristics which would associate them with their minority group. They want all homosexuals to achieve the same. Homosexual assimilationists attempt a balance in behaviors, interests and expressions which allow them freedom of movement between both heterosexual and homosexual worlds. The psychological rationale is taken from the heterosexual interest in the androgynous ideal. The homosexual suits this ideal to his own needs. For both, it is merely an exercise in personality utopianism. Androgyny has a long history of variations in thought and use—for both ancient and contemporary people.

Androgyny implies a balance between male and female characteristics. In Plato's *Symposium,* there were originally three sexes, according to early legends; men, women and androgynai. Zeus chopped the androgynai into halves which were scattered among men and women. Heterosexuals were originally androgynai with one male half and one female half; homosexuals were two halves of the same sex. Both searched for reunification with their severed halves.

From early myths then come the idea that males search for their other half in females; homosexuals adopt a similar mode of thought. "Soul-mates" implies that a single person is incomplete without his/her supplementary partner. The Romantic ideal became locked into later literature, social politic and personal imagination with the search for the perfect mate. Androgyny thus argued for dualistic thinking, as well as dualistic roles. Masculine role combined with feminine role to achieve wholeness in coupling.

More modern thinking moves androgny into personality utopianism. Men and women recognize the negative potential within role dichotomy. Many want to define their personhood singularly by achieving androgyny within themselves. Men explore their feminine characteristics, women wish to activate their masculine potential. Simone de Beauvoir, a feminist author, argues for an androgynous world in which women transcend current psychological restrictions by accepting masculine values. Sociologists and psychologists commenting on American interests in polymorphism, use such terms as "unisex," "neutership," "flattened sexuality," and "sexual thinness" to describe deactivation of sex role rigidities. Fasteau views the androgynous potential within men and women with the word "and" as the alternative to "either-or."

The mythical search for the ideal mate to complete one's "missing part" (dominant theme in Romanticism) and the ideological recognition that individual freedom includes the androgynous potential within each person, lend the heterosexual male interesting but often conflicting enlargements of his vaginal space.

For the homosexual male, the ideology of androgyny gives him an intellectual basis for assimilation into the heterosexual concern. Bisexuality, as a behavioral offshoot from the androgyny concept, even affords the homosexual (and heterosexual) a screen of social validation for same-sex activity.

Yet, bisexuality is merely sex object rotation, rather than a so-called sex object amalgamation. Until American society radically changes its myths, rituals and images, it will always link concept and behavior—through name and expectation—to sexual role. Androgyny currently exists as a Romantic ideal linked to popular psychological methods of personality enlargement. Perhaps it has become our new ideological "norm"—something perfect worthy of attainment.

Such a phenomenon finds a paradigm in religious, i.e., spiritual pursuits. The human seeks to imitate the divine—to even assimilate the self into divinity—to transcend the baseness of the human condition. Androgyny then becomes self-assimilation through an amelioration of masculine and feminine opposites.

Thus, the homosexual finds access to an ideology that socially permits a positive self-consciousness. He fits in with contemporary experimentation by men with the feminine in themselves. He can explore his vaginal self with less guilt and social judgment.

Another adjustment to homosexual membership which carries a stronger challenge to heterosexuals, and more inner and outer directed militancy than assimilation, is that of clowning or humor. Homosexuals frequently resort to "camp" behavior and repartee. Their outrageous behavior and use of language emerges from a sense of social and personal outrage. Camp regulates the pain of being vaginal, through rituals of irregularity. It tends to caricature the very stereotypical caricatures which heterosexuals ascribe to homosexuals.

The lisping, wrist flipping mincing, the exaggerated costumery, the emotional overloading of a scene to achieve dramatic effect, all help the homosexual to dramatize his distinctions. Such dramatizations range from drawing room farces to guerrilla theater waged in public places. Feminine overtones become personas and vehicles, as well as targets, for the male homosexual's anger and need for self-acceptance. Camp then assumes spiritual and psychological aspects based on style or theatrics. Camp combines theatrics into a minority statement against the political majority. It dares to mock what society mocks in the homosexual. Thus, camp carries a form and tradition similar to Greek theater.

The Greeks believed the *theatron* (a show taking place in one's own city) was a festive show to which the gods and men came as spectators. The subject within the spectacle often showed men the way to achieve godliness. Invention became the way to reveal truth; theater was like a mirror which revealed what was concealed within the show. Gods watched the contradictions in human experience, contradictions which separated men from the gods and each other—and the gods laughed. Men are entertained, too, by their own ruinous and often miserable interactions with each other. "Before Zeus, the laughing onlooker, the eternal human race plays its eternal human comedy."[19]

Because both gods and men shared real contradictions, as well as watched them theatrically represented, there was an implied fraternity of existence. Differences between the two was through confrontation of idea-of-divinity with idea-of-humanity. The Greeks believed the confrontation of god and man made them become One.

Related to theatrical festivals was the element of representation and sacrifice to the god of a particular cult. The cult attempted to represent the performers in a festival as divine—and also as a gift to the divine. Cult members played, sacrificed and exaggerated in excess, to elevate themselves above the level of humanity into the free play of the gods. Such ecstasy carried playfulness to extremes, but also sadness and tragedy.

Thus the atmosphere of theater, as well as the spirit within camp offer the homosexual a mode to celebrate the tragicomedy of the existence judged by heterosexuals, as well as created by heterosexuals for their homosexual "brothers." Camp regulates as well as equalizes the alleged difference between heterosexuality and homosexuality:

The man at play shapes the whole world to a world of his own and becomes thereby its creator and god. Play is power. . . .[20]

If heterosexuals play the god to homosexuals, camp provides the homosexual with a celebrational moment of his own creation. He mocks the rigidity of sexual politics with a double-edged parody.

Another form of behavioral camp is that of camp rhetoric. Homosexuals who normally appear high in masculinity quotient, often relax in repartee which includes substitution of pronouns—"he" becomes "she." The pejorative term "Mary," the reference to other homosexuals as "girl" or "sister" all reflect a deliberate gender confusion usage which symbolizes the identity confusion the homosexual feels he has been given by heterosexuals. The homosexual has no positive role model offered to him in American society. He has been given a vaginal ascription which contradicts his knowledge of himself as a man.

Resistance to such subordination, as well as attempts to regulate pain through shared mockery, occurs in camp language. The homosexual feels caught in between; he says so through gender rhetoric. Gender confusion—or diffusion—also represents the heterosexual male's perception of men who can sexualize other men. Heterosexuals thus use feminine terms to categorize homosexuals. The terms are usually vaginal.

A typical judgment of how homosexuals depersonalize each other through language occurs in *Beyond Success and Failure* by Willard and Marguerite Beecher. In the chapter, "Homosexuality," they see "languaging" as apparently different from that of heterosexual males:

> At cocktail parties of homosexuals, or in their social evenings together, there is no tendency to explore subjects in a serious way below the surface. Things must be kept light and gay in the gay life. A prize is placed on cleverness and sarcasm; the process of taking the hide off a victim is called "bitching" him. This shallow, uncharitable form of conversation prevents homosexuals from finding any warmth, or human understanding, for an impersonal friendship that might otherwise arise if they were not competitive.[21]

Heterosexual males also use language content and forms for competition. One could easily parody the Beechers to comment on the nature of language between American men, regardless of sexual orientation.

> At cocktail parties of *hetero*sexuals, or in their social evenings together, heterosexual males discuss women, sports scores and

recreational accomplishments. Heterosexuals avoid expressing personal feelings about anything in an effort to keep communication light, distant and controlled. Heterosexuals prize cleverness, authority and sarcasm; the process is called "oneupmanship," "razzing," or "bullshitting" their victim. This shallow appearance of camaraderie prevents heterosexuals from achieving any depth to their male friendships. Emotional closeness might arise if there were not such socially ingrained competitions expected where such men gather.

So much for the Beechers' stereotypical analysis of stereotype.

What most heterosexual male semanticists miss in their analysis of homosexual conversation, is the deeper psychological structure of sarcastic wit in camp rhetoric. The lightness, pace and aggression within some homosexual repartee help regulate and release an anguish most homosexuals share in their socially denigrated "sisterhood." Shared self-mockery lessens the power of terms used by heterosexuals against them. Terminology and usage detaches homosexuals from themselves in momentary sprees of verbal catharsis. Behavioral and verbal self-effeminizing rejects, as well as accepts, those fellow victims of heterosexual subordination.

Blacks employ similar verbalization techniques. They use terms on each other, such as "nigger," "boy," and "brother," in ways which isolate them together and confirm their sense of extended family with all black people. In *Black Rage*, William H. Grier and Price M. Cobbs note that black patois, or special minority group language, helps the black American convey to whites and to each other ". . . That he is aware that he is perceived as inferior. . . ."[22] Black patois serves as an adaptive function ". . . Even though the circumstances to which adaptation must be made are less clear-cut and the nature of the adaptation itself may be unconscious."[23]

The "jive" language and the "hip" language, while presented in a way that whites look upon simply as a quaint ethnic peculiarity, is used as a secret language to communicate the hostility of blacks for whites, and great delight is taken by blacks when whites are confounded by the language.[24]

Thus, the "sisterhood" of the homosexual and the "brotherhood" of the black both stem from an adaptive function achieved through speech forms. While camp language is hostile to majority groups with flaunting and privilege, it also tightens in-group affiliation.

The play *The Boys in the Band,* by Mart Crowley, best illustrates camp language and behavior used in an apparently lethal manner. Long time homosexual friends gather at a birthday party where they ritualize language and behavior into an analysis of each self caught between polarized feminine and masculine role assignations. The rituals become verbal challenges to penetrate each other in order to find essential truth within their lives. They strip away subterfuge to reveal essences; they achieve a deeper and more honest commitment to each other through revelation of level after level of fiction and feeling.

Michael, the host, expects a heterosexual friend to arrive. He begins to lecture his friend Donald about the need to pretend they are heterosexual. Donald interrupts:

> Michael: . . . Now listen, Donald. . . .
> Donald: Michael, don't insult me by giving me any lecture on acceptable social behavior. I promise to sit with my legs spread apart and keep my voice in deep register.
> Michael: Donald, you are a real *card-carrying cunt.*[25]
> [emphasis in original]

Later, Alan, the straight friend arrives to witness the "Geriatrics Rockettes" dancing in chorus line, led by effeminate Emory. Events pass and Alan and Michael talk about Emory. Michael tries to camouflage homosexual Emory's camp behavior, which includes frequent exchange of masculine for feminine pronouns:

> Alan: I just can't stand that kind of talk. It just grates on me.
> Michael: What kind of talk, Alan?
> Alan: Oh, you know. His brand of humor, I guess.
> Michael: He can be really quite funny sometimes.
> Alan: I suppose so. If you find that sort of thing amusing. He just seems like such a goddam little pansy. I'm sorry I said that. I didn't mean to say that. That's an awful thing to say about *anyone.* But you know what I mean, Michael—you have to admit he *is* effeminate.[26]
> [emphasis in original]

Later, Michael turns against Alan in a savage attack; he points out Alan's repressed homosexuality and then dangerously proceeds to bind his homosexual group more closely together through forced revelation of their love objects. The savageness does not disintegrate, but rather solidifies their understanding of themselves and each other. This birthday party ritual of camp achieves an *esprit de corps*.

Such clannishness, achieved within *esprit de corps,* is an attempt to provide strategies for homosexual minority members to protect themselves from outside attack. *Esprit de corps* is a sharing of a special inferiority given homosexuals by heterosexuals. By cohering, homosexuals alleviate some of the burden of their "problem." This vaginal coping strategy employs camp language and behavior. It also provides a type of safe preference for one's "own kind" and thus activates prejudice against out-group members. One resulting characteristic is gravitation towards appreciation of symbols, events and expressions which are rejected by the stereotypical heterosexual male. Clannish support, either actual or affectional, for those elements considered feminine, enhances *esprit de corps* and allows the homosexual to accept his vaginal ascription with style and a feeling of greater social value.

The following activities and interests explore trends in homosexual achievement of *esprit de corps;* they do not represent all homosexuals—they often characterize heterosexual males as well. But for the heterosexual male, attachment of significance does not strengthen an in-group affiliation as is the case with homosexuals.

Homosexual males attach significance to the performing, graphic and fine arts. The opera, ballet, design, fashion, drama, the symphony—all have appeal for homosexuals who spectate, as well as create. Art Deco and Art Nouveau appeal to homosexuals. The fashion designs of Erté and Beardsley, historical films softened by nostalgia, certain literary works of emotional intensity, collection of antique *objets d'art,* biographies of famous homosexuals, recordings of Jazz Age blues singers—all are items selected as insignia for homosexual value.

Attachment of significance to events, items or expressions from the general cultural contributions, evidences general patterns of the homosexual male. He selects out what is beautiful, passed over by time, passionate and frequently vaginal in character or atmosphere, to create sub-culture insignia. Such insignia tend to elevate the homosexual above the general cultural milieu, even as he elevates those elements he chooses for admiration.

An illustration is the cultist attitude attached to film stars or specific films in which they starred. "Gone with the Wind," "A Streetcar Named Desire," "The African Queen," "The Sheik," "Sunset Boulevard," represent people who faced disaster with style and intensity. Vivien Leigh, Hepburn, Valentino, Gloria Swanson, have become cult subjects. Singers Judy Garland, Bessie Smith, Helen Morgan and Billie Holliday were adored by their public, as well as abandoned to live out their own forms of self-destruction. Lists of performers or performance vehicles are numerous and varied. Yet, a specific psychological attraction to, and affection for, artistic people and productions indicate reasons for identification by homosexuals exploring the vaginal they learn to accept.

Many homosexuals select out the remoteness of Garbo's beauty, the exaggerated grandness of Swanson, Garland's repeated salvaging of herself from disaster, the premature deaths, the victimizations by the public; homosexuals use such people and plots to represent their own tenuous existence in society. Most of these women, or men like Valentino, were used and abused by men. Escape into drugs, alcohol, suicide, or madness by cult figures was understood by many homosexual males. They face similar exploitation by men. The pathos within nostalgia, the romance within artistic creation attracts many homosexual males because such energy inspires an emotional renewal which contradicts the general heterosexual male disdain for emotional display.

Such emotional intensity and display of feminine style by homosexuals not only contradicts general heterosexual male interests, but also those of homosexual males eager to deny their vaginal assignment. At this point, an adjustment strategy occurs within the general homosexual minority group—in-fighting.

In-fighting among homosexuals is affected by so-called masculinity and femininity quotients valued by the heterosexual majority. The homosexual who denies his self-as-vaginal, feels shame for possessing the despised qualities of his group, e.g., effeminacy. Such self-hate turns against those members of his minority group because they possess those undesirable qualities to varying extremes. In-fighting is most commonly based on the heterosexual masculine-feminine acceptance and denial. Class distinctions occur within male homosexual groups. "Butch" homosexuals often avoid association with "fems." The "fems" resent the more masculinized homosexual for his attempts to lose his homosexual distinctions within the heterosexual male mystique. Both arguments appear based on choice of style.

All male homosexuals must explore the vaginal assignment given them by heterosexuals. Experimentation with style is necessary for self-definition. Appearance often indicates the degree of vaginal commitment the homosexual can tolerate. Appearance becomes a choice one makes to achieve psychological equilibrium according to the homosexual's current role conception. Appearance can shift from macho attire to transvestism.

The "drag" motif indicates a deeper trial merging into the feminine mystique. Some men become "drag queens" and appear or entertain publicly. Other men cross-dress privately within the dimension of their own fantasy. Some are occasional cross-dressers. New Year's, Halloween, or drag balls offer license for feminine costume. The "queen" aspect of attire presents a momentary relief from psychological contradictions implied in heterosexually polarized sex roles.

The women that heterosexual males venerate most are the movie queens, royalty at proms or other social ceremonies. Exaggerated feminine auras make such women desirable and socially approved. They are ultra-vaginal. They command male respect and dangle their favors before admiring males as a gift or trophy to be sought after, perhaps to be awarded if a man is worthy. The homosexual transvestite thus embraces an ultra-vaginal experiment in role definition. He enters into the feminine mystique to which he is banished by heterosexual males, and by which he is inauthentically defined.

Inauthentic vaginal ascription can indeed be converted into an authenticity by the homosexual, in order to achieve psychological equilibrium. The transvestite is in touch with the reality of gender division. Walter C. Alvarex speaks of such division as an ability to be a man for a while and then to forget his manhood while he becomes his female self.[27] Yet, such an explanation implies an impossible compartmentalization of the psyche. It becomes personality alternation.

What some homosexuals are capable of doing is really more of a dissolving of gender polarities. The masculine merges into the feminine to balance and relieve the inner tension experienced by social demands to be one or the other. *Simultaneity of gender* in transvestism symbolizes a wedding of body and mind; physical symbols express a masculine parody of the feminine. By expressing the ultra-vaginal in dress, or the effeminate through degrees of mannerisms and affectations, the homosexual achieves coalescence of vaginal mentality learned from the heterosexual milieu. Personally, the homosexual's vaginal mask worn on a male body does not mean he *is* "both." Simultaneity in transvestism is a cathartic revelation of paradoxical social roles. These roles camouflage and confine all males and females. The catharsis of revelation occurs within the apparent mutual exclusiveness of transvestism. It implies courage to attempt reconciliation with gender differences. It also implies vulnerability once the catharsis of revelation is acted out in public.

All women are vulnerable to men, within American society. Psychologically, socially, sexually and physically, many homosexual males feel or experience similar vulnerability to heterosexual males. To cross-dress publicly is to invite attack, scorn or misunderstanding. Public transvestism also challenges heterosexual gender stereotypes. As it attempts to reconcile the division between male and female roles, it seeks to come to terms with one's given or assumed effeminacy.

In an interesting and important article, "Sissies," written by Mark Thompson for *The Advocate,* the author explores the issue of homosexual male rejection of effeminacy. Many homosexuals enter the macho competition and politics of heterosexual males, and reject those men who experimentally probe the meanings of their vaginal assignment. Thompson argues that acceptance of vaginal assignment can be a positive opportunity to explore the feminine characteristics available to all people. Acceptance need not be a socially destructive behavioral set, but could offer the homosexual deeper emotional strength by acting out the full range of his human complexity:

> "Sissy." Chanted, inferred, denied. Few words in the male lexicon so universally hit the emotional bottom-line. It's a word with which to grow up and, for gay men in particular, a word to pray that "It doesn't mean me," although it usually did. . . . Our sisters have taken the rhetoric of "Don't" and have turned it into the power of "Why not?" For gay men it has become the plea-bargaining of "Are not," and it has left us emotionally crippled.[28]

Effeminate men face an in-fight within the homosexual group which attempts to assimilate into the heterosexual male motif. Effeminate men also face another strategy of acceptance of their vaginal role given by heterosexuals. *Out-fighting back* becomes minority frustration converted into aggression. Homosexuals refuse to tolerate further abuse of their vaginal assignment. Aggression occurs within homosexual ranks designated as more or less masculine and feminine. Aggression occurs against heterosexuals by both "masculine" and "feminine" homosexuals. Regardless of recipients of aggression, such aggression symbolizes a tacit acceptance of the homosexual identity and a rejection of its status.

Thus, the transvestite challenges heterosexual as well as the more masculine homosexual judgments against such effeminacy. The effeminate homosexual challenges the double standards of sexual attitude and behavior held by macho homosexuals. To them, any attempts to falsely claim androgyny implies sexual oppression. Such men falsely want to enlarge the space of their sexual capacities so they may claim everything which is male, as well as everything considered female. "The idea of 'swinging bisexuality' is part of it. Now, men have twice as many objects to fuck and still remain 'men.' "[29]

While effeminacy is an embarrassment to many homosexuals, as well as most heterosexuals, it is a militant statement in the style of counter-agression. Thus, many homosexuals wish to avoid such compulsive or sexually imagistic statements. Yet, homosexuals have difficult making distinctions between what is necessary or "right" forms of out-fighting back. They turn to political or activist organizations to improve their position in society. Within each activist homosexual group, a variety of images and styles, as well as often conflicting philosophy and strategy, provides additional opportunity for in-fighting and out-fighting back.

Such political and activist groups as the Mattachine Foundation, the National Gay Task Force, ONE, Inc., and the Gay Activists' Alliance provide legal counsel, public information, organized protest and legislative lobbying on behalf of homosexual needs and interests. Sexual minority counseling services and "community" centers provide one-to-one sharing of minority problems to help fortify the homosexual against self-defeat. Task forces exist to achieve liaison with other minority groups, churches, public schools and media outlets to counterattack negative images, information and judgments about homosexuality.

At the smaller group and individual level, out-fighting back assumes a variety of strategies and style. In 1969, the Stonewall Riot attained national attention when homosexuals fought police harrassment for three days on Christopher Street in New York City. They publicly declared gay pride and used The Stonewall bar incident to arouse militant homosexual consciousness. In 1973, the Lavender Panthers formed in San Francisco to combat homosexual beatings by roving heterosexual adolescents. *Time* Magazine reported that "Besides their goal of halting the attacks, the Lavender Panthers want to gainsay the popular notion that all homosexuals are 'sissies, cowards and pansies' who will do nothing when attacked."[30]

Additional forms of guerrilla warfare occur in public statements which both entertain and insult. They are a vulgarization of gender dichotomy, and a self and social satire. An entertainment group known as the "Cockettes" employed a militant art form to achieve the shock value of deformity in a camp manner:

> . . . The Cockettes present excellent imitations of our society's female "sex queens"—but with an ironic difference: either by sporting beards or by displaying their genitals, these performers make obvious their own masculinity. The result is what might be called "mind-blowing," both disorienting and satirical in impact. At a time when society has been sensitized by women's liberation to its problems with sex roles and gender identity, the gay community has produced an art form to illustrate our cultural ambiguities and contradictions.[31]

An offshoot of the Cockettes is the phenomenon of "gender-fuck," in which a man publicly and simultaneously combines aspects of male and female attire. A beard or mustache, hairy chest, earrings and make-up combine with skirt, motorcycle jacket and a woman's wig to "fuck" gender.

This conglomerate attire surfaces the range of a homosexual male's feelings and ability to perceive himself concurrently within gender extremes. The shock value to heterosexuals, as well as the political statement achieved, comes from parody of the either-or dichotomy. To have a penile role simultaneously linked with a vaginal one, is to fuck with oneself. Shocking. Impossible?

The heterosexual's angry dismissal or make-yourself-invisible is—"go fuck yourself." The homosexual male who publicly gender-fucks, argues against that banishment. He disobeys the command for remaining an invisible man for the political convenience and comfort of the heterosexual majority.

One group of male homosexuals select sexual invisibility and thus choose to submerge themselves totally into a vaginal role. The strategy of coping with a negative vaginal ascription, is to identify with it so strongly that one comes to find one's male genitalia unbearable. To correlate an internally admired, emulated or accepted vaginal self-concept requires a more complete alteration of visible male characteristics than transvestism offers. Transsexuals thus choose surgical mutilation of male genitalia, to compensate for their sense of sexual-social disassociation. Compensation through substitution offers the homosexual transsexual vaginal legitimacy and status.

Many transvestites and transsexuals argue that they are basically heterosexual. Perhaps what they believe they are is a legitimate definition for what they are. Perhaps their mental set is stronger than sexual assignment through anatomical and hormonal structures. Yet, the homosexual transsexual has possibly subscribed in some complex manner to a strategy for viewing the self in a masculine-feminine dichotomized society.

The male homosexual who wishes a vagina to be surgically substituted for a penis, intellectually achieves an organic balance to internal desire, social definition and role expectation. Moral and traditional conflicts are resolved. The society which disapproves of men sexualizing other men, offers approval to women sexualizing men. The homosexual transsexual thus becomes an invisible homosexual who remains attracted to men as sexual objects. Such an illusion of being vaginal results from the strong need to reconcile oneself to social demands that anatomy dictates sexual role, and that sexual role constitutes one's sexual identity.

The illusion of being vaginal thus emanates from social dictation of sexual monologues. Transsexuals act them out to the extreme. Perhaps an answer exists to the question, " '. . . What does cutting your penis off change? Isn't the whole thing all in your head?' "[32] Acceptance of the vaginal through sexual surgery achieves a form of status fantasy. Inability to tolerate male-to-male sexuality, inability to cope with social denigration, perhaps lead some male homosexuals to elevate their sense of minority status through genital substitution. Such status fantasy then serves as a paradigm for the American male's tendency to make vaginal all that he uses or does to ratify his phallic identity.

In the article, "Mixed Singles," by Andrew Kopkind, the author comments on transsexuals who mutilate their bodies and practice exaggerated feminine behavior to pass for women. He notices that American sexual labels tend to correlate genitalia with identity. In speaking of Renee Richards nee Dick Raskind, the ophthalmologist and tennis player who chose surgical sex re-assignment, Kopkind concludes:

> . . . Her story becomes a metaphor for America right now: the sexual ambiguity, the identity crisis, the instant renewal, the complete retooling, the self-absorption.[33]

Gender cannot be established by genitalia, transvestism, hormones, surgery or behavior. Gender identity remains an individualized response to one's self-concept in tension with the images, concepts and expectations mixing together in one's society. Given the American penchant for clear cut categorizations, then status fantasy, out-fighting back, in-fighting, *esprit de corps,* humor, assimilation, claims to bisexuality and androgyny form negative strategies for men coping with the vaginal status of homosexuality.

Yet, these strategies drain the full human potential of male homosexuals in America. Once they accept themselves as value violators, they also accept the heterosexual male's devaluation of them as vaginal. The following dialogues speak to the male homosexual's degrees of vaginal ascription by the heterosexual majority. They offer rephrasing of heterosexual monologues which many homosexuals struggle to deny, or accommodate to accept. Rephrasing of such monologues is necessary to the psycho-social well being of homosexuals within their minority milieu.

The necessity is whimsically, as well as tragically, caught in the comment of Christine Jorgensen, an older transsexual of equal fame to Renee Richards. In speaking of attempts to align psychological sex orientation with social definition of role, Jorgensen says:

> "All in all," she told a friend not long ago, "I've got all the problems of a middle-aged woman, along with all the problems of a middle-aged man."[34]

Many homosexual males share the burden of varying degrees and kinds of Jorgensen's sexual paradox.

Yet, the heterosexual monopoly of sexual behavior through privilege, command and social pressure can be resisted. Conversion to dialogues of such heterosexual monologues, help reveal the illusion within alleged sexual paradox. Dialogues contradict the political dream and psychological wish of heterosexual males to render the other as vaginal. The homosexual thus figures in reality as another, rather than merely an expedient other.

3/DIALOGUES: The First Series
Exits from the Men's Room of
Vaginal Space

> . . . If man stops developing his consciousness of
> freedom it tends to weaken for lack of exercise.[1]
> —Bruno Bettelheim, *The Informed Heart*

The following dialogues for the homosexual male do not offer a panacea for personal and social difficulties he experiences in life. They do not provide foolproof formulae to reconstruct the realities of existence in a homophobic society like America's. They do offer forms of rephrasing negative images, behavioral structures and value judgments which thwart the homosexual's potential realization of himself as a positive person.

The homosexual need not be reactive to internal or external pronouncements against his affectional preference. The homosexual could be more active in initiating his own self-concept, his own guiltless interaction with others, and his own choices for his life as he wishes to construct it. Modern technology, mass production and growing anonymity within a mass society, create problems for the individual. They also provide many benefits which make personal problems seem tolerable, or at least resolvable.

Technology offers the individual dependency on experts to solve social and personal problems. The option exists to give up autonomy to others and find relief in personal problem solving through dependency on others. One who does not resist the convenience of submission to others is apt to be easily governed by his society, as well as by personal desires which find no outlet except through fantasy.

American society is constructed by beliefs and values transmitted through symbolic language. With language, we consent to construct external realities to match the interior structures of our minds. We consent to create, construct and control for the good of society. We consent, individually, to match the social good by personally representing that social structure within ourselves. There is no real need to do this. Such a casually accepted social contract is assumed through early growth and maturation into conformity to our social models. We imitate, rather than create our sense of identity.

The imitated self receives social approval if it conforms to socially defined good. Imitation becomes the convenient mode of living for many Americans. Inconvenience occurs when internal desires, feelings and concepts do not match the current social contract to reflect valued norms, which help locate the social contract as being real. That such reality is often visionary, utilitarian and always political, does not occur to the individual as he compares himself to norms.

In America, the social good is proximity to imaginary norms. Average is the range of comfort, convenience and acceptability for thought and behavior. Average is the beginning point for construction of category, creation of value hierarchy and ratification of the social contract.

Homosexuals dislocate the forward flow of society through its normative structures of thought and behavior. Homosexuals disrupt society's attempt to categorize and control reality. Any disruption to a normative flow of conceptual beliefs—whether by race, religion, sex, age or any other minority qualification—requires the concerned majority to relocate such disruption imaginatively and actually.

Relocation can be achieved by sharply defining dislocation as an obvious positive, negative or neutral proximity to consensual norms or averages. Such definitions are always monologues of evaluation, which originate in the imagination and extend into society as laws, rituals, traditions and normative expectations. Because men tend to describe through evaluation, in relation to artifically selected norms, one could argue that the terms homosexual and heterosexual do not exist except as evaluative conveniences.

Homosexual describes nothing which is superior or inferior to the term heterosexual. They are both behavioral labels which serve as categories. Both carry categorical imperatives which command an individual to imitate characteristics of either classification. Imperatives thus serve as behavioral guides.

Behavior also serves as judgment. The homosexual becomes socially dislocated from the heterosexual majority. By social consent, he is taught symbolically and actually to imitate socially prescribed monologues which guarantee his chronic sense of dislocation. The homosexual then acts out his imitated self which is conveniently provided by society. He conforms to the good representation of the bad homosexual; such conformity makes life tolerable as he learns to depend on others' definitions for himself.

Dialogues contradict heterosexual monologues of distortion, despotism and defeat. Dialogues challenge the comfortable consent to imitate internal norms through external behaviors, which often leave the individual feeling alien, artificial and without control of himself. Dialogues establish personal location for the self.

The homosexual male can energetically become more self-loving and other-loving, by sharing himself as he is, rather than as he is told he should be. Being, is the ultimate responsibility of one person alone. In becoming, one draws from the many social resources each person shares with others. Becoming what one could be is the adventure in living, the challenge of self-fulfillment for the homosexual.

Dialogues between self and others, provide the *beginning* of self-renewal for the homosexual. From thought proceeds action. From creative manipulation of ideas, proceeds the dynamic re-creation of the self. Through each hour and event, one confronts and absorbs one's self forward into life. The unique integration of thought with being, is captured in the wisdom of an Old Testament appraisal of man's nature:

For as he thinketh in his heart, so is he. . . . *Proverbs* 23:7 (KJV)

1. As a homosexual male, how should I view the world of people, events and things around me?

I live in two worlds; the one is inside my mind and feelings, and the other is the one I share with others. There are similarities between both worlds as well as differences. The world inside of me is primary. I must be careful to select the best *for me,* from the shared world. I must internalize such friendships, loves, activities and desires for material goods which fulfill me, rather than confine me in states of longing, frustration or confusion.

I do not need everything. I can have something. I do not need to shape myself identically to the commercial theories of my social world. I do not need to emotionally impoverish myself according to social standards of success. I can select out such values, experiences and things which I think necessary for my own enrichment.

Why I select what I do does not require that I believe social definitions of purpose or motive. Such definitions of purposeful living are purely arbitrary. There is no purpose to life, beyond my own choosing. I must become more conscious of which standards are socially constructed, and which are personally constructed. Social standards of value and success are received, rather than conceived. I learn them from others, who then judge me by them. I must learn to refuse. I must learn who and what to accept for myself.

As I begin to restructure my interior world, I also desire to reveal inner facets of myself to my world around me. My sexuality is one facet of my whole identity. How I communicate and share the whole of me depends on my recognition of appropriateness to context or occasion. Conscious degrees of self-revelation must be balanced against the absence of absolute certainty in any social interaction. I must become accustomed to the discomforts of anxiety. Such feelings follow my rejection of security that could be maintained by repeating imitations of social norms.

If I attempt to repeat majority modalities, I am tempted to hide in heterosexual models of the self-as-majority. If I embrace characteristic homosexual models, I tend to resign myself to alternation between acceptance and denial of self-as-minority. Both extremes direct me towards a passivity of consciousness. My being is paralyzed. I caricature myself. I imitate what others design for me.

In contrast to passive consciousness, the active consciousness penetrates my internal and external worlds with a growing sense of integrating both environments. Conscious inner control creates my own sense of significance. I carry that significance into my shared world. Such dynamic penetration does not allow me the right to phallically argue others into vaginal confinement. Penetration requests the privilege of congruency. A state of mutual accord or agreement is the ethical territory in which I must function. The phallic state is one of domination through self-seeking gratification. Its ethic is that of expedient relief.

Thus, vaginal conversion of others, or even of myself, maintains the politico-sexual illusion of dominance and submission. In vaginal contexts which I create or allow, I then become a master or slave in what converts to ultimate sexual struggles for power. Such dichotomy becomes convenient within relationships. Dichotomy reduces the struggle and ambiguity always present in the balance between equals. There exists the tendency to identify with whom I confront. Identification carries the potential for imitation. The slave and master, jailed and jailor or the discriminated and discriminator, need each other for identity. Those who are discriminated against learn early the techniques and rewards of discriminating against others.

Therefore, I must resist the comfort of dichotomy and accept the efforts towards balance in relationships. My world model for myself—and others—exists between the phallic and vaginal polemic. I am more than either; I include aspects of both. The right to model myself with my own beliefs and images, includes the rights of others to construct themselves according to their own design. If my right is denied, then the authenticity in any relationship is diminished. If I deny others, then I impose a constricting monologue of imperative upon them. Sexuality has no imperative. The phallic or vaginal vehicle of sexuality contains no intrinsic power value by itself. Conversion of people or contexts into sexual imagery redesigns reality to suit the dominant phallic mode. The operation of that mode assumes imbalance. Perpetuation of that mode thus occurs within the institutionalized beliefs of the male majority in America, which attaches power values to sexual imagery and performance.

When I locate myself freely within my social institutions—as a homosexual male—I enlarge the narrow definitions by which many are forced to live. I enlarge the world of possibility by confronting the tyranny of sex for what it is. Illusionary value judgments are attached to the many perplexing series of opposites which comprise our lives. Such value judgments become tyrannical when they stop defining opposites, and attempt to control the threatening ambiguities in them.

Ambiguities are not controlled; *people* become the monitored, the diagnosed and the discriminated. When such ambiguities are resolved by labelling them as deficiencies, weaknesses or aberrations, the tyrant then plays the role of benefactor. The benefactor reasonably protects society by "helping" the "helpless" deficient, weak and aberrant victim.

Thus, homosexuals are judged as opposite to heterosexuals. As opposites, they carry an ambiguous quality. Their qualities are allegedly diagnosed, criminally charged, treated or otherwise relocated in the heterosexual institutional framework. Such logic emerges from the self-serving rationale within the tyranny of sexual politics.

My world view must include a conscious resistance to the false benefaction of my heterosexual tyrant. I am not helped when I am involuntarily relocated into negative roles which imitate the illusions of the phallic state. I must refuse my vaginal role, even as I refuse to impose a parody of that role on others.

I must rephrase the opposites within myself to achieve an integration of my potential personality. Integration includes the viewing of myself as complementary to those opposites beyond myself. Opposites will continue to exist. I cannot wish myself to be other than what I am. I cannot will others to become expedient to my desires.

I must generally expect heterosexuals to prefer to define my "sexual opposition" as dangerous. Their definitions confine me within imaginary conveniences which act as vaginal monologues. I am morally obligated to resist their tyranny over the existence of opposites, and over the natural progression of life's innumerable variations.

As a homosexual, I am necessary in our social biosphere. I contribute myself as one human being among many, sharing my unique existence in concert with others to design the best possible destiny for humanity.

2. *Heterosexuality and homosexuality are constructed as categories of extreme. Categories then label people with role expectations. How can a homosexual male avoid the confinement of labels?*

Division of people into groups, by using labels of male or female, homosexual or heterosexual, creates a "groupthink" reaction. The individual person is eradicated, and is conveniently treated as a label. Labels allow the user to recreate people for biased interests, needs and desires. Labels do not demand discriminating thought. They permit emotional reaction to replace logical decision. They minimize the potential range of interaction between two persons, who are really more than what their arbitrary label describes.

When I, as a homosexual, label a man as "significant other," "lover," "trick," or "number," I convert that man into a categorical series of behaviors which I wish to fulfill my expectations. I often eroticize men to suit my sexual fantasies or emotional desires. Their own self interests become submerged in the utility of function I create for them. I can also serve the self interests of other homosexuals, if I merely become a functional instrument which satisfies their momentary interest.

When the label or role I give other men becomes attached to such task accomplishment, they are converted to sexual instruments. To typecast other men is to tempt them to believe they are not reacting to labels, but are really playing themselves. As I respond to their role, I authenticate their performance.

Yet, often the performance is only impersonation—an imitation of labels a man acts out according to the characteristics of his category. Thus, as a homosexual, I can help another homosexual engage in fairly competent performances. Then the probability exists that we grow unable to distinguish between the imitation and the genuine, within ourselves and between each other.

When I meet a man, I must practice eroticizing his whole person, without designing a limited agreement to know each other sexually. Relationships do not have to be performances of style or skill, which serve as means to our private ends. A male-to-male relationship begins with initial recognition of the other's freedom to be more than a phallic object which performs on command. Friendship develops as I consciously control and deny my preoccupation with phallic competition. Friendship deepens on multiple levels, if I resist converting another man into a vaginal territory subject to my domination, pleasure or control.

Eroticization of the whole personality of another requires my own wholeness within a mutual social contract. I feel security because he does; I experience the energy of involvement, because he moves into the same field of consciousness which I provide. I take love, because I offer it in a reciprocity of freedom from imitation of erotic elements which I have falsely learned as part of a sexual program.

Sexual programs contain the props and themes which promise relief from anxiety, loneliness and insecurity. The misleading certainty of labels only deceives me to require patterned responses from another man. They distort my own expressions into repetitive attempts to duplicate a genital contract that matches my fantasy expectations.

My fantasies imitate those behaviors I have learned to attach to labels which I give to other men. Overdependence on fantasy attachments restricts them, and myself, to a psychological confinement—the trap of habit. If I reject the convenience of labels which others give to me, I must also reexamine those labels I impose on them.

Thus, even as I initially view a man as heterosexual, homosexual, lover or trick, I lose the man within the category. He disappears into an impersonal realm of sexual fragmentation, rather than erotic wholeness. He must imitate the traits which I attach to a suitable performance—meaning the burden of chronic arousal of each other to act and act again.

Perhaps when I encounter each man I meet, I need to practice meeting him without expectation. I need to learn that unconscious labeling falsely guarantees a certainty to expectation. The dynamic within my presentation of erotic wholeness is really that of uncertainty. To expect nothing, to withhold nothing, is to create the framework for anything. The infinite possibility of everything surmounts the limitation of categories and their attendant labels.

"Groupthink" promises a compromise between the anxiety of uncertainty, and the impossible ideal of total knowledge. It argues for a resolution of opposites and control of extremes. Groupthink has always hindered heterosexual thinking and interacting with homosexuals. Adoption by homosexuals of this mode of discernment by group conclusion, only distorts potential knowledge of one man by another. It confines each man within his tiny role, and habituates him to gradually forget who he could be—to someone else.

3. *How can the homosexual reevaluate the confining vaginal aspect to male space?*

I recognize that heterosexual males have defined the vaginal ethic as, "Fuck, or be fucked." Such an ethic socially and erotically divides people into two categories: the passive and the active. As a homosexual male, I am included within this traditionally socialized male view. My thinking and acting often alternate between these socio-sexual identity extremes. Alternation retains the element of conflict between opposites. Yet, mere integration of both views also offers conflict of interest—mine with someone else's.

In the vaginal style of passivity, I become oriented to outside sources for gratification of my needs and desires. I want to be loved, rather than act as lover. I "fall" in and out of love, or what circumstantially substitutes for appearances of love. I drift from one man to another, because I am paralyzed when I don't receive constant attention, confirmation and security from my external sources.

Since I cannot say "yes" for myself, I say "yes" to others without anticipating the consequences of my indiscriminate encounters. I reject making decisions by myself. I avoid responsibility for sexual involvements. I need others to sexualize me, so that I can believe I am not alone. I depend on chronic reinforcement from words and actions which prove I am desirable. I am afraid of losing sexual resources which act as reasons for my being alive.

My anxieties reduce my efforts to create myself. I allow others to use me sexually and socially, and then I know—for a while— who and what I am. I fear withdrawal of others, because I fear to lose the security their definitions give me.

I constantly search for a "lover." Until "it" arrives, I masturbate my fantasies. I wait for someone to create a context for me—often casual, usually sexual—and I watch time pass within a mirror of frequency.

I contain a corresponding aspect to my vaginal passivity. It also makes me actively search outside myself for personal gratification. I lack the ability to be original. I copy style and mannerisms. I perpetuate the appearance of activity, because I use whomever or whatever is good looking, interesting and vogue. I cruise and hustle. I want to take what others have, because I believe I don't have much inside of me to offer others. I am body conscious. I stress performance. I entice men away from their security in a lover, friends or a crowd of alternatives.

I tend to fall in love with those who are able to be exploited. I know these relationships won't last. That is why I choose them. I quickly become annoyed or disappointed with another man. I claim he bores me, because I drain him of what little personal or sexual variety he is able to offer. I call his deficiency my logical reason for release from a relationship that offers no future. I justify my freedom and my supremacy each time I conquer and quit what I begin. His worth did not match my continued efforts. I rationalize, and thus ignore, my own feelings of worthlessness.

These active and passive polarities within vaginal ethics, stem from heterosexual models which helped socialize me. Images of ideas, imitations of ideals which my society values, shape my own modes of relating to others. Like heterosexual males, I reflect social values which have utilitarian popularity. As a homosexual male, I must examine my tendency towards reflexive operation of phallic attitudes within a vaginal frame of reference. If heterosexuals use this attitude with me, perhaps I unconsciously use it against other men, and myself. "Fuck, or be fucked," is the political concept within a sexual metaphor. Its false dichotomy creates a psychological ethic for males who wise to serve, or be served. It is *unconscious* desire, shaped to imitate a phallic self within a vaginal other. The correspondences between "male" symbolic values and social operations, are then defined by penile and vaginal concomitance.

This vaginal aspect to male space alienates me from others, as well as potential dimensions of my own person. I tend to socially absorb the propaganda of sexual technique. Images of masculine success become my authority and pattern for behavior. If I fuck, or seek to be fucked, I reinforce alternating patterns of dependency, by searching for self confirmation through others. I become dependent on social illusions, which I mistakenly and habitually designate as my own thoughts or beliefs.

I learn the messages of social propaganda: I should appear chic, have sex often, acquire possessions, travel, stay in shape, be socially active, behave appropriately to my context, and consider taking a lover . . . and yet not be overly serious about it. I should become a reasonable facsimile to all that my society says is desirable or desired. Thus, I forfeit myself to pursuit of illusions of myself. Such manufactured social illusions, I imagine I create for myself.

Productive reevaluation of the male aspect of vaginal thought, activity and existence begins with examination of my self knowledge. Do I exaggerate my focus on imitating or conquering external style, feeling and other beings? Do I disunite myself from whom I could be, as I simulate who, and what, I am told I should be? If I "fuck my brains out," I remain unconscious to the vaginal fallacy. If I attempt to integrate the passive-active dichotomy, I only rotate conveniently between opposing perspectives.

Specific expressions of who I am, generally tend to correspond to those objects or subjects of my will to be. Who I am, can exist individually—without imitation. When I respond, I exchange. If I love, as an expression of who I am, but am not loved in return—I need to reassess the validity of my self expressions. If I am unable to exchange love, perhaps I operate in my vaginally active or passive dimension. Then I only simulate a limited form, rather than essence, of loving. If I cannot become a *beloved* person, I also need to evaluate the validity of the other's expression of himself. I must not permit partial participation. Synthetic exchanges do not substitute for truthful mutuality of feeling, action and appreciation.

Self knowledge is only the beginning point of vaginal denial. It is recognition that I am human, and I must exchange myself in human ways with other men. Such humanity implies an individual growth towards completion. The mechanics of technique, energized by the logic of submission and domination, are only artifices of momentary gratification. Technique offers no guarantee for success within a relationship. Quality becomes lost in the concentration on performance. Capacities for human completion diminish to transient arenas of win or loss. The paradigm for such passionate seeking of completion, is the restless quest for possession, maintenance and momentary enjoyment of the elusive erectile state in self and others. The transciency of erectile projection, matches the limitation of a vaginal attitude. Both promise an imaginary shortcut to human definition.

To be passionately human implies an unflagging devotion to every aspect of personal growth. Growth appears through change, as well as exchange. Loyalty for loyalty, love for love, trust for trust, balance internal realities with external possibilities. The inner balance of my self, can only help to balance my relationship with other men. We are then both released from the imbalance of male space. We are freed from the unfairly divided portions of social roles—the categorical imperatives—which separate us into active-passive, phallic-vaginal or insertor-insertee.

Rejection of masculine motives and denial of sexual power decrees, can then dissolve "male space" into limitless human possibility. To act, to be, to love without illusion—frees the homosexual from emotional entrapment in isolation defined by roles. Such roles mark the utilitarian borderlines within the imperfect imagination of heterosexual males. They impose their imagination upon social reality, to contain such human differences which seemingly appear to threaten the logic of their vaginal illusion.

The homosexual need not accept this logic as his own. I am vaginal only if I imagine I am. I do not exist within the narrow logic of the heterosexual dream. I can resist participation as a shadow person who appears consistently within the heterosexual nightmare—upon command.

4. What happens to me, if I attempt to deny my capacity for loving other men?

My capacities for love are as diverse as any heterosexual male's emotional ability and expression. As I seek loving companionship with other men, I recognize my outreach is made tenuous by my society's fear of men who love other men. The reality of my own capacities and desires is called into question by heterosexual males who cannot act out their own affections for their sex. They wish to contain or destroy what they do not understand. They hesitate to allow the legitimacy of my existence, because I threaten the legitimacy of their masculine mythology.

Heterosexual mechanisms of sexual vigilance and hypersensitivity towards maintenance of masculine norms, often become mechanisms of my own defense. I am what heterosexual males consistently reassure themselves they're not. The manifestation of homosexuality—in whatever manner—challenges the validity of American maleness. Thus, I am socially enjoined to deny the appearances of my own identity. To do so distorts the essence of my reality.

In addition to my threat to heterosexual males, I am also a symbol of anxiety to *homosexual* males. They are conscious that our public interaction with each other sometimes becomes a social confirmation of their homosexual identity. Our interaction always internally confirms the sense of tension within the homosexual's self concept. I represent the opposition to the heterosexual ideal; I represent the ambiguity of sexual definition within most homosexuals' unconscious accommodation to heterosexual expectations.

I tend to adapt myself to both heterosexual and homosexual males with degrees of camouflage—which become self-destructive techniques of survival. This is the crux of paradox in my homosexual existence. To survive, I practice modes of pretense even as I yearn towards authenticity. I notice that pretense to survive with heterosexuals, merges with my dealings with homosexual men. Perhaps this is why confirmation of lasting love with another homosexual, seems to fail to last . . . so often.

In repeated casual encounters with men, I sometimes hide behind the facade of sexual performance. I maintain degrees of anonymity beneath the sexual cosmetic of calculated subterfuge. No one notices *me;* my reality is in *what I do.* As I hide, I gain distance from myself, as well as my sexual partner. Forms of withholding then block the liberating possibilities of love.

When I choose a man, and live with him, I attempt to isolate myself with one whom I think can release each aspect of my human capacity. Yet, the heterosexual expectations for maleness often habituate my responses to my companion. I continue to hide the range of feelings, ideas and goals which could possibly incorporate another into myself. I remain selectively anonymous within the safety of mere sexual activity. Sex is the safer dimension.

I play at experiencing the daily events which people share in growing together. I have little experience with the larger dimensions of life shared with another. My social models are transferred to the structure of my shared reality—with difficulty. Such models do not prepare me to love another man. I model myself in imitation; I sense my partner's recognition of the synthetic quality of my performance. I rely on sexual performance to fortify our bond. I steel myself against his discovery that he really doesn't know who I am. I want to tell him, but I don't always know how to argue against an illusion.

Another self-destructive survival technique related to that of withholding, is one of self absorption. The anxiety of rejection by other men, is countered by my becoming lost in endless preoccupation with a search for self confirmation in others. I become absorbed in a restless ritual of despair. What I claim I look for, I hope I will not find. Discovery would necessitate commitment. It would stop the process which has become a mode of my existence. I am anyone to everyone. I adapt to serial circumstance. My existence is relative to sexual intensity within each new encounter. I must have many encounters which make me feel accepted and desired.

I sleep with many men. Yet to sleep with one, in a perpetual commitment to responsibility as someone, frightens me. I restlessly continue to redefine the meaning of myself in opposition to heterosexual definitions of denial. I absorb myself into the many variations in role which characterize the homosexual milieu. I experiment with trial identities which perfectly simulate the heterosexual ideal of masculine behavior. I attempt achievement of the androgynous posture, by alternating between playing the masculine and feminine part. I experiment with various caricatures of vaginal roles adopted by homosexuals. Each alternative to self denial absorbs me more deeply into concern for display, into imitations of myself which offer others discreet denial of my real capacity for love.

I yearn to legitimize myself to other homosexuals. I wish to love against the anxiety that argues me away from myself, that keeps me distant from others. Unless I learn to legitimize my sense of existence for myself, I cannot exist for others. And then I will have reached the final stage of self denial—that of habitual annihilation which love cannot redeem.

I cannot truly love another homosexual as he is, until I learn to love who and what I am. Because who I am has no necessary connection to what I do, my capacity for loving men speaks only partially about my identity. To overly enlarge my sexual activity with men, in my mind, is to succumb to the sexual distortion of me within the heterosexual's mind. To rationalize that activity is to destroy the possibility for love to motivate what I do, as well as to energize the personality I share with others. To embrace the fulness of meaning within any sexual expression with another man is to accept one small beginning to the complexity of my identity.

My complexities are formed by multiple differences in my character structure. No two human structures are identical. Social character does not exist. Character is uniquely personal and individual. Social character attempts to reflect and dictate the arbitrary ideals chosen by the majority as politically serviceable. Human character contains the variations and mutualities which allow me my place within the human context.

If I allow myself to be convinced that I threaten the social character, I will spend my life denying my humanity because I live and love differently from the male majority. Self denial of my character structure causes me to selectively dismantle myself in obedience to conformity. Self acceptance of who I am, inspires self confidence to act out appreciation of my own complexities. I am freed from the necessity of paradox which tempts me to search for an excuse for myself.

I am my own reason for being as I am, for doing what I do. My acceptance of my own reason, rather than the negative techniques of rationalization, helps other homosexuals to accept themselves. The logic of self love lends reasonable freedom and spontaneity to others gripped by habitual self denial. Love offered reveals me, to them, intruding into the monotony of lonely rituals of denial. Love seeks out and holds to those hidden, valuable differences we share. One man loving another, constructively.

5. *How can I achieve honest relief from the coercion of mass homophobia?*

Homosexual males represent a form of honest independence which frightens heterosexuals. If honesty represents freedom from deception, then many homosexuals threaten to reveal the deceitful oppressiveness within the sexual-political structure of the heterosexual majority. That sexual behavior actually is the basis for social politics, is underscored by the excessive fear, hysteria, hatred and forms of punishment created for homosexual men.

Male-dominated society creates rules for voluntary sexual behavior, then attaches values to these rules to create consensual control through personal feelings and group sanction. Voluntary sexual behavior is made involuntary through the design of image and ideal transmitted into society through law, religion, artistic structures, the media, science and folkways.

The motive behind the design is psychological and social control of behavior. The hidden rules attempt to convey to all that there are constants to which each person must adhere—to be "normal," to be "good," or to be "masculine."

The homosexual, as anyone might, participates in his society through contact with immediate experience. Intervening between him and his own experience are the mythical patterns of social context containing images and ideals which act as rules or guides for appropriate living. Such guidelines for testing one's experience are heterosexual definitions which describe and categorize people and their behavior into status hierarchies. These function together to give coherence and progressive thrust to social life.

Homosexuality is then a form of *rule reversal.* When I have sex with another man, I am trained to feel I have broken various rules, and therefore I am not playing the social game correctly or fairly. Yet, my own sexuality in voluntary association with another, is realistically defined by the rules of my own nature. Such independence challenges the various forms of relationship management used by heterosexual majorities against minorities. Relationship management is based on the logic of predeciding the differences between the real and the counterfeit.

Such predetermined logic is frozen within social consciousness and activity through construction of metaphors, which present behavioral ideals as real. My imitation of ideals, or my likeness to metaphors, supposedly helps me and others to decide whether I am real or counterfeit. "He plays like a girl," "You bitch," "I can't stand fairies," are all negative metaphors which can compare homosexuals to women, and which brand homosexuals as counterfeit men.

Metaphorical logic is merely a language tool used by heterosexuals to define, control and condemn the homosexual who reverses masculine rules for sexual behavior. As a homosexual, I represent the real potential within heterosexual males to eroticize men also. I reveal the artificially manufactured character to the strategies they use to block emotional and physical contacts with other men. I depict a legitimate reason for their illegitimate *subliminal* forms of same-sex interest.

They must not appear to be like me, or the whole dishonest framework of the masculine conception will be shown as nothing more than imaginary metaphors for masculinity made obligatory. Even if heterosexuals wish to avoid being "like me," they ironically enter this metaphorical trap by symbolically elevating masculine features to admire. Their dictum: "Look, but don't touch!"

Approved symbols of masculinity are used to define manhood on the basis of *distance*. Proximity towards or away from women—as socially dictated—and from other men—as socially provided by competition—forms the psychological parameters of masculine symbols. As a homosexual, I threaten clear delineation of psychic distance in both emphases on proximity. I appear to destroy the necessary difference between the male-to-female behavioral mode. I seem to shrink that psychic distance considered necessary between men.

Heterosexuals deny what they internally fear. They project intolerable desire and socially false assumptions onto their external threat factor—the homosexual. Thus, my honest attempts to respond behaviorally as a person—to either heterosexual or homosexual—become distorted by heterosexually projected fears and judgments. My responses become contradictions to the majority "game plan" for social strategies of survival, production and profit.

As a homosexual, I cheat and I soon learn that people expect me to be morally, psychologically, legally and socially dishonest. Homosexuals then share the burden together of successfully or unsuccessfully proving to each other that they can honestly create viable, meaningful and satisfying relationships. That so many homosexuals succeed, is a tribute to the active integrity of the human spirit. That so many homosexuals fail perhaps points to the potency of heterosexual relationship management to force personal congruency to social ideals.

I can twist my natural inclinations and attitudes to suit, or become congruent with, those heterosexual laws, religious pronouncements and social traditions which evaluate me as deviant or dishonest. My own attempts at honesty can become warped by secrecy, tainted by guilt, repressed through fear and stifled by self doubt. The result: the heterosexual fear of losing access to their masculine identity based on rules for sexual behavior, converts into *my ownership of fear.*

Once I have learned to fear others, as well as myself, I have accepted the dishonesty of heterosexual logic as a lie for myself. I have voluntarily given up management of myself. The fatigue factor of fear, allows me to feel that I must hide, deceive or seek help from others. I fatigue myself with patterns of congruency, as I attempt to imitate the truth or lie of social logic. The available benevolences which concerned heterosexuals offer me, give me minimal comfort and keep me psychologically dependent. The available punishments extend my fatigue of fear.

There are current opportunities for homosexual males to resist submission to dishonesty. I do not need to continue to learn defeat. I do need to understand how to discriminate between truth and negative atmosphere, between honesty and subtle capitulation to false metaphors. Such distinctions are finely drawn in intrahomosexual writings, activities and commercial productions. Imagistic differences can be even more subtly conveyed within heterosexual sources concerning homosexuality. Both often carry psychological and social messages which again entrap the homosexual in a dishonest frame of reference.

I need to comparatively and critically read fiction and nonfiction about myself as a homosexual. I need to view films and plays with homosexual themes. I need to select productive opportunities for participation with other homosexuals. Discussion groups, volunteer work, bowling teams, sailing clubs, religious endeavors and college campus meetings provide some alternatives to share myself with other homosexuals in typical social structures.

I need to observe, listen and discuss varying interpretations of my identity. Then I should intellectually compare differences between my real and socially defined expectations for myself. I would profit from emotional and ideological support systems which could fortify me against destructive forms of fear. I must recognize such destructive forms are often transmitted between homosexual males, as well as from heterosexual males. My alertness to myths and stereotypes shared by my whole society concerning masculinity, help me to understand my unique position in relation to all men. Understanding at least allows me a conscious defense against my social and personal vulnerability to systems which appear to offer me support, and those which contain none at all.

My sharing with other homosexuals what I think, feel and perceive can then enlarge our collective consciousness. Yet, in sharing with homosexuals, I must also be aware that *collective consciousness can easily become institutionalized into collective conscience.* Heterosexual norms can be exchanged for new homosexual prescriptions, which homosexuals use to bind each other together in rules for appearance, behavior and belief.

Homosexuals need to become sensitive to American social trends which measure and control human behavior, according to technological patterns of predictable norms. Behavioral modification is the concern of most social institutions in America. Business, schools, the armed services, marketing, applied research and the media all shape American males towards the mythologies of normative social-sexual behavior.

In the shared process of learning and testing one's position in society, each is consciously and unconsciously modified into a personal translation of collectively held averages or norms. The negatively normal homosexual models are included in collective heterosexual patterns, to emphasize heterosexual superiority, legitimacy and integrity.

The major theme of American masculinity is acquired distance from femininity. Its corollary is homophobia. Heterosexuals attempt to understand their exaggerated fear. They treat the homosexual phenomenon by applying deterministic thinking in yet another form of political protection through normative strategies. Heterosexuals search for antecedent "causes" for homosexuality, in order to predict negative "effects" of homosexuality. As a homosexual, I am logically understood and treated within metaphorical constraints imagined as medicine, law, religion and tradition.

Identity achieved through fear of self and others is a common feature to heterosexual life. Attempts at honest evaluation of social hypocrisies and mythical content is an additional feature. As a homosexual, I can share both features with all men. I can incorporate the metaphorical "graphics" of homosexuality—conveyed through the media, film, literature and daily social scripts of my society—and continue to depict myself as unhappy, self seeking, emotionally unstable and genitally oriented. I can allow myself to be pitied, "understood," banished or tolerated according to the relative effect I cause within those contexts I appear.

If I absorb such negative thematic scripts for homosexuality, I act them out with other homosexuals. Then together we perpetuate our tendency to learn, believe and fear the overwhelming "insights" of heterosexuals concerning allegedly normative behavior.

Homosexuals establish a form of defensive egomania to cope with their unique sense of inferiority. It is marked by hypersensitivity towards gaining appearances of successful normality. How we achieve such appearances matches those extremes of our denial or acceptance of the masculine-feminine character traits created by heterosexual males.

However, the egomanic homosexual is not much different from the egomanic heterosexual. Both are concerned with achievement of narcissistic uniqueness. Both seek appearances of success in their own social contexts. Many images of success are available to grant both a false sense of unique individualism to their efforts.

In American society, all men are encouraged to produce the self in the image of a socially defined ideal self. The heterosexual definition may match the homosexual male's productive imitation of that ideal self. Frequently, the homosexual's ego validity hinges on masculine overcompensation, or else various degrees of submission by default to feminine imitation. Any form of self production is almost always integrated with other consumption. Self interest then marks the dominant ethical feature in American relationships.

At the same time I strive to become independently unique, I also become dependent on others to achieve that uniqueness. I consume those apparently admirable traits of others as products to be enjoyed and incorporated for self benefit. Despite our awareness of learned American tendencies to "capitalize" on people; despite our alleged sensitivities accrued from rap groups, consciousness raising seminars, readings of "humanizing" books or private therapy, we continue to produce and consume personal traits as though they were marketable commodities available for our use and pleasure. Egomanic concentration on production and consumption of success features manifests an appetite for synthetic reassurances to nourish our famished desire for recognition of our human worth.

Within the production-consumption ethic is the illusion of obsolescence. To be obsolete is to be deemed valueless according to style, function, familiarity or complexity. Americans value something new, entertaining, novel and simplified to reduce effort and guarantee an optimum of pleasure and benefit.

Obsolescence then implies the momentary quality to my marginal value for others. It describes the potential fear in any relationship. If I cannot produce myself interestingly, fashionably, quickly and consistently, if I cannot sell myself to other men, my product becomes obsolete. Things may become obsolete. I am more than a thing, a tool, or a toy for others' idolatrous pleasure.

If my egomania moves me to imitate social norms that homosexuals are taught blindly to follow, I superficially idolize myself as a representation of others' false values. I become an appearance of dubious ideals, without substance or character. Various personality idols which have been socially created for us to imitate increase my tendency towards self idolatry.

Exaggeration of egoistic self idolatry carries a fear of those who do not conform to my own image. We tend to reject what we fear threatens our private concepts of perfection. Idolatry then militates against the beliefs, practices and personalities of those whom we term other—not like us. We compete within the current forms of masculine idolatries. The competitive spirit becomes cultish. Thus, many homosexuals divide against each other into cliques of conformity to mutually shared principles and objects of self-worship.

Yet, homosexuals often notice they cannot hold new acquaintances; they quickly exhaust their product service and are cast aside; they become paralyzed in cliques—retaining their membership if they continue to reflect the shifting value images consonant with their sub-cult's objects of imagination. Cult membership becomes lonely, tenuous and frightening.

Fear reduction has always motivated certain beliefs in man. Various beliefs have assumed ritualized behavior, once the objects of worship have been selected for imitation. Contemporary Americans worship social success images in themselves and others. Their ritualized beliefs assuage their fears of self failure and other domination.

Fear of homosexuals by heterosexuals only exemplifies the paranoia, distrust and rivalry which exists among most American men, regardless of sexual orientation. Americans need to believe they are "making it," sexually, economically and socially. They fear failure. Yet, the hollowness of momentary success haunts them.

As a homosexual, I have broken one social idol of the ideal image of American masculinity. I have sexualized other men. I do not have to believe what I do is frightening; I do not need to reflect heterosexual fear of me, as my own. If I accept myself as an honest individual, forsaking my egomanic idolatry of my society's false values, I can better accept others still caught in the production-consumption cycle of false economy. Since I have broken one idol, I can continue to break the falseness of others.

I can iconoclastically smash false logic and mythical images used by one group against another. As I consistently strive to live my life with integrity and honest daily reappraisal, I can smash those marginal values which apparently entrap both sexual polarities.

I disbelieve the heterosexual lie about myself, and free myself to recreate my daily life apart from false idols which others create, in worship of their various forms of fear. I can create myself in my own image, even as I release myself from the comfortable bondage of the familiar and secure.

Only in this manner can I offer other homosexuals relief from the icons in historical social trends, beliefs and practices by which heterosexuals too long have dominated our position in culture, time and sexual politics. My own image, honestly created by me, is in responsible rebellion against the social patterns of imaginary fear.

PART III / The Toilet

4/Voiding the Disadvantages of Early Toilet Training

Men who frequent "tearooms" . . . expose themselves to fairly constant danger—danger of being
arrested or maybe beaten—yet it seems that it is
often the danger itself that attracts them. . . .[1]
—Dennis Altman, *Homosexual: Oppression and
Liberation*

As for us, we shudder in our cells . . . for, merely
suspecting that debauch of males, we are as excited
as if we saw a giant standing with his legs spread
and with a hard-on.[2]
—Jean Genet, *Our Lady of the Flowers*

The heterosexual male psychologically and actually toilet trains
the homosexual male. Such training exaggerates symbols, attitudes and practices exclusive to the function of the public
restroom. Space communicates.

Americans need to locate their sense of "place" in space; then
they attach position or rank to selected places. They internalize
territorial space, as well as spatial components, arrangements,
functions, and atmospheres. The public restroom, as any other
territory, becomes symbolically internalized as a toilet "complex."

This public territory then provides a paradigm for male
heterosexual location of the homosexual in conceptual and actual
space. It communicates heterosexual relocation of homosexuals
to define, confine and humiliate them. It is a major metaphor in
heterosexual monologues against homosexuality.

In this particular men's room, one anatomical need of the penis occurs—elimination of waste. Assignment of homosexuals as human refuse achieves a similar purpose for heterosexual males. Thus, the toilet becomes a scurrilous definition and emotional outlet for heterosexuals seeking relief from tensions which homosexuals seemingly arouse in them.

Relief from tensions is a common desire and expected requirement in America. Tension relievers are built-in factors for drugs, hobbies, fads, recreation and sexual activity. Heterosexual "needs" are generally accepted as rational and natural aspects of living. Marketing, advertising and psychiatry argue that need relief is necessary to mental health. To do so is profitable.

Need for relief permeates contemporary thought on sexual behavior. Such a psychological fallacy offers a rationale for personal profit—need for relief legitimizes male sexual interest, requirement and frequency. Phallic release, according to majority thought patterns, provides men a necessary physical and emotional homeostasis. A man can become nervous, tense, irritable and sick unless orgasms relieve him of his stress. Apparently the male's psychological fulcrum is his penis.

However, heterosexual males argue against homosexual needs and relief options. Male homosexual needs are neurotic, illegal and unnatural. Homosexuals have lusts, rather than needs. Their relief patterns are considered perversions. Heterosexuals psychologically castrate male homosexuals; then, homosexuals do not require similar penile gratification to that of heterosexuals. Thus, heterosexuals reduce their own tensions by rendering homosexuals as vaginal.

They find relief by psychologically persuading homosexuals to view themselves as biological freaks. They confuse biology with sociology. They shift fact to value, according to their social goals. The heterosexual goal is to train homosexuals to seek their aberrant need relief only in "appropriate," isolated and demeaning areas. One major area of isolation is the toilet. Ironically, heterosexuals share this territory with homosexuals, as they share most penile concepts, interests and functions to a degree they attempt to deny, in order to control their own same-sex fascination.

Heterosexual males' denial of homosexual needs carries a chauvinistic tone and purpose similar to that by which males have traditionally defined the sex life of females. Women, at least pure, decent wife-mothers, do not have sexual needs of the same kind and intensity as men. If they do, such women are deemed unnatural and neurotic. Their suspected potency challenges the masculine need for sexual domination; forfeiture of such domination by men renders men impotent. This monologue of psychosocial oppression, serves male needs to dominate women.

Similar logic is used by heterosexuals on homosexual males. Heterosexual chauvinism towards homosexuals is reinforced by jingoistic monologues designed to create differences and distances between similar penile need relief.

Heterosexual tensions are seemingly relieved by viewing homosexuals as: unnecessary (they do not reproduce); unseemly (they offend public decency, i.e., morality); unstable (they are fetishistically preoccupied with penises); unnatural (they do not share majority male orientation towards vaginas as penis objects); and illegal (law and religion regulate sexual behavior based on male-female genital exchange). These heterosexual tension relievers serve as an intellectual placebo. They calm anxieties that heterosexuals have about their own penises, as well as their chronic interests in the penises of all other men.

Assignment of homosexuals to a toilet context affords intellectual and emotional reduction of heterosexual anxieties based on *urgency*. Relief of fear is an urgent human need. Relief from homophobia causes heterosexuals to identify (locate) and contain their fears. Homosexuals create an irregularity in the sexual order of majority males. Heterosexuals regulate their homosexual fear sources by symbolically attaching them to a social position and function permeated with humorous pity and personal disgust. The heterosexual mythology of sexual behavior designs the space for his view of homosexuality. The homosexual then learns how to use it.

The toilet training is successful, because the homosexual has already learned to hide, withdraw and furtively reenact heterosexual phobias about himself. As Allport notes, "It is far easier to project an inner state upon an outer object if the outer object lacks a firm structure of its own."[3] The inner states which homosexuals then assimilate, are those heterosexual attitudes and fears attached to them in metaphorical monologues. However, such monologues arise from dominant social necessities beyond the attempt to structure the existence of homosexuality. The toilet metaphor contains homosexual behavior in a demeaning frame of reference, but its components also reveal majority attitudes about sex itself.

Partially because the sex organs serve to eliminate bodily waste, there is an initial and general social equation with sexuality as being somehow "dirty." Children are admonished not to use "bathroom words." They are told their genital manipulation or exploration is nasty, not nice, and should be hidden. Adult experimentation with sexual variety often carries guilt that one could possibly equate love with combinational contact of mouth, rectum and genitals. Guilt arises from lack of imagination; sexual behavior is regulated by institutional patterns of image and belief.

However, "romance" intrudes into the institutionalization of sexual behavior, to ameliorate the sweat and smell of biological function with love. We call it passion. Violent feeling allows the intellectual rationalization for physical excess. We can feel better about feeling. Yet Havelock Ellis states that ". . . The organs of sex and excretion are on the surface so closely adjoined any attitude of disgust towards one is likely to embrace the other."[4] In spite of currently liberal attitudes of Americans concerning avoidance of sexual "hang-ups," there remains an association with sexuality as a guilt laden and rather unseemly practice.

Thus, the elmination faculties of our sex organs and our moralistic attitudes dictate avoidance reactions to help us maintain a comfortable self image. We search for new terminology, technique and rationale to help us believe we can also enjoy our disgusting sexual interests and practices.

Avoidance reactions are uniquely contrived in the terms we apply to palliate our sexual behavior. Instead of intercourse, we "lay" or "get layed." We "ball" or "bang" others. We replace coitus with "fucking." These terms speak frankly and openly about our sexual liberation. They also limit the range of our attitudes and emotions in sexual encounter.

To fuck, ball, or bang is to avoid involvement. Involvement is so messy. To fuck is to describe an event of brevity and personal insulation. Fucking eliminates the other, but retains the self inside a sheath of remoteness from the complications of close contact. Screwing condenses the person into an impersonal action, similar to that of an instrument merely doing its job. Technology is cleanly, automatically and operationally guilt-free. American sexual technology thus offers guiltless terminology for sexual avoidance reactions. Simultaneously, as Robert N. Whitehurst notices, we remain ". . . Sexually obsessed, tending by indirect and subtle means to give sexual messages. . . ."[5]

One social device to alleviate the tension of sex was the

Victorian mode. It not only represented historical confusion regarding sexual behavior, but served men well in dominating, regulating and isolating the sexual behavior of women. Thus, "Males and females dealt with each other as though neither possessed sexual organs."[6]

Kate Millett analyzes the male oriented novels of Henry Miller and conclude his Puritan ethic causes his male characters to see fucking as contemptible. Women degrade themselves through intercourse. Sexuality is obscene; "cunt stinks . . . and sex is cunt."[7] Millett believes Miller's puritanical response to women is shared by many contemporary men:

> . . . Since sex defiles the female, females who consent to sexuality deserve to be defiled as completely as possible. What he really wants to do is shit on her.[8]

Millett considers male territorial psychology to be one primary source for Miller's sexual graphics. She claims, "The men's room has schooled Miller in the belief that sex is inescapably dirty."[9] She refers to his frequent use of the term "genito-urinary"; his sexual framework implies that his ". . . Sexual comfort station is a pay toilet whose expense is great enough to constitute its own reward."[10]

While our historical changes in attitude towards sexuality appear to have evolved into greater frankness about our bodies, it is dubious whether we have achieved freedom from guilt or more gratifying sexual encounters with others. Rollo May argues that such apparent sexual freedom from puritanical sexual attitudes and Victorian behaviors is deceptive:

> . . . Our highly vaunted sexual freedom has turned out to be a new form of puritanism. . . . I refer to puritanism as it came down via our Victorian grandparents and became allied with industrialism and emotional and moral compartmentalization. . . .
> I define this puritanism as consisting of three elements. First, *a state of alienation* from the body. Second, *the separation of emotion from reason*. And third, *the use of the body as a machine*.[11] [emphasis in original]

Thus, American males have an historical and psychological tendency to create avoidance reactions to sexual encounters. Language, sexual attitudes towards women and a toilet complex towards sex, disassociate heterosexual males within their need relief corollaries. Inadvertantly, heterosexual males move closer to homosexuals in a mutual male bid for sexual comfort stations.

One major method of disassociating the self from guilt about the double function of genitals, is to concentrate on the penis as instrument, and the sex act as technique. If a man views himself as a phallus, and what he "owns" as phallic extension, he can disassociate himself from why he does what he does. We now notice the modern emphasis on how to do what we do. The mind then becomes severed from the penis.

However creative, penis stimulation to various forms of ultimate orgasm possibly limits the human emotional range to one of momentary sensation. Construction of opportunities for successful penis function, reduces the sex act to mechanical solutions to emotional problems. Mirrors, video cameras and the intensity of our partner's gasps and moans let us step back from ourselves to evaluate objectively, how well our penile performance registered on our slide rules of activity criteria. Did our penis measure up to the occasion? Did we "fuck ourselves senseless" in a momentary emotional plunge? Did we sufficiently gargle and wash away the taste and smell of the messy closeness?

Alienation, lust and mechanical rituals define much of sexual behavior and resulting self attitudes. Such definitions are not necessarily limited to the rest room metaphors attached to sex. They *are* enlarged there. Heterosexual males share them, along with homosexual males. Lawrence K. Frank notices in *The Conduct of Sex:*

> Our attitudes toward sex have reflected our feelings of shame and guilt about all our organic needs and functions. Anything "below the neck" has been considered unclean, not to be thought or talked about, not to be recognized unless urgently necessary. . . .[12]

To cope with our uneasy ambivalence concerning our penises and buttocks, heterosexual *and* homosexual males resort to humor and insult in language. Anxiety is relieved by alienating ourselves or others through power references to bodily parts. Friends are encouraged to avoid foolish extremes with enjoinders not to be an "ass" or "dumb butt." A good time is a "kick in the ass"; a bad time, or an irritating person is a "pain in the ass." An enemy is an "asshole," or a reduction to nothingness. One can dismiss an inferior with a "kiss my ass."

All men use the phallus to achieve masculine display of dominance, power and challenge. The penis is symbolic of what we think of ourselves, or what we think of others. The "Roman gesture" of the extended middle finger, with the clenched fingers representing testicles, has worldwide popularity. When the erection of the penis is used to assert dominance by implied threat, the larger the phallus, the greater the threat. Desmond Morris describes phallic traditions in *The Human Zoo:*

> The average length of the erect penis in real life is 6¼ inches, which is less than one-tenth of the height of an adult male. In phallic statues, the length of the penis often exceeds the height of the figure. . . .[13]

Thus, traditional phallic art, behaviors and masculine self concepts lend themselves to depersonalization of the male body. We become penile representations separated by exaggeration from thought and emotion. What the penis does, represents what we are. Where the penis does it, becomes psychic or real locations of interest. While the male heterosexual monologue claims that the toilet enshrines homosexual phallic opportunity, the toilet also typifies heterosexual interest in male genitalia.

When heterosexual males institutionalize the self as phallus, they do so within a trilogy of psychological phallic enshrinement which offers the ambivalence of desire and guilt. First, phallic *narcissism* provides the exaggeration of self, idealized in parody of various fantasies attached to the phallic state. Narcissism gives impetus to the American male's value of competition, frequent indifference to others and a preoccupation with size. The American male values self-englargement in a quest for individualism. Yet, such values create a sense of deprivation, a feeling of isolation, even as the male yearns for privacy.

Secondly, *exhibitionism* accompanies a narcissistic desire to inflate the self; men like to exhibit what they have, to reveal who they are. Homosexuals learn to value "the basket" as a primary exhibit of narcissistic self esteem. Tight fitting clothing, levis brushed or bleached in the crotch to simulate penis size, uplifting underwear and other devices help to stimulate phallic attention. Heterosexuals apply creams, suction cups, genital exercises and vitamins to enlarge their penises. While homosexuals seek to arouse men to admire what they exhibit, heterosexuals wish to arouse women's admiration and the *envy* of other men. Envy follows the male competition factor in exhibitionism, and arouses a third aspect of phallic enshrinement which increases the ambivalence of desire in conflict with guilt. *Voyeurism* is an invasion of another's privacy. Men like to see what other men have to boast about. They check the competition against their own abilities and acquisitions.

To watch bigness, or size in action, inspires admiration of—and identification with—an insatiable hunger to view power personified by the male instrument. The chronic delight in spectator sports, the salacious interest in pornographic viewing, the continual comparisons of male achievement, all signify a masculine taste for the trilogy of narcissism-exhibitionism-voyeurism.

Americans have a ceaseless appetite for experiencing or watching activities within phallic institutions. Appeasement of such desire arouses degrees of guilt that they have somehow over-indulged themselves in masculinity. Men need to reassure themselves and others that such interest demonstrates admiration and affection, but never sexuality.

Myron Brenton interviewed working-class men for his book, *Friendship*. They were conventionally masculine, "strong, tough, self-contained, little emotion showing through."[14] The author drank with them at a V.F.W. post and watched them become less unemotional:

> "I love this guy, I really do!" exuberantly cried a telephone company lineman . . . after he had introduced me to his buddy for the third time. . . . It was clear he meant what he said, especially when he added, "But you know, not, like, in an effeminate way."[15]

All heterosexuals practice forms and appearances of phallic narcissism through the comparative vehicles of exhibitionism and voyeurism. They have an almost pathological fascination with male bodies—their own and others'. Heterosexuals equate symbols of masculinity as aspects of penile power and status. Since heterosexual and homosexual males receive similar socialization content, rituals and values in America, heterosexuals know homosexuals are unaware of the degree to which heterosexuals eroticize males.

To disavow their own phallic preoccupations, heterosexuals conveniently label homosexuals as fetishistically imbalanced. Their unnatural crime is male-to-male genital contact. This then leaves heterosexual males free to rhapsodize, idolize and indulge their psychological penis envy in socially approved, often covert, manners. Elements of narcissism-exhibitionism-voyeurism exist in all heterosexual male-to-male relationships. When men are not busy building their own bodies into a tumescent state, they turn to envy or admire their comrades' physiques. The ninety-pound weakling of the magazine ad gets sand kicked in his face. He loses the girl to a larger male body. He is punished because he has carelessly forfeited membership in the desired majority male power group.

The heterosexual narrator in Dickey's *Deliverance* looks at his friend standing nude in the river:

> I looked at him, for I have never seen him with his clothes off. . . .
> Everything he had done for himself for years paid off as he stood there in his tracks, in the water. I could tell by the way he glanced at me; the payoff was in my eyes. I had never seen such a male body in my life, even in the pictures in the weight-lifting magazines. . . .[16]

In *Scavullo on Men,* the photographer asks Bruce Jenner, the 1976 Olympic Decathlon Champion, to describe his favorite kind of male body: "Wrestlers. They're very lean, more wiry than bulky . . . to me, a really good body is functional."[17] Scavullo interviewed Alan Bates, concerning his nude wrestling scene in the film, *Women in Love.* Bates' performance was the first time two men had appeared nude together in film:

> It's a great expression of physical closeness that is not necessarily sexual. Sometimes there is a need to actually fuse with someone that you feel for, but it doesn't have to be a sexual thing. Sensual, yes. Physical, yes. There's a difference.[18]

Whatever the fine line might be between *sexual* fusion, and *physical* fusion, must be left to the imaginative disavowal definitions men use to objectify and give distance to their affection, admiration for, and contact with other men.

Racial minority myth and stereotype also contain elements of phallic idolatry for the white heterosexual male. John Howard Griffin, a white author posing as a black in the Deep South, wrote of his hitchhiking experiences with white heterosexual males in *Black Like Me:*

> All showed morbid curiosity about the sexual life of the Negro, and all had . . . the same stereotyped image of the Negro as an inexhaustible sex machine with oversized genitals. . . .

> The significance lay in the fact that my blackness and his concepts of what my blackness implied allowed him to expose himself in this manner. He saw the Negro as a different species. He saw me as something akin to an animal in that he felt no need to maintain his sense of human dignity. . . .
> The boy ended up wanting me to expose myself to him, saying he had never seen a Negro naked.[19]

Griffin captures a moment in which exhibitionism and voyeurism occur simultaneously to gratify the male interest in penises. The white man exposes his curiosity, while encouraging the black man to exhibit his prodigiousness.

Eldrige Cleaver, reformed rapist and writer, attempts to sexually explain the white-black male dialectic through his theory of "primeval mitosis."[20] In *Soul on Ice,* Cleaver claims that the white man is intellectually separated from his body. The white Omnipotent Administrator is characterized by ". . . Effeminacy . . . with the affectations of demonstrative homosexuals."[21] The black Supermasculine Menial represents the sexually erotic power source which white males admire, but fear. They emulate masculine image activities to exploit or camouflage their own deficient virility. They spectate through Cleaver's conception of ultra-masculinity—the boxing match:

> The boxing ring is the ultimate focus of masculinity in America, the two-fisted testing ground of manhood, and the heavyweight champion, as a symbol, is the real Mr. America.[23]

Cleaver's point is that white males must frequently identify Mr. America as a black victor, underscoring his claim that the effeminate white male must feed from the physical achievement of black masculinity. Thus Bates' "need for fusion," is contradicted by Cleaver's mitotic division of mind from body, of white from black.

Heavyweight champion Muhammed Ali reflected actor Bates' murky delineation between physical closeness and sexuality. While campaigning in Detroit, he returned to Cleaver's mitosis to defend himself ". . . when an ardent male admirer rushed up and threw his arms around him."[24]

> "You kissin' on me like that, you blow my whole thing," cried Ali, who then countered with a limp-wristed monologue about "sissies."[25]

Norman Mailer, ever the advocate of virile heterosexuality, forever on guard against the spectre of homosexuality, adapted Cleaver's mitotic division in his essay, "The White Negro." In writing about the hipster as a possible vanguard for American erotic freedom, he claims the hipster is a White Negro who lives on the margin of the Negro and white world. The hipster absorbs the existentialist synapses of Negroes and achieves meaning from experience, through the dialectic of the orgasm.[26] He is society's true rebel against organized sexuality. Yet, Mailer cannot concede such inspirational individualism to the homosexual.

Thus Mailer considers the orgasm, hipster-style, to be a liberating communication of self to self, or other. The physical orgasm becomes Mailer's metaphorical fusion of white stagnation to Negro vigor. Cleaver used mitosis as the image for men to unite mind to physical function. Griffin used drugs to cover his white reality with black skin. Each experimented with racial forms of sexual narcissism-exhibitionism-voyeurism; each revealed types of heterosexual preoccupation with male genitalia and masculine virility.

Homosexuals may observe, but they must not intrude into, the delicate structure that heterosexuals erect for their same-sex philosophy. Homosexuals threaten sexual reality which heterosexuals safely idealize through the filter of competitive racial difference—necessary psychic distance is maintained by heterosexual white and black males who must always view each man as other.

The heterosexual voyeur relies on the exhibition of phallic narcissism. Penile ideals vacillate between fantasy and reality, to create interest and anxiety in one's own penile performance, as well as in others'. The problem is that ideals represent one's desires. In America, men tend to sexualize their desires. Imagination and emotion are often converted into physical action, which is covertly or overtly manifested in erotic expression. Such a propensity for erotic expression begins early in each man's life.

Expressions of love appear to share a common motive or psychological mode. One person projects a part of himself which is highly valued (narcissistically), onto another person, whom he can then love as though this person were an extension of himself. When I say, "I love you," in effect I am able to continue loving my projected self values in you. Thus, a parent has a potential conflict in loving his child. "The desire to experience vicariously and to indulge projected child-like facets of the self is one of the basic ingredients of parental love."[26]

The desire also exists to *repossess* projected aspects of the self; the parent then faces the potential desire to physically unite with the child and love one's self in a sexualized manner. Incest taboos block such desire, yet taboos rely on internalized guilt for what one actually wishes to do. The father thus carries high anxiety about his affectional expressions, especially towards his male child:

> The American father is generally more inhibited in fondling his children than is the mother. He is also more prone to assuming that his interest in physical contact with them is sexual in nature. He is likely to practice a studied avoidance of physical contact with any child past puberty. . . . And in the case of a male child, the father's fear of homosexuality is added to the fear of incestuous desire.[27]

The male child, as the female child, likes to be fondled warmly and affectionately. He receives early cues that male-to-male touching is diminished with his increasing age. It is altered from holding, hugging or kissing by his father, to one of wrestling, handshaking, shoulder jabbing and other distancing techniques which substitute for emotional-erotic desires for closeness.

With such learned distancing, the growing male child interacts in boy-culture, learning also to distance his self image from anything feminine. Male camaraderie contains elements of misogyny contradicted by socially approved uses of females as ratification for masculinity. Male camaraderie contains elements of homophobia contradicted by socially selected rituals of masculine aggrandizement. Such rituals are typically genital in atmosphere, value and kind.

Genital rituals begin with autoerotic manipulation or masturbation, by the young heterosexual male. Curiosity, boredom or impulsiveness accompany early touching, comparing or reference to another boy's penis in youthful sex play. Boys in groups then compare, appraise or compete with peers covertly through voyeurism, or overtly through degrees of exhibition. Boys measure themselves and each other with rulers, spy through the soapy lather in gymnasium showers, feint crotch attacks in a game of flinching, joke with the boy playing "pocket pool" because he has his hand in his pockets, flick each other's genitals or buttocks with locker towels, play strip poker and thus creatively enjoy genital gratification in the dubious comfort of psychically distancing rituals.

As men, they can recall their same-sex interest filtered through the hazy nostalgia of pubescent brotherhood, preparing for their "real" interest in women. A member of a men's consciousness raising group speaks of "recollections of early camp experiences such as the 'circle jerk' and penis measuring. . . ."[28]

> . . . Did you guys ever have a Boner's Club? It was just about the time a lot of us were getting our puberty hairs. In the evenings, around bedtime, we would all sit around and try to get a boner. We'd sit and think and think as hard as we could about some girl we couldn't quite get all the way with, and hope we could get it hard. The Boner's Club was in the next room, behind a sheet; as each guy got a boner he could enter the area behind the sheet. Everyone already in the club would look at the new guy's penis to see if he really had a boner—and if he did, he made it into the Boner's Club.[29]

The Boner's Club illustrates narcissistic value in penile performance. Performance is exhibited to other males; they ratify the masculine stance. Admission to the male club hinges on mutual agreement that the novitiate has indeed "passed the penis test." Women are used as intellectual rationale for erectile interest and motivation. What is really important is that such penile performance is practiced in the presence of other males; it is not necessary for females to be present. The real concern is genital competition and comparison. Women camouflage heterosexual male interest in other-male capacities.

Lionel Tiger, anthropologist and author of *Men in Groups,* has constructed a scientific rationale for the Boner's Club phenomenon. His theory of male bonding is based on study of monkey behavior and imaginative speculation concerning male hunting and gathering bands' aggressiveness and natural superiority over females.

Tiger believes that biological complexities encourage males to ". . . bond in a variety of situations involving power, force, crucial or dangerous work. . . . They consciously and emotionally *exclude* females from these bonds."[30] Tiger allows homosexual males a traditional position in his "natural" caste system, typical of heterosexual design of "social policy":

> From a strictly biological viewpoint, there is no good reason for forbidding or even discouraging homoerotic activity, though in terms of Euro-American family structure and sexual attitudes there may be sociological reasons. . . . There are important inhibitions . . . against

expressing affection between men, and one result of this inhibition of tenderness and warmth is an insistence on corporate hardness and forcefulness which has contributed to a variety of "tough-minded" military, economic, political and police enterprises and engagements.[31]

Tiger's desire to "reason" heterosexual male-to-male interests from a genetically verifiable position of innate aggression, is as "reasonable" as the Boner's Club member's inclusion of women in men's socially acquired phallic competition.

Rather than exclusion of females from male bonding, as Tiger believes, women may metaphorically substitute as object or motive for much of what men do together in phallic bonding. Initiation of men into phallic intimacy has the safety factor of disavowal. Thoughts of wife, girlfriend or female sex object stimulate erotically phallic behavior between males.

Perhaps male-female intercourse benefits male camaraderie in a uniquely verbal manner. Each man has intercourse with a woman, "for the guys." Each man's sexual gratifications with women last momentarily. Sexual enjoyment of other men's performances can be shared and extended through verbalization. All-male company traditionally engages in endless discussions of details concerning what each male did do, or plans to do sexually to a woman . . . "for the guys."

Men use epithetical means to focus on male sexuality, as they attach penile terms to friend and foe, to define attitude, behavior and evaluation of each other. Depending on tone of voice, "You prick," or "What a cocksucker," define emphatic approval or disapproval of another male. One "Gets it up," for the appropriate occasion which is then an opportunity to really "Get off" on a pleasurable experience. Acts of skill and daring mean a man "has balls"; withdrawal or mishandling of self converts a man into a "weenie." The genital epithet thus renders the individual and his performance as genital in tone and content. Language serves to punish or reward; men frequently employ the genital label to distinguish the argot of men in groups.

Visual images are connected with verbal ones to distinguish the phenomenon of heterosexual male interest in other men. Literature and film, as well as advertising, depict same-sex interest within the male club context of Tiger's "natural" segregation—and call it friendship. Such friendship between paired males allows close affectional, sometimes physical, ties within the aegis of "buddyism." Historical and contemporary literature record the legendary friendships as being between two males; legendary romances are male to female.

Stories of excessive closeness between two males provide all men with comforting, reinforcing and often romantic versions of two buddies sharing and caring in the contexts of adventure, a college dormitory, prep school, a woman, a drink, a foxhole—but never their bodies. In the film, *Butch Cassidy and the Sundance Kid,* the male couple challenge and reinforce their masculinity as mutual masturbatory, mutual congratulatory vignettes of "raising hell." The film, *Easy Rider,* replaces horses with motorcycles to update the man to man odyssey culminating in suicide revenge against "straight" male intervention in two buddies' mutual pact.

On television, *Route 66* serialized two men's adventures on the highway of life together in a Corvette. Their attachments to women were resolved with a "kiss them goodbye" attitude; their permanent constructions were moments spent together probing their male relationship on-the-move. *Starsky and Hutch* allow themselves more physical contact and display of affection than the older *Route 66* series.

The buddy theme permeates film and television in cop shows like *Freebie and the Bean,* where two men share violence and danger, passionately and with relish. Cowboy themes show buddies with more sophistication than the Lone Ranger and Tonto, but the image is the same—men, real men, prefer the company of another male. The river raft buddyism of Tom Sawyer and Huckleberry Finn assumes added dimension in the film, *A Separate Peace.* Phineas and Eugene, roommates in a private boys' school, learn the intensity of love for each other distorted by the element of jealousy, and lost by death. All the pathos of Romeo and Juliet is caught in Eugene's trying on of Phineas' shirt before a mirror, and for an instant Eugene "becomes" Phineas in a way he could never tell him.

The foxhole buddies of war films and novels relate the emotional dependency and intimacy between men, tolerated and idealized by the public because of the intensity of danger, mutual need and the unnecessity of women in waging war. Buddyism is visualized in medical, scientific, corporate, political and even marital stories in film and literature. Yet the one element which all male companions (buddies) share is a basic repugnance for homosexuality, even as hypermasculinity is lauded.

Feelings by heterosexual buddies for things or events they

share often revolve around instruments for phallic self-conception. Skill in using a gun, a car, a woman or their entire intellectual or physical expertise lend buddies their masculine ratification which they mutually exhibit and observe. They can share everything but sex with each other. As one cowboy succinctly put it, when asked if homosexuality existed among cowboys (and despite historical documentation to the contrary):

> No, cowboys don't want anything to do with that. They absolutely hate those kind of people. And it's funny, you know, that cowboys stay together all the time in the same room, we share double beds together all the time, and nobody does anything like that at all.[32]

Recent pronouncements against homosexuality by the Church of Jesus Christ of Latter-Day Saints (Mormon), includes forbidding of missionary companions (spiritual buddies) from sleeping in the same bed. Church elders are apparently not as trusting as the cowboy. In a letter from a homosexual student to his anti-homosexual psychology professor at Brigham Young University, the anonymous writer cites from ". . .*The Teachings of Joseph Smith:*"

> "When we lie down, we contemplate how we may rise in the morning; and it is pleasing for friends to lie down together, locked in the arms of love, to sleep and awake in each other's embrace and renew their conversation" (p. 295). This statement, made in all innocence, is in sharp contrast to the preoccupation the "brethren" now have forbidding missionary companions to sleep together for fear that their affection will turn physical.[33]

Thus, the rituals of visualized and actual buddyism formulate heterosexual phallic projections into male groups for exhibition and admiration. Exhibition of homoerotic behavior carries unwritten and written sanctions; "indecent exposure" of heterosexual genital behaviors also carry sanctions. Such are deemed socially unhealthy or unlawful. Such sanctions seem hypocritical in view of ambivalent American attitudes towards obsessive interests in the body. Consider the anomaly of current manic attention to physical development, in the guise of health. This potentially psychological fetishism is nonetheless glossed as normal by the American public.

As the ninety-pound weakling "indecently" exposes his physical failures, sanctions are imposed by a "real" man. He notices that ultra-masculinity guarantees a sexual payoff for inflation, adulation and emulation of the male body. The proliferation of televised spectator sports, physical regimen of jogging or work-outs at the "Y", increase of Little Leagues for children (and their parents), Yoga derivatives and other group celebrations of the body-in-action, all provide men a type of actual or vicarious support for masculinity as healthy, character building cama-raderie—in a competitive framework. Women may participate also, but in a secondary fashion.

No woman in America can succeed in sports to the financial or popular extent that men may. In tennis or golf, women athletic "personalities" achieve fame for their physical skill; their finan-cial remuneration never matches that of male counterparts. Women are not as important to men, as are other men. Women do not command million dollar contracts in baseball, football, bas-ketball. Their participation in athletic events parody that of men's. Few women are recruited from high school into collegiate or semi-professional sports; no woman is offered as much money in sports scholarships, as is a man. While women have gained additional opportunity for participation, the real recognition of achievement is given by men to other men. According to the average male mind, women then basically imitate men in the male sports arena.

Thus, the growing fascination in America with physical de-velopment and athletic activity offer heterosexual males another aspect to their narcissistic-exhibitionistic-voyeuristic fascination with what they can do with their bodies, in concert with other males.

If exhibition of what one has or does carries an element of competitive challenge and aggression, then to observe another's masculine prowess carries an element of invasion, and possession of another. Thus, heterosexuals widen the "circle jerk" to include all aspects of the body as phallus. They value mutual performance: arousal, technique and culmination—recounted by memory to match against a bigger, better achievement in the future—become the psychic and physical rhythm of the sports-as-health buffs. It's chic to be physically sporty, it's chic to care about health. Yet with so much attention paid to the accoutre-ments of style—the incorporation of sports clothing into popular apparel, the frenzied devotion to hours of workouts (so one can talk about it at cocktail parties or in *People* magazine)—these still create the suspicion that American males engage in a compulsively stylized form of mutual masturbation of the whole body.

From stylized chic, American males move into the "heavy metal" of physical culture magazines, beef-cake competitions and "pumping iron," which all serve to inflate the male muscle, i.e., ego. In the book, *Man's Body: An Owner's Manual,* each reader is told:

> The average human body is between 16 and 27% efficient—which compares badly with several products of the human mind. But by regular exercise the body's efficiency can be raised to 56%, which is better than many machines.[34]

The concern for efficiency is noted through American equation of people producing themselves as products. Comparison of the self to a machine, is perhaps an apt paradigm for masculine concepts of sexual performance, or at least elements of physical activity.

As sports activity may indeed represent something else, Myron Brenton notices in *The American Male* that sexual activity can be as removed from love as physical activity can be removed from interests in health:

> . . . Much of what passes for sex (even in so-called love relationships) is really a way of proving something, a way of being competitive, a way of rationalizing fears, a means of controlling, a device used for exploitation, and a technique for not being left out of things, so that it's essentially removed from love, affection, *or* desire.[23]
>
> [emphasis in original]

Whatever the motives of sport-as-health participants, there appears to be a heterosexual construction of a body cult of significant proportions—on a national scale.

The epithet "jock," regardless of context, remains rooted in the crotch. Heterosexual males display the insignia of the jock with pride; so do homosexual males. The former may wish to disqualify the latter, but American (physical) culture is available to both.

In the section, "Gays, Sports, and the Macho Trip," from *Gay Source,* Dennis Sanders explains that homosexuals are stereotyped as unathletic because they reject the aggressive, insensitive macho trip of the straight athlete. Then he offers a way for homosexuals to join the heterosexual power group which shuns them:

. . . There's the whole mystique of the subliminal sex of sports, especially contact sports—and most gays are turned on to the athlete type. Again, the fascination has to do with our need to survive; our greatest need is survival, and that need is satisfied through sports, especially football. People see there's a kind of life-and-death struggle out there. . . . There's a kind of conquering, and I think the fascination with athletes has to do with so many lives not having that kind of thing.[36]

While Sanders has struck upon the obvious subliminal sexuality in American contact sports, "most gays" are not necessarily turned on to athletic types.

Equating football to survival perpetuates the myth that life skills are mystically present in the strategies of a mere game. The life and death struggle represented by athletes for the passive, bored spectator (gay or straight), is simulated fantasy acted out by players symbolically through cooperative strategies, employment of skill and aggression, emasculation of male opponents, behavior confined to male one on one contact which is exciting, erotic and repetitious. Sanders appears to describe images, rather than realities, in his invitation to homosexuals to join the heterosexual sports fraternity for social survival. Allport defines such efforts of minority members as "symbolic status striving."

People admire the cripple who has persevered and overcome his handicap. Such direct compensation for an inferiority is the type of response most highly approved in our culture. Accordingly, some members of minority groups view their handicap as an obstacle to be surmounted by an extra spurt of effort.[37]

Submersion into a sports mystique will not turn a homosexual into a heterosexual.

John Rechy scathingly reveals the subliminal sex aspect in body culture through a scene in *Numbers*. Johnny, the homosexual hustler, meets heterosexual Danny who invites him to "muscle beach," where men exercise in couples. Men sitting on each other to help a buddy do situps or "donkey raises," aid the other in achieving *inflation* and a *lift*. "Each couple—in brief trunks—appears to be performing a distinctly recognizable sex act."[38] Surrounded by admiring, bikini-clad women, envious straight men, and homosexuals (whom the straight adonises hate), one muscleman calls to heterosexual Danny:

". . . Blow us a great big goodbye kiss, beautiful." The faggy words, the determinedly masculine tone—the latter again meant to obviate the former and render it acceptable.[39]

Danny invites Johnny to work out with him, admiring his physique which he needs to *maintain,* bringing to mind Brenton's statement that ". . . the male is obliged to walk around with a perpetual psychic erection."[40]

Johnny imagines the scene: He'd want me to sit on his butt while he does "donkey raises" like that guy on the beach . . . for his calves. I'd "spot" him on the bench press, standing over his face . . . for his chest, triceps, and deltoids. I'd sit on his legs to keep his movements strict . . . for his abdominals. And then he'd want to do all that for me. And we'd rub each other down afterwards, all sweaty and breathless.[41]

Rechy captures the subliminal eroticism between male partners engaging in serious physical development approved by heterosexuals. The narcissism peaks in rituals of exhibition and observation of themselves and their partners. The rhythmic contact is obviously sexual, almost a ballet of resistance and submission alternating within the safety of body mechanics. One strokes the other body-as-phallus; the ego remains intact because the penis is seemingly ignored. Sweat becomes semen?

While Sanders' football logic employs a fantasy of danger in American living (which automation and police alleviate for us), Rechy illustrates the fantasy of surrogate sex, which many heterosexual athletic activities represent. Phallic domination becomes paramount: the phallic need is survival (echoes of Tiger); the call is to participate, not spectate, to conquer, and not wait to be conquered. We can all share the joyful, healthy mechanics of phallic participation. The restroom mentality becomes portable.

Where heterosexuals take such subliminal interest in their own penile functions, as well as those of other males, they are ritualized in behavior and institutionalized into imaginative thought. The majority of all-male heterosexual groups subliminally incorporate same-sex interest in a variety of methods which ratify pleasurable masculinity as "healthy fun." We commonly acknowledge that initiation into membership in all-male groups provides masculine solidarity, status, protection, economic support for participants. We don't commonly acknowledge the sexual ambivalence of heterosexual male interaction, or comfortably accept that much of it is homoerotic.

To do so, would threaten the vaginal construction of the male's psychic conception of his world as other. Masculine is only defined in contrast to feminine. Yet the homosexual male often assumes degrees of vaginal roles, which then define him and confine him in heterosexual politico-sexual submission; but the heterosexual male *also* assumes degrees of vaginal roles to symbolically satirize the weakness of the feminine in relation to everything masculine.

Initiations into sports groups, fraternities, gangs, the armed services, social clubs, adolescent play groups, or celebrations before or after important male group efforts—often carry elements of sodomy, bestiality, simulated male-female intercourse, fellatio and variations of romantic activity of lips, hands, buttocks and groin.

Perhaps emphasis on reduction of initiates to vaginal status, before elevating them to phallic status, does serve as a dramatic rite of passage into an all-male group. Perhaps simulation of male-female sex activity in all-male groups does provide a vehicle of control and definition which ultimately sets men apart from women, or "lesser" men who do not enjoy group membership. Yet through the dramatic representations for camaraderie, fun, and satire is revealed a subliminal interest in sexual components of men by other men. The rationales exist, but so do the sexual realities.

In the film version of *Bless the Beasts and Children,* by Glendon Swarthout, a summer camp for wealthy boys carries the slogan, "Send Us a Boy—We'll Send you a Cowboy!" Forty-two Cabins divide into tribes, ranked by number of points accumulated in weekly competitions, and symbolized with animal head totems. The under-achievers were ranked as the "Bedwetters"; they received a chamber pot. The film showed the adolescent winners urinating into the chamber pot, which would then be thrown on the adolescent losers.

Candidates for college fraternities often have "dinging" sessions with fraternity members which are attempts to match candidates with fraternities. Ding is a slang term for penis. Male initiation rites for fraternities are highly sexually charged. Nudity is a frequent ingredient. Focus on buttocks and penis have many variations. Pledges strip and have bricks tied to their penises as they are blindfolded. Then they are told to throw their brick, without knowing that the strings have been cut. Pledges are asked to bend over and expose their buttocks to senior men—not atypical of baboon behavior in which lesser members of a troop expose their rumps to baboon leaders. Marshmallows are stuffed into the rectum, which pledges then must eat. Lubricated nails are employed with spoken vows, pledges bending to receive the nail from a senior member, who substitutes a beer can for it at the last moment—and the pledges are elevated into the ranks with a celebrational drinking party.

More daring fraternities actually sodomize their pledges; others require seniors to be fellated. Some fraternities place their pledges in gunny sacks and beat them; others prefer to whip bare buttocks or brand their pledges. Carloads of fraternity boys "moon" or "hang B-A's" from moving vehicles to shock passers-by with bare buttocks hanging from windows. Ceremonial variations differ only by imaginative zeal of each year's fraternity membership.

Entrants to military academies or various boot camps of the armed services, expect to endure the process of "fagging" by senior officers. Physical and verbal abuse, to humiliate the initiate to the status of woman or "grunt," is supposed to *harden* the candidate into manhood according to the unique traits valued by a particular male group. From the weakness of novice as woman subordinate, the candidate allows other men to erect him to the superior phallic state. Apparently only men can give other men a psychic hard-on.

Sports team participants celebrate together in less rigorous manners than more exuberant collegiates, or more serious militarists. Soccer teams, bowling clubs, and other sports groups drink together in hotel rooms or taverns closed to females. Antics carry overtones of sexuality which are funny, titillating and crude. "Gross-outs" include the elephant walk, in which men hang one hand under their crotch, for the man behind to hold elephant-style, "trunk to tail," or strip tease contests staged on table tops, which reach the jock strap at about the same time the song ends.

Jim Bouton, baseball player and author of *Ball Four,* spoke of a kissing game his team members would play for laughs:

One of our jocko things is to mince around like a fairy, which is pretty funny sometimes, especially while wearing baseball underwear. . . .

After a while some of the guys began to walk up to each other and pretend to kiss on the lips. . . . Then it began to spread. As a gag, of course. You'd be walking down the aisle of a bus and all of a sudden a guy would clamp his hand over your mouth, kiss the back of his hand and continue on down the aisle. . . .

Then we got a little drunk on a bus one night and the guys started kissing without bothering to put their hands up. And then *that* became a joke. We'd kid about how many guys had kissed other guys and then there was this little club, and only guys who had kissed and been kissed could be members.[43]

There appear to be many variations in the rituals of the Boner's Club mentality.

Where men collect together to engage in athletics, share social companionship in clubs and fraternal organizations, group together in skill or goal pursuits, create male-to-male friendships in the mode of buddies as depicted in film and literature, or verbally share sexual stories and innuendo—there is a phallic atmosphere permeating their interaction. Guilt tempers desire to display heterosexual insignia of masculinity for other males to observe and compare themselves against.

The American heterosexual male seeks narcissistic reflection of himself in other men. He desires a social exchange of mutually shared phallic recognition and admiration. His phallic rituals define his status in male rank. Status is achieved through matching the self against other males, as well as against socially selected images of masculinity. Thus, masculinity is earned or achieved, in phallic comparison to other males. Masculinity is always imitative.

Given the penchant for heterosexuals to value all-male company, one can only postulate why more heterosexuals do not sexualize what they idealize, or why they *do* evidence strong homophobic reactions against men who do sexualize each other. Several issues simultaneously converge in American society to complicate heterosexual males' concepts of their sexual behavior.

American heterosexual males are traditionally uncomfortable with sex. They view sex as dirty, because of their misogynist attitudes towards women. Female sexual functions have historically been considered by males as impure. The menstrual flow arouses universal male disgust and disassociation. It smells and supposedly contaminates.

Women are associated with men in myth and legend, as evil

temptresses who deplete male power, create anxiety that his property will be invaded or won by another male (through rape or enticement), and negatively intensify intramale competition for self ratification via a vaginal subject. Male hostility—as evidenced in rape, pornography, ribald humor, or physical and mental abuse—perhaps occurs because males resent seeking masculine ratification through a feminine source they historically view as inferior or secondary. If females must be penis objects, then other males assuage such psychological compromise by existing as the "real" penis *subject* of male values, interests and behaviors.

An additional complicating factor in heterosexual males' sexual behavior, is the shifting social view of personality as defined by culturally shared images of success, purpose and performance. The female in America now has greater access to masculine behaviors, pursuits and expressions. Her orgasmic needs and capacities are viewed as just as important to her as helping the male achieve his orgasmic fulfillment. Some men refuse to acknowledge they need women to help their penises perform. Some men compromise in an egalitarian concern that both male and female sex partners achieve satisfaction at the same time. The pursuit of the simultaneous orgasm reflects male democratic idealism, or at least the desire to break even. Yet some men become dysfunctional as evidenced by increasing instances of impotency among heterosexual males.

Cultural images overstimulate all American males to believe that personal freedom is linked to sexual freedom. Success is based on numbers of orgasms; purpose to life is pleasure-centered (the sex-is-fun syndrome); and performance rests on a win-lose battle to outdo the self stylistically in each successive sexual encounter.

> Thus, the message from Madison Avenue is now: "Mister, can you lay 'em good?" And, increasingly, the advertisers play on that other deep-seated fear of the American male: "Mister, sure you're not a homosexual?"[44]

Now, historical misogyny redefined by changing male and female sexual role definitions, blurs the masculine-feminine dichotomy. Heterosexual male anxiety occurs because he must compete even harder than before "sexual liberation" to delineate and achieve his psychical masculinity.

Such delineation is necessary to the heterosexual who suspects he is being rendered as vaginal. His penile exhibitions become more inclusive (body as phallus); to borrow aspects of feminine child nurturing, cooking, employment descriptions, emotional display or leisure activity is to *enlarge the male territory voluntarily*.

And yet there lurks the anxious feeling that such male tokenism diminishes the male's phallic self concept in his vaginally conceived environment. The heterosexual male fears being described as vaginal, i.e., as feminized; he also fears becoming vaginal, i.e., impotent, through comparative competition with other males. At this point in reason, the homosexual male poses the greatest threat to the heterosexual male's phallic image.

While heterosexual males are intrinsically interested in the phallic potency of other males, they must psychologically and actually isolate themselves from sexually willing males. Most heterosexual males imagine they risk becoming an overt sex object for sexually willing males. Heterosexuals then face an imaginary vaginal self concept within their own class-status-subject construction of their social arena, based on penis-to-vagina, master-to-slave, employer-to-employee or winner-to-loser.

Where heterosexual male erotic interest in other males exists, then phallic narcissism, exhibitionism and voyeurism compensate for social taboo against male-to-male genital contact. When heterosexual same-sex interest is more demanding, rituals of erotically flirtatious play can regulate, rationalize or occasionally permit intermittent satisfaction of such interests.

Homosexual males frighten heterosexual males, because they challenge heterosexual phallic and vaginal role concepts as quasi-political designations confirmed by the dominant male group. Homosexuals alarm heterosexual males, because they actualize those homoerotic tendencies which heterosexual males subliminalize. The homosexual creatively intrudes a sexual anarchy into the total male group. Heterosexual male group members must reject or not recognize such intrusion, which merely reflects the potential sexual diversity and ambivalence in themselves.

Heterosexuals then artificially create rules of order for their vaginal world. These, in effect, work to control role proximity to males, by subordinating women, racial minorities and various competitive stratifications of men. Such rules of order parallel definitions of what the penis may penetrate, and where and when it may privately or publicly appear.

Heterosexual male rules of social order emerge from historical concepts of *penile encroachment as crime*. Rape, in the average male mind, is not so much a personal violation of a woman's person or right to autonomous integrity, i.e., consent, but is rather a penile violation of another man's property right. Father, brother or husband of the violated woman, is psychically the violated man. The woman's male relative has been rendered vaginal through other-male trespass. Rape by a male, of another male, is an aggressive act of trespass, but also an act which retains the rapist as phallic, and the raped as vaginal.

Laws have amalgamated myth, folkways, biology and religion into majority opinions concerning the "naturalness" of penile penetration into specific bodily orifices. Certain orifices are forbidden to the penis because of social convention, sexual guilt and arbitrary attachment of sin or sickness to body contact activity. In America, most state statutes consider male-to-female fellatio and sodomy to be illegal. Apparently, such sexual behavior prevents procreation, and is therefore unnatural. The age of orifices also helps define *when* penises may enter them.

Laws control *description* of penile activity through rules concerning sex in print. Pornography exists as a relative index to erotic arousal. Such arousal is apparently possible due to the state of mind of the observer, rather than to intrinsic capacities within erotic representations. Penile activity viewed on film, is similarly labeled illegal by erotic degree and decree—depending on the observer's point of view.

Legal control of context or occasion for public penile appearance, is defined by crimes of "indecent exposure," "lewd and lascivious conduct," and the like. Legal control of the penis in private behavior includes incest and homosexuality. Freud examines socio-sexual taboos and reaches an interesting awareness of the psychological purpose of such laws:

> The law only forbids men to do what their instincts incline them to do; what nature itself prohibits and punishes it would be superfluous for the law to prohibit and punish. Accordingly we may always safely assume that crimes forbidden by law are crimes which many men have a natural propensity to commit.[45]

The social ramifications of Freud's thoughts on the purposes of sexual law hinge on agreement as to society's general welfare. Incest would create rivalry and divisions within families; rape would generate competition and threaten male property concepts. Public display of genital behaviors would flaunt public anxiety with sexuality *per se*. Private variations in sexuality would defeat general efforts to "normalize" and control sexuality. Imagistic portrayal of phallically erotic activity might have an "imitative" effect leading an observer to experimentation outside of accepted sexual norms. Homosexuality could reverse heterosexual male conceptions of other as vaginal—or at best, reduce the phallically competitive support males need from each other, even as they seek personal success by rendering other males as vaginal subordinates.

Thus, male heterosexuals rely on rules of social order for phallic activity, in order to regulate their social conceptions of vaginal contexts for phallic participation. That heterosexuals share phallic preoccupation with homosexuals, is not the essential issue. That heterosexuals sublimate what homosexuals actualize, is the necessary mode in a heterosexually dominated social hierarchy. Homosexuality threatens with psychic anarchy, which inverts, perverts, or subverts necessary penile control. If the penis is a power symbol, it is also a fear symbol. The heterosexual male entertains both symbolic considerations within himself.

Many heterosexuals construct private, imaginary obsessions with selected, socially defined phallic images. Their *autistic* reasoning (self-oriented fantasied thinking) struggles to parallel socially shared interests and rewarding preconceptions concerning male power symbols. Heterosexuals fear another male's power symbol, unless the other male's visible interests tend to match their own. Obviously, homosexual self-interests visibly appear to threaten or subvert heterosexually shared self-interests. That some homosexuals may also reason autistically, does not usually occur to heterosexual males. Homosexual minority behaviors appear not to match heterosexual visible interests.

Thus, in the heterosexual's autistic reasoning, symbol mania and symbol phobia can tenuously and concomitantly coexist. Heterosexuals alternate ambivalently between private phallic fantasy and socially defined reality. Their symbol mania and symbol phobia, often exaggerated, excite them to move on a homoerotic continuum of symbolic and real possibility.

Yet, for the heterosexual, desire and fear must counterbalance. Social concept can then control self-interest. Thus heterosexual penis envy is regulated in ritualized sublimation, and sanctioned by social rules of order. Heterosexuals can then actually camouflage, or psychologically repress, the disturbing dynamic which they experience because of same-sex interests implied by penis envy. And so their sexual ambiguity apparently is relieved.

To illustrate heterosexual male ambivalence in regard to penis erections made visible, the crime of indecent exposure reveals much more than the crotch. Lance Rentzel, the professional football player, exposed his penis to several young female passers-by. His superior later confronted Rentzel with the police report; his male superior was ". . . embarrassed, a little ill at ease . . . but he was also amused."[46] Rentzel's "crime" ultimately cost him his marraige, much psychological distress and public humiliation. It is not necessary here to analyze the uniquely personal reasons why Rentzel needed to expose his genitals. He explains the moment in his autobiography, *When All the Laughter Died in Sorrow:*

> On this day, for some reason, I needed someone to play with me in a childish game I was making up. Look at me, look at me. Look at what I've got. I sat in the car and they came over and I exposed myself. It took maybe ten seconds; then I drove off, strangely relieved.[47]

Rentzel's "crime" was essentially no different than the learned needs displayed in the Boner's Club, or the white male curiosities about black male genital size and ability. As Karl Menninger argues, ". . . most sex-crimes . . . are impelled . . . by a need for reassurance regarding an impaired masculinity."[48] Perhaps most laws originating from males to regulate male genital behavior (display), are really punishments for phallic failure. While many of our penis laws are designed to protect women, children or the general public, perhaps it is really the sensitivities of corporate males which are being protected.

The threatening aspects of penis envy are codified in various gentlemen's agreements. A man may display his penis in shower rooms, barracks, college dorms or all-male rituals of sport, initiation or other phallic extensions. A man may not violate his camouflage of narcissistic exhibition, or he violates written and unwritten gentlemen's rules of phallic conduct. Such violation is actual or symbolic flaunting of context for phallic behavior. Flaunting is questionable sportsmanship. Covert penile competition becomes too threateningly overt, as in Rentzel's case. He violated heterosexual moral codes of phallic conduct, with blatant visibility, i.e., exposure.

Thus, the heterosexual covers himself and his phallic interests (penis envy), either actually through ritual, or psychically through rationalization. Inappropriate exposure of penis erection, or erectile substitutions, is illegal behavior. Men must legalize their genital cover, in order to regulate their vulnerable phallic sensitivities. Phallic mania must counterbalance phallic phobia.

In the fantasy dominated autistic reasoning of most heterosexual males, homosexuals stand guilty of flouting the general phallic code of conduct—by "flaunting." They break the gentlemen's agreement to regulate penile mania. Homosexuals' alleged penile mania is too overt; heterosexuals react with penile phobia, in an effort to cover homosexuals. Homosexuals are thus considered immoral, illegal or unnatural, in order to define and confine—and thus achieve relief for heterosexual homophobia.

Such relief is designed to eliminate the inordinate phallic tensions which heterosexuals attach to masculinity values. Partial elimination of phallic tension is achieved by eliminating the homosexual, thus voiding the homosexual's claim to male membership. The toilet becomes the actual arena for this heterosexual psychic need.

Yet, even in the male space of the toilet, heterosexual phallic interest prevails. Autistic reasoning prevails. To cover homosexual behavior in public restrooms, heterosexual undercover policemen attempt to expose homosexuals by becoming decoys—or phallic enticements. Such toilet morality allows the decoy to offer money for sexual services; if the homosexual accepts, he is arrested by entrapment. If a decoy manipulates his genitals at a urinal and a homosexual approaches him with a proposition of sexual exhange, the homosexual is arrested via enticement. If a decoy asks a homosexual what are his sexual preferences, verbal suggestion can lead to arrest. Sexual contact between two or more homosexuals in a public facility can lead to arrest. Indecent exposure, lewd and lascivious conduct or solicitation of sexual favors—are possible breaches in phallic codes of conduct.

An undercover agent with the Seattle police vice squad "was trying too hard" when he engaged in an act of prostitution, said police Captain Dale Douglass. A confidential police report . . . told how Agent 227 "dated" two men in a car and had sex with them for which he received $20. . . .[49]

The officer's enthusiasm for his work has been experienced by many homosexuals within restrooms. Arrest follows sexual overtures or enticements by decoys; in effect, the police agent enters the phallic ethic of the homosexual, and then withdraws, claiming legal right to simulate the phallic mode by which the homosexual is judged illegal.

Such expeditionary missions into the homoerotic atmosphere of the toilet, parallels previously mentioned rituals and modes of male phallic interest in other males. Co-mingling such mania with phallic phobia, whether in the locker room, the bar room or the restroom, men seek to compete with, control or dominate each other's phallic identity.

That homosexuals frequently act out their psychological confinement within the toilet context—to the derision and expectation of heterosexuals—comes as no great surprise. Homosexual personalities are not indifferent to social expectations or social abuse. Homosexuals are disparaged, discriminated against and isolated within the rest room context of heterosexual imagination. Forms of ego defense against such maliciousness vary uniquely within each homosexual. Fighting back, compensating with a mixture of desirable and undesirable traits, or capitulating to abusive expectation, generally form homosexual defense reactions.

Yet, the toilet stigma given to homosexuals—and accepted to whatever individual degree—tends to reproduce facsimiles of that stigmatic metaphor in the homosexual's reaction to himself and other homosexual males. Allport's theoretical illustration of ego defense reation by one who is hated, applies too frequently to the homosexual minority's dilemma:

A child who finds himself rejected and attacked on all sides is not likely to develop dignity and poise as his outstanding traits. . . . He develops defenses. Like a dwarf in a world of menacing giants, he cannot fight on equal terms. He is forced to listen to their derision and laughter and submit to their abuse. . . . He may withdraw into himself, speaking little to the giants and never honestly. He may band together with other dwarfs, sticking close to them for comfort. . . . Or he may out of despair find himself acting the part that the giant expects, and gradually grow to share his master's own uncomplimentary view of dwarfs. His natural self-love may, under the persistent blows of contempt, turn his spirit to cringing and self-hate.[50]

5/Evacuating the Self from the Habit of Incontinence

As he looked back upon man moving through history, he was haunted by a feeling of loss. So much had been surrendered! and to such little purpose! There had been mad wilful rejections, monstrous forms of self-torture and self-denial, whose origin was fear and whose result was a degradation infinitely more terrible than that fancied degradation from which, in their ignorance, they had sought to escape. . . .[1]
—Oscar Wilde, *The Picture of Dorian Gray*

Love . . . Screwing . . . that's not a man's whole life. A man lives for what he can personally create in this world . . . the recreation of this world, his environment. . . . If all men lived their lives for the next world, man would never have invented the flush toilet. He'd be up to his ass in his own shit.[2]—Robert H. Rimmer, *The Harrad Experiment*

We tend to recreate our world in the image of our distorted perceptions of our external realities. We filter through our intellect those experiences we select to think about, within the emotional framework unique to each of us. We thus fabricate our existence according to the resources of our imagination. Much of our internalized reality is redirected to our external world of experiences in the form of inner-directed acting out of images we have in our heads. What we "think" tends to "appear" as we act upon our environment—or each other.

We classify our images, in order to assemble our inner logic. We classify our shared external realities, selectively, in order to create coherence within our changing circumstances. Images of reality are subject to exaggeration. Nothing is neutral, but rather assumes selected value according to our needs and desires. We judge. We evaluate. And thus we relate to things, events and people.

When we classify people, we group them. To simplify perception, thought and emotional reaction, we stereotype—or attach fixed clusters of mental pictures—and then construct beliefs from ideas. Beliefs justify our ideas and conduct towards others. Others can become projection screens for the fixed pictures in our minds. We can share stereotypical generalizations with others and thus gain social support for what we think we see.

Heterosexual white males generally see women as dependent, passive, gentle, yet somewhat threatening erotic corespondents . . . in relation to themselves. Blacks are seen as low in motivation, inferior in intelligence, entertaining, carefree and sexually vigorous . . . in relation to white males. Homosexual males are seen as promiscuous, immoral, emotionally unstable, sad, threatening and deviant from social and biological norms . . . in relation to heterosexual males.

To place such imagistic stereotypes upon others often reduces inner anxieties about these characteristics within oneself. We project what we find uncomfortable or unvaluable in ourselves. Thus, the relationship between heterosexual and homosexual males in America resembles an *ego* to *alter ego* relationship. The homosexual male is the heterosexual male's second self.

Psychically, the homosexual is prototypical of the heterosexual's actual homoerotic interest; existentially, the homosexual matches the heterosexual's phallic interpretation of his being; and socially, the homosexual is profitably *subordinate* to the heterosexual male in value and power. The heterosexual male constructs ideological distance from his homosexual counterpart. He stigmatizes the homosexual with distinguishing marks, in order to discredit his masculinity, his personal credibility or his social claim to male equality.

The homosexual stigmatic is marked by heterosexual image projections into law, religion, folk lore, the media and other reflectors of identity. The homosexual stigmatic learns to internalize available images of himself. The homosexual male contemplates such negative stigmata, and reproduces the stereotypical expectations of his heterosexual "superior" within himself.

The phenomenon is not unlike that found in religious traditions;

in humble self-denial, various people have contemplated the suffering and wounds of the crucified Christ, to the degree that they have claimed to have reproduced Christ's marks upon themselves. Such close identification marked them as belonging to their spiritual superior; they were distinguished from average men, and set apart from the world they commonly shared.

The heterosexual majority produces distinctive images of homosexuals, who in turn reproduce themselves in those imagistic patterns of self-concept and behavior. The heterosexual majority creates the rest room space for homosexual containment. Stigmatic monologues are socially disseminated as ideologies, to toilet train the homosexual. Such negative monologues are often internalized as belief and practice, and the homosexual marks himself with generally available prejudices, anxieties and rituals stemming from the male majority concept of self-as-phallus. The homosexual reinforces his sense of belonging within the toilet complex of heterosexual construction. Fulfillment of such expectation of others damages the homosexual's self esteem. He fragments himself into replications of various stereotypes about himself.

His ability to function as a whole person is often limited to exaggerated repetitions of several major behavioral patterns or to an over-focus on few, rather than many self-concepts. The dominant theme to his life becomes a sexual one—furtive, guilty, aberrant and rapacious sexuality—which affords little esteem, security or comfort.

To illustrate the poignancy, savagery and exploitation which homosexuals share by "belonging" in the toilet conception, Yukio Mishima's *Forbidden Colors* depicts the ambience of the homosexual who merges personhood with context. Though writing of Japan, Mishima accurately describes the meaning of each American homosexual's life defined within the space of the rest room:

> He entered the dim, clammy lamplight of the rest room, and saw what is called an "office" among the fellowship. . . . It was an office where the tacit office procedure is based on winks instead of documents, tiny gestures instead of print, code communication in place of a telephone. This was the dimly lighted, silent office whose activities here greet Yuichi's eyes. . . .
>
> They are all my comrades, Yuichi thought as he walked. Rank, occupation, age, beauty notwithstanding, they are a fellowship welded by the same emotion—by their private parts, let us say. What a

bond! These men do not have to sleep together. *From the day we were born we have slept together.* In hatred, in jealousy, in scorn, coming together for a short moment of love just to keep warm.[3] [emphasis in original]

Mishima's perceptions of the homosexual bond, achieved by an emotional attachment to penises, is similar to Tiger's study of secret societies. Mishima describes hatred, jealousy and scorn as being both inner-directed and other-directed. Tiger notices that general antipathy towards a secret society is a negative reaction to imagined aggression by that secret society against the larger social group:

. . . Any group of persons who join together and agree to hold certain secrets, whatever these secrets are, and who permit their secrecy to be known or suspected, are committing an aggressive act which is bound to invite hostility and fear.[4]

Both Mishima and Tiger imply that the rest room bonding of homosexual males is general, rather than personalized. The "moment of love" is anonymous; warmth comes from anyone, momentarily. Such moments are emptied of identity, but charged with contempt for the self, as well as other men within the group. Perhaps "love" is a euphemism for occupational skill or property. Thus, the rest room context provides the individual male with performance training as a "professional" homosexual.

The office metaphor of Mishima employs the homosexual in competitive exploitation of other homosexuals' phallic skills and anatomical resources. The self-contempt one might feel in such impersonalized business is assuaged by projecting that contempt on others. Contempt is also lessened by the brevity and anonymity of sexual contact.

Yet, such self-preservation is achieved by reserving the self from others. The potentially whole self engages in phallic activity, with the penis functioning in place of the withheld personality. If one is reduced to a penis, one's personality structure may be defended, but potential expressions of a whole, intact self are diminished and distorted.

While both heterosexual and homosexual males share the fellowship of the phallic bond, male homosexuals are unique in the form of secrecy which their society must assume. The homosexual exists within a psychosocial context fraught with greater emotional intensity than heterosexuals. The toilet training of homosexuals confirms their sense of belonging in a milieu ascribed as typical of their monomanic need to relieve their penis fixation. Heterosexual males also use the toilet to achieve their penile relief—voiding the homosexual threat, by confirming the homosexual as human offal to be discharged from the social system. Thus, the homosexual's sense of life often becomes marked with three major phenomena which reinforce the penile expectations designed for him by heterosexuals: sexual marketing, sexual cannibalism and sexual suicide.

The individual homosexual's engagement in these three areas may vary according to his intensity of participation within his secret society. Yet, all American males are touched by elements within these sexual attitudes and ethics, because they spring from interpretation of the self-as-phallus.

The marketing mentality within American sexuality is generated from combinational sources of historic trends, pragmatic philosophy, technological advancement and economic exigency. Millett notes that Victorians used the term, "to spend," when alluding to sexual orgasm. As though semen were money, what is commonly alluded to as the American money morality can also transmute into a form of economical sexual morality.[5] Our society encourages and lauds accumulation of number and kind of sexual experiences. Sexual exploits may then burgeon one's ego account.

When men seek status through commercial forms of leverage, they often employ the symbols or ethics of sexual currency. "When executives are 'fucked' by the company, they can retaliate by 'fucking' their secretaries." ". . . In business, 'it's fuck or be fucked.' "[6] The main concern of men is whether or not they can "fuck over" the male opponent within their phallic competitions. Sex-as-economics is a residual ethic stemming from the larger technological requirements of a commercially oriented society.

Currently popular philosophy and psychology view man as an end in himself. This view concomitantly exists with the practical reality of our technological society, which demands that man become a means to his own end . . . or, more frequently, a means to someone else's end. As we pragmatically learn that ". . . Man exists only as a function—as an exchangeable part in the larger machine of society,"[7] we learn to make emotional and ethical adjustments to the processional momentum of American social life.

Because we have drives which demand personal responsibility

for how such drives are acted out, it becomes easier for us to abandon ourselves to the techniques of technology. Comfortable expediency becomes the *modus operandi* of self-fulfillment. J. Herbert Fill addresses himself to the danger of the technician internalizing his technique, in *The Mental Breakdown of a Nation:*

> Drives, those that emerge from our intellectually disowned will, dominate today's technology and encircle men in an increasingly illusory world. . . .
> We bcome depersonalized automatons, mere robots manipulated to keep the machinery running smoothly.[8]

If men become instruments of techniques which serve to keep the economic machine running smoothly, they then abstract themselves so that their personal humanity becomes secondary to larger, more personally debilitating social necessities. Erich Fromm, in *Marx's Concept of Man,* cite's Marx's belief that what and how a person produces often becomes internalized and then expressed as qualitative of the person's whole life.[9] Fromm continues to examine Marx's consideration of persons becoming their own raw material. Thus, each individual becomes the product of his own history. Given the social requirements of personal production, each man who views himself as ". . . his own product,"[10] can as easily consider other people as products also.

In *Man for Himself,* Fromm extends his marketing analysis of interpersonal relationships. He discusses the person with a receptive orientation to other people. Such a person feels the source of all good things is external to himself. To get them, he gives himself to others. In the area of psycho-sexual encounters, such an orientation becomes the marketing barter system. Fair trade rules change according to age, physical resources, commodity deficiencies or surplus of bartering parties—marketing principles now parallel social exchange principles.

In contrast to the person with a receptive orientation, the exploitative person also views sources of personal benefit as external—but this person hostilely manipulates others for personal gratification. Fromm considers both receptive and exploitative personality types as evidence that most personalities in American society function as exchange value for a personality market.[11]

It is obvious that the white homosexual male has little or no market value to his heterosexual counterpart. The homosexual male is dismissed, rather than competed against. The sexual market value of the homosexual male to other homosexuals is the chief concern here:

> Inside the homosexual world there will, of course, be Status Sex competition as vigorous as that found in the heterosexual sphere. . . .[12]

Within the socially defined toilet complex of homosexual adjustment, the homosexual male—as the heterosexual male—views himself as a phallic entity which requires and depends upon oral and genital contact for ratification of its function. Public display of penile attributes in toilets, bars, parks, movie houses, steam baths—or anywhere penile sexual contact is accompanied by degrees of anonymity—permeates the trade ethic using self-as-product in the sexual market place.

The techniques of such trade require the sexual technician to view others as mere exchangeable components within a covert social location. These locations then serve as the sexual department store of Fromm's statements concerning the dynamic between one who produces himself to be consumed, by another who shares a similar mercantile attitude about himself.

The variety of commodities displayed in homosexual department stores, often cause the individual to feel relatively unimportant, competitive, anonymous and potentially obsolete. "As an abstract customer he is important; as a concrete customer he is utterly unimportant. There is nobody who is glad about his coming, nobody who is particularly concerned about his wishes."[13]

Thus, as the homosexual male ratifies his identity as penile, his sense of self becomes identified with his function. The homosexual defends his ego structure, by learning to abstract and make anonymous the personalities of other homosexuals. They are rendered mere functional components in the endless search for gratifying penile contact. The number of contacts, rather than the potentially rewarding quality of such contacts, often becomes a measurement of how well one functions in the flesh ("meat") market. Yet, such concentration on number, makes the person another number in the competitive continuum of sexual possibility. To be just another "number," means one is just another penis to be manipulated indiscriminately in the ritual of sexual change.

Everett L. Shostrum interprets such behavior, in *Man the Manipulator,* to mean that ". . . the person who regards another as an 'it' becomes an 'it'."[14] The potential for the homosexual is then to experience disassociation from a healthy self-regard, as well as alienation from others. That the homosexual's life becomes disvalued and manipulated by others, reflects his own phallic concept and technique which he employs on others. Trade values in external units, force homosexuals to concentrate on acquiring or simulating visible commodities for exchange. What one looks like (virility of phallic self), how one acts (phallic style) and one's ability to arouse to penile agreement—as well as be aroused— (phallic confirmation) revolve about the penile marketing in sexual economics.

In the homosexual novel *Butterflies in Heat* by Darwin Porter, the author indulges in the tendency to disown or deny who one is, even as one exploits another person as a thing. Numie, the male hustler, meets Lola the black transsexual. Numie needs "her" for economic support. Lola wants sex in return for Numie's rent:

> The bedsprings were rusty and creaky—just the kind of rhythm he needed to do his job. She'd brag later. . . . But the joke would be on her. She'd never really have him. He gave them sex, but he'd never give of himself.
>
> Ignoring her at first, he started to pull out. His job over, he'd earned his supper. After all, he didn't like to kiss fags. . . . He was quick and efficient. But also thorough, competent in his job.[15]

Sex as work; work as technique; sexual technique as currency: sex moves from self-as-product, to penis-as-logic. The performer merely needs to ignore the self and other. The performer is only a penis doing its job, dispassionately and remotely, with no need to consider anything more about one's partner than where to put "it."

The need (or habit) to block the mind from self-consciousness, or even other-consciousness, helps the homosexual reduce himself to a narrowly defined organ within the whole complexity of potential personhood. He thus conforms to the larger sexual ethic of "fuck or be fucked." The "rhythm" of the "job" is the repetition of the penis in action. Such a sexual technician then levels his intrinsically multiple capacities, as well as reduces another individual's differences, to automated responses. He submits to harmony with the core of technology—machines. Jacques Ellul comments on larger ramifications of sexually technological logic, technique and self-concept in *The Technological Society:*

> The machine tends not only to create a new human environment, but also to modify man's very essence. The milieu in which he lives is no longer his. . . . He is acquainted only with the machine. His capacity to become a mechanic . . . has occasioned profound mental and psychic transformations which cannot yet be assessed.[16]

Yet, homosexuals continue to adapt and transform within the toilet space assigned for them by heterosexuals. They were not created for this world, but rather such a male space was designed by majority phallic politico-sexual needs, and minority homosexuals must now assess their unique degree of adaptation to it.

Homosexuals must also recognize that the new world that Ellul describes—given the logical mechanics of heterosexual males—is not particularly new in relation to any male's concept of the world-as-vagina. Technological metaphors apply to both heterosexual and homosexual males in their psychic orientation to space.

If the homosexual feels he is used, he often views other homosexuals as things to be used. Such instrumental operationalism falsely alleviates personal feelings of worthlessness at the moment of desired penile contact. The contact, the mechanical operation, contains its implicit body language. The message given and received is, "I am not me. I am what you want me to do." To tolerate that, "I shall play with you as a gadget in a game of simulated intimacy." These players rarely expect to win; most experience a sense of something lost. All hope, at least, to break even.

Such sexual gaming seems related to personality marketing, or the game/anti-game philosophy, so popular in American society. We are inundated with self-help books which attempt to formulate techniques for successful interpersonal relationships, or suggest systems for normative self-improvement. Most employ terminology and ethics of the sexual marketplace metaphor. Most seem written by heterosexual males whose frames of reference reflect a concentration on mechanical manipulation of self and others to make "people (and yourself) *work* for you." The end result is better feelings through better control of personal circumstances, i.e., other people.

Such self-help formulae contain marketing principles as well as forms of covert masturbatory satisfaction. Such formulae become how-to manuals of personally fulfilling manipulation of self and others, conceived by psychological and medical experts. Authors seeking to make human relationships more personal, more productive and more real—often reinforce what they claim to argue against.

Shostrum states that ". . . manipulation is a *system* of games or a *style of life,* as opposed merely to *playing* an individual game to avoid involvement with another person."[17] His argument implies the virtue of at least playing with others versus playing alone. Shostrum's life-style as gameboard, claims the role of therapy to be a technique which is a systematic approach to helping people become actualizers, rather than manipulators. Such a change occurs through increased awareness of one's manipulations, which leads to a "transformation"[18] or integration of one's polarized abilities. Thus we consciously substitute one technique for another, to manipulate people for the "good," rather than the "bad."

Agreement as to the good, apparently rests on the judgment of the expert-facilitator guiding such "transformations." One notes the spirit of the faith-healer, as well as the either/or logician. One also notes an objective distancing of the self-in-process, from potential attachments which might block the competitive fun in personal relationships:

> Most interpersonal relationships are games of domination or control, in which for the manipulator the need to win is paramount. The actualizer's alternative may be described as "creative excitement." He sees conflict as something exciting from which, win or lose, he can grow. He doesn't permit himself to become *attached* to what he might win or lose, for he knows that he is *changing,* and he identifies instead with what he can *become* from the creative conflict. Involved in this, naturally, is *faith:* faith that both parties will prove adequate to the resolution of the conflict.[19] [emphasis in original]

Good and bad thus become convenient dichotomies for viewing people, relationships, events and choices. One writer, however, emphasizes a trichotomy system for personality simplification, in order to view one's feelings as "positions." Thomas A. Harris sees life as composed of "tasks," defined by social metaphors of the self as Parent-Child-Adult, in his book, *I'm OK—You're OK.*

Similarly to Shostrum, Harris makes pragmatic, ". . . the faith we have in a new way to live. . . ."[20] For Harris, becoming "new" requires time. Change also occurs through three-way dialogues that clarify which of the three roles of Parent-Child-Adult happens to dominate the moment.

These dialogues contain potential "systems" which become semantic games to be played for greater self-understanding. Dividing the self into such apparent roles becomes similar to a game of "Guess who I am now?" Its value perhaps rests in helping our "adult" become a more effective reality computer to monitor behavioral transactions[21] which we can then call "real." In effect, we manufacture our own reality by rethinking it.

If we manufacture reality by transacting together, then the transaction analogy for human involvement fits nicely into the marketing mentality of personality. Such commercialism of self and others remains popular as a "positive" game-plan strategy, which allegedly oppose the unconsciously "negative" games. We ameliorate opposites by trading off the "good" for the "bad."

C. A. Tripp, who wrote the highly astute analysis, *The Homosexual Matrix,* also borrows marketing principles as metaphors to explain his theory of the origin of homosexuality. He substitutes "import-export" for the nature of personal transactions, and uses his economic image to explain how or why homosexual males get together. Simply put, his argument appears to rest on complementation: "I need what I don't have (or think I don't have), and I think you can supply it." Thus, homosexuals have

> . . . Eroticized and come to desire same-sex partners. . . . This desire means that the person wants to import admired same-sex attributes and thus that he has a felt-shortage of them. Sometimes this felt-shortage implies an actual shortage, as in the case of certain effeminate males. But what about the large majority of homosexual men who have an abundant (often superabundant) masculinity; how do they manage to retain a felt-shortage of it and thus a desire to import still more?
>
> Nobody wants to import more of exactly what he already has. . . . What he wants to import are the differing qualities which have made his partner attractive. Thus, the items of highest import-priority are characteristically those which a person has never tried to develop on his own.[22]

To attribute Tripp's reasoning to the worn-out psycho-social myth of "opposites attract each other," would do injustice to his theory. But he does seem to echo the sex-as-business psychology by implying that the "differing qualities" that make a homosexual's partner "attractive," is a sense of deficiency in those personal "items" which both partners attempt to acquire. Tripp implies that homosexual transactions can continue indefinitely, due to the insatiable nature of such homosexuals' eroticizing of brands of maleness.

Tripp thus appears to equate masculinity to brand items which can be borrowed or owned as commodities. Relationships become founded on superfluity or deficiency. The insatiability of the erotic capacity (or appetite), compensates for any imbalance in trade—any deficit or surplus of brands of maleness—when such masculinity characteristics are exchanged.

Tripp's explanation of homosexual relationships collides with Fromm's "receptive-exploitative" terms for people who look outside themselves for confirmation of their identities. The receptive and the exploitative person both barter themselves in the sexual marketplace. Perhaps Tripp's enthusiasm for his commercial explanation of sexual behavior underscores the majority male view of people as markets, relationships as often temporary incorporations and human characteristics as items to be used as products or currency in the competitive sexual marketplace. If individuals are resource components, then import-export relegates human sexuality to mere commercial technique.

As Tripp alludes to the insatiability of homosexuals' eroticizing brands of maleness, Maxwell Maltz also employs references to satiation of emotional hunger through the consumption of desired characteristics available in the personality marketplace. Mechanical techniques, technological imagery and product consumption, continue to frame masculine strategies for goal accomplishment.

In *Psycho-Cybernetics,* Maxwell Maltz denies the negative thought that man is mechanical. Yet, he describes the inner mechanism which operates each man as a device or instrument seeking a "target." The analogy to self-as-phallus could easily be substituted for Maltz's psychological system for self-gratification. Maltz illustrates each person as a "self-guided torpedo, or interceptor missile." The "target" or goal is "an enemy ship or plane." One's objective is to reach the goal with one's propulsion system, by using information about one's target through one's "sense organs." If one receives negative feedback from "an enemy ship," one uses these as signals to guide the self through personal errors. Then the "torpedo accomplishes its goal . . ." as "it literally 'gropes' its way. . . ."[23]

Maltz's torpedo paradigm could also illustrate the phallic attitude which homosexual transactions share. In the rest room of Mishima's *Forbidden Colors,* the "tiny gestures" and "code communications" resemble information signals about the phallic target. By trial and error, the homosexual's "torpedo-self" is guided by his sense organ to conquer the phallic enemy.

The sexual marketplace becomes a munitions factory. Personalities are produced to conquer others in a pleasurable and gratifying manner. That the manner describes the technique of sexual warfare, is perhaps due to Maltz's choice of terminology urged by a masculine conceptualization of penis or person-as-weapon.

To the images of machinery, marketing, and war that male writers use for interpersonal relationships, Eric Berne adds sexual appetite to explain his version of a transaction.

In *Games People Play,* Berne claims that "An exchange of strokes constitutes a *transaction,* which is the unit of social intercourse."[24] He believes that all people yearn for recognition, which he calls "recognition-hunger."[25] He considers mutual stroking as the technique to fulfill each person's need to be stimulated:

> . . . Not only biologically but also psychologically and socially, stimulus-hunger in many ways parallels the hunger for food. Such terms as malnutrition, satiation, gourmet, gourmand, faddist, ascetic, culinary arts, and good cook are easily transferred from the field of nutrition to the field of sensation.[26]

The curious combination of nutrition and psycho-erotic well-being, as well as Berne's "hungers" for recognition and stimulation, perhaps illustrates a unique relationship between food and sex, in the American male's self-concept.

If a man conceives of himself as a product to be selected from the sexual marketplace, he exists as an appetite appeaser for others. Such a man's value becomes subject to popular taste appeal. Berne's "hungers" require satiation. Satisfaction of phallic capacities then becomes paramount within "social intercourse." In the logic of sexual nutrition, then, "we are what we eat." Such logic requires that self-as-product will be consumed by others. Thus, we arrive at a *symbiotic* metaphor for such a person-to-person transaction; sexuality becomes a mutual act of cannibalism.

From the marketing of personality, as defined by self-help psychology books, the devouring of personality as a source of erotic nutrition is encouraged by sexual cookbooks. In *The Lonely Crowd,* Riesman speaks of the fairly recent proliferation of cookbooks, such as *The Joy of Cooking* and *Food is a Four Letter Word,* which raise food preparation and appreciation to new sensual heights. We do not merely cook or eat; we experiment to broaden and refine our exotic tastes. We are offered more exciting stimulus-hungers to illustrate what we possibly lack in erotic ability or appreciation.

Riesman also defines the contemporary person as one who in his "approach to food, as in his sexual encounters, is constantly looking for a qualitative element that may elude him."[27] As gourmet cookbooks transform the act of cooking to joyful ecstasy in more experimental self-accomplishment, so the excitement and pleasure of each man's increasingly imaginative sexual recipes are used "for reassurance that he is alive."[28] Riesman illustrates the restless search for self-meaning achieved through the constant need for excitement, whether that appetite is defined as food-hunger or sex-hunger. The search for self-meaning usually implies such a quest involves a need for personal security.

Riesman uses cookbooks as a paradigm for the need to unite the self with another in order to feel the pleasurable security of being alive. Erich Fromm uses a consumption metaphor to illustrate a person's search for security in union with another. Fromm believes such a mutually consuming symbiotic union devours the personal integrity of each individual. As a man is swallowed by another, his sense of self dissolves:

> . . . Instead of seeking security by being swallowed, he gains it by swallowing somebody else. In both cases the integrity of the individual is lost. In one case I dissolve myself in an outside power; I lose myself. In the other case I enlarge myself by making another being part of myself and thereby I gain the strength I lack as an independent self.[29]

In Gordon Merrick's novel, *The Lord Won't Mind,* young Peter admires his more experienced future lover, Charlie. Peter depends on Charlie's confirming attention; Peter needs to unite with Charlie's power—both emotional and sexual—and that power is

Charlie's penis size and function. To ingest Charlie's essence, Peter swallows Charlie's semen. As he swallows, he in turn is metaphorically swallowed by his consuming passion to become "lost" in Charlie. While Charlie drives the car, Peter fellates him, and ponders the food element in what he does:

> Peter's shoulders contracted, he retched once, but he held the sex in his mouth until Charlie's final spasms had subsided. . . .
> "Was it all right to swallow it?" he asked, his lips brushing against the dwindling sex.
> "Yes, sure."
> "I thought it might make me sick." He kissed the sex with lips and tongue and gentle teeth and lifted it back into the trousers and buttoned it in.
> "Actually, it's supposed to be good for you," Charlie assured him.
> "You taste wonderful. It is something people do, isn't it? I mean, with the mouth? I've heard of it."[30]

Food metaphors for sexual activity help define our tastes in physical experimentation, as well as help us to abstract another person to menu components. Language expressions for sexuality are replete with innuendo concerning eating, nutrition and health.

Heterosexual males refer to women's breasts as watermelons, cantaloupes or lemons. Her buttocks are transformed into buns or cupcakes. Her vagina carries a fruity essence by reference to its "juices." Her total person is frequently captured in euphemisms such as, tomato, dish or tasty morsel—she is generally described as a piece of meat. Robert H. Rimmer allows a female character to have intercourse with a male "dietician" in *The Harrad Experiment:*

> Last night, with Harry deep inside me, my face snuggled against his neck and shoulder, I was in a blissful, talkative mood. "It is incredible to me, that I lived twenty years and never tasted Jewish food until I knew you. . . ."
> Harry interrupted my breathless recital by kissing my breasts and gently probing them with his tongue. "I like the taste of your breasts better than any food. What's more, this diet is not fattening!"[31]

Later the woman refers to her childhood memory of making her ice cream cone last. She tells her sex partner, "Your lips and mouth taste better than any ice cream cone . . . You won't melt will you?"[32]

Such romantically cannibalistic images turn from the playful, "You look good enough to eat," to the more visceral "I want to eat you out." Thus heterosexuals and homosexuals attach romantic food value to various aspects of sexuality. Homosexuals often joke about getting their quota of "protein," or ingested semen, from the act of fellatio. Many believe that semen ingestion draws one closer to one's sexual partner, or that one becomes a part of the person one "eats." If semen somehow represents the male "juices," and the penis is the "meat" of the matter, the rectum also carries a nutritional, as well as a "therapeutic" factor.

In *The Joy of Gay Sex,* authors Charles Silverstein and Edmund White explain the delights of *rimming* (tongue in rectum) as ". . . a prime taste in sex. Among gay men, it is usually a prelude to fucking and is not only fun in itself but is a very effective way to relax the muscles of the anus."[33] The heterosexual counterpart to this book, *The Joy of Sex,* more blatantly equates sex with food, by designing "recipes" for sexual pleasure which reinforce the idea of sexual technique-as-content. Alex Comfort edits *The Joy of Sex* into divisions of "starters," "main courses," "sauces" and "pickles":

> But still the main dish is loving, unselfconscious intercourse—long, varied, ending with both parties satisfied but not so full they can't face another light course, and another meal in a few hours.[34]

While such sexual cookbooks represent "mealtimes" as loving opportunities for all participants to satisfy their psychological or physical appetites for each other, Kate Millett notes more savage cannibalistic themes which describe the sexual hungers of heterosexual males.

In *Sexual Politics,* Millett reviews two popular American male novelists, Henry Miller and Norman Mailer. She notes that Miller's female characters are consistently represented as "cunt," a crudely biological abstraction of female humanity. Miller's males are simultaneously biological animals, but superior intellects, who can achieve admirable cultural contributions. Miller's male suffers from the inner division between intellect and biological drive. "His appetite for 'cunt,' recurrent and shameful as it is, is, nevertheless, his way of staying in touch with his animal origins. It keeps him 'real.' "[35] If eating "cunt" keeps Miller's male characters "real," Norman Mailer "spiritualizes" the sexual devouring of the female by the male. For Mailer, sexual symbiosis becomes cannibalistic through his belief in "the old maxim of 'eat what you kill.' "[36]

Mailer's metaphorical cannibalism is epitomized by a form of sexual transsubstantiation, which is "enhanced by the macho Eucharist, 'bull's balls,' which he recommends with manic earnestness not only as a 'delicacy' but as 'equal to virility.' "[37] If Mailer's "macho Eucharist" consists of eating male sexual components, he glosses over the real intention of such ritualized cannibalism of masculinity. The logic to his sexual eating becomes suspect.

If we become identified with what we eat, Mailer's male characters who eat "cunt" would assimilate femininity; he cannot allow that. If the ultimate delicacy is "bull's balls," Mailer implies the better diet is phallic; however, his homophobia will not allow such a concession. Therefore, he must create a spiritual symbiotic union of male to male-part. The method of union still remains ingestion.

Without reference to moral value judgments, the oral assimilation of another's penis into the self contains significant psychological meanings, if not the "spiritual" tone of Mailer's meaning. Homosexuals inadvertently perpetuate mythological aspects of sexual cannibalism. An understanding of the cannibalistic mythos within one's ingestion of another could perhaps elevate the contemporary homosexual's attention from a bodily part, to consideration of his partner as a whole person. Mere swallowing of another does not achieve a viable symbiosis of two people, as noted by Fromm and Riesman. Emotional union of two people can even be thwarted by one conceiving the other as a sexual "portion" which can be pleasurably consumed.

The consumption of parts of people is a phallic construction in symbolic logic. Perhaps Norman O. Brown, in *Love's Body*, achieves greater accuracy in his eucharistic theory than Mailer does in his more "macho" rendition. Brown discusses the mystical meaning of eating the sacrificial body; he attaches his metaphors to the Eucharist of Christ, as well as the eating of sacrifices in ancient myths. Brown considers that our major "reality-principle" must acknowledge that all men are of one body. When they treat each other as separate parts, they thwart or corrupt the sacrificial element to their consumption of, or union with, each other:

The true sacrifice is total, a making holy of the whole; the false sacrifice sacrifices a part . . . a part cut off, bitten off; *the* part;

castration. Partial incorporation is castration; the part eaten, when the eating is partial is always a penis. Castration is mitigated (symbolic) cannibalism; the original aim is to eat, and to eat all.[38]
[emphasis in original]

Geza Roheim cites many cross-cultural legends associated with the god, Zeus, which incorporate aspects of castration-cannibalism. ". . . The cannibal ogre . . . is really the castration complex and 'to be eaten' means to be castrated by the father or to play the female role. . . ."[39] The implication here is that the participant in the sacrificial meal, eats of the phallic parts. The eaten one undergoes a transformation, or role exchange, which is played out as a woman.

James Frazer notes in *The Golden Bough* that a majority of tribes and cultures ate such parts of animals and humans which they believed to contain a particularly admirable quality. Ingestion of such physical parts supposedly gave the eater a valued capacity latent within the eaten part:

> . . . There are cermonies by which the youths are formed into guilds or lodges, and among the rites of initiation there is one which is intended to infuse courage, intelligence and other qualities into the novices. Whenever an enemy who has behaved with conspicuous bravery is killed, his liver which is considered the seat of valour; his ears . . . the skin of his forehead . . . his testicles which are held to be the seat of strength . . . are cut from his body and baked to cinders. The ashes . . . kept in the horn of a bull . . . during the ceremonies observed at circumcision, are mixed . . . into a kind of paste, which is administered . . . to the youths.[40]

Such traditions appear similar to Mailer's selection of "bull's balls" as appropriate food for enhancement of masculine virility. Other contemporary writers additionally notice that shared eating and drinking construct a context by which men are incorporated into each other, rather than (or in addition to) the meaning of the sacrifice which they eat. In William Golding's *Lord of the Flies,* the castaway British schoolboys kill their first pig; it is important that they all eat the significance of the killing, even though all were not involved. Jack, the hunter-leader shouts, "I painted my face—I stole up. Now you eat—all of you. . . ."[41]

Additionally, Tiger focuses on the importance of the drinking of alcohol within men's groups, and considers the possibility that sharing of ritualized drinking enhances the incorporation of men into a recognizable bond.[42]

Thus, Tiger's male role bonding, Golding's schoolboys sharing the act of killing by eating the pig's flesh and Frazer's infusion of qualities achieved from consuming significant animal or human parts, all point to an assumption of role. In consumption, each participant's sense of manhood is derived from an ultra-masculine source or action.

When men participate together, whether in hunting, warfare, sports, business or other fraternal companies, they personally seek to enhance their own, or ritually reinforce each other's sense of masculinity. Their ideal represents an ultra-masculine set of references, from which they assume or derive mutually shared images of masculinity. Each man attempts to imitate shared ideals. Such male affiliation achieved through shared erotic activity or belief, creates a male kinship group similar to that of fraternal brotherhoods, teams, squadrons, political parties or religious groups. The possibility exists that modern male kinships, bonding, or sharing of goals, values, images and ideologies are rooted in the much older psychic components of historical totemism.

Totemism was apparently a world-wide mystical belief in one's kinship with a totem object or animal. The character of the totem was inherent within human affiliation with the emblem or object. The emblem was only a representation of another, more mystical object or subject.

Festivals were held in which men imitated characteristics of their totem. Some groups sacrificed or symbolically ate their totems; others refrained because they felt they would eat themselves. Religious significance of totemism shifted into sociologically defined rituals and behaviors. Yet, one of the oldest taboos continued to exist psychically in relation to totem belief, which was ". . . to avoid sexual intercourse with totem companions of the other sex."[43]

Sigmund Freud, in *Totem and Taboo,* believed that historical taboos attempted to prevent acquisition or touching of the forbidden other, and worked against the human desire to imitate what was deified. Thus, Freud considered that "The basis of taboo is a forbidden action for which there exists a strong inclination in the unconscious."[44] Apparently all men share inclinations to violate the actions they forbid. Those who do violate socially held taboos, then contain a *disease* (contagion) factor in relation to taboos originating from totem conceptions:

An individual who has violated a taboo becomes himself taboo because he has the dangerous property of tempting others to follow his example. He arouses envy; why should he be allowed to do what is prohibited to others? He is therefore really *contagious,* in so far as every example incites to imitation, and therefore he himself must be avoided.[45] [emphasis in original]

There appeared a psychic conflict between prohibition and impulse, in relation to a person, a totem object, or an action regarding that object. "The individual constantly wants to carry out this action (the act of touching), he sees in it the highest pleasure, but he may not carry it out, and he even abominates it."[46]

In modern American male totemism, heterosexual males evidence a strong tendency to imitate socially valued male virtues. The character of various emblems of masculinity is socially shared by men, as they attempt to affiliate with the male mystique towards which these male emblems point. As heterosexuals affiliate with each other, and thus reinforce emblems of masculinity, Tiger compares such behavior to ancient totemistic urges, ". . . to the sense of personal manly validation individual men feel in terms of their male groups, and . . . perhaps the chief effect . . . in this matter is to specify object, instrument, and mode for the validation of individual maleness and group power. . . ."[47]

Thus, there exists the possibility in American culture that *heterosexual male totemism is framed within the object of the phallus. The phallic instrument is images and activities associated with masculinity. The phallic mode is the posture and style (psychic erection) attached to individual and group maleness.*

Male members observe and exhibit masculinity emblems. Yet, heterosexual males also share anxiety and conflict between Freud's "prohibition" and "impulse" to manifest touching behaviors towards their totem members. Perhaps at this point in logic, we arrive at the heart of the male heterosexual-homosexual conflict of interest.

In America, same-sex touching is highly regulated. Men may imitate each other, but not sexualize other males. Homosexual males violate this same-sex taboo. In effect, homosexuals tempt heterosexuals to do what heterosexuals are psychologically inclined to do—sexualize each other. Even within the psychic structure of heterosexual homophobia, one notices the contagion aspect in totemistic thought. Contagion implies that one imitates a forbidden visible behavior. Attorney Robert M. Brake, writing in *Skeptic* magazine, echoes one heterosexual version of homosexual contagion when he says, ". . . Role models can have an effect in seducing children into a homosexual lifestyle. . . ."[48] Freud details Brake's "modeling" concern as indicative of more historical characteristics of "taboo disease":

> Anything that leads the thoughts to what is prohibited and thus calls forth mental contact is just as much prohibited as immediate bodily contact; this same extension is also found in taboo.[49]

In the heterosexual disease framework of homosexual definition, contagion is obviously behavioral imitation, rather than a biological reality. Heterosexual males must create homosexuals into a taboo disease, in order to maintain political balance within the male kinship group, as well as to prevent such same-sex activity towards which each man is inclined. The argument against such a theory might rest on the idea that taboo existed to prevent sexual activity within totem families, and, in effect, control incest. However, Freud notes that members of a totem were originally ". . . *associations of men* consisting of members with equal rights, subject to the restrictions of the totemic system. . . ."[50] They were considered kin to each other. Other rules of totemism required that only kin could eat the sacrificial meal together. ". . . A kin is a group of persons whose life is so bound into a physical unity that they can be considered as parts of a common life."[51]

Thus, kin were male groups in common identity with their totem emblem or god—and were quite distinct from familiar blood ties, or family. While taboo controlled cross-sexual incest to prevent social rivalry and aggression, taboo also served to regulate homosexuality. Taboo merely socially blocked what individuals unconsciously desired to do.

While incest taboo continues in modern times to regulate intrafamily conflict and protect the real sexual abuse of children, the homosexual taboo no longer provides a social reality for containing a psychic capacity. Homosexuality as birth control, or as a realistic threat to tribal population and power growth, is an unnecessary consideration in a modern world. Yet, as a psychic threat to contemporary masculinity structures (totem emblems), homosexuality continues to be a chronic consideration of American males. It represents a behavior which heterosexuals covertly parallel in subliminally shared phallic objects, instruments and modes which ratify and reinforce male kinship.

That heterosexuals deny, confine and punish the homosexual potential within them, might be due to masculine configurations within *socially designated* maleness. Modern complexities of determining one's sexual identity, definitions of power structures of males in relation to sexual-politico stratifications via masculine/feminine dichotomies, and the unique American association between sexuality and guilt—all converge to create degrees of anxiety for males.

These components within American male-dominated sexual mores, include forms of sexual marketing, in which technology defines a man as a commodity to be produced and consumed. Such consumption of one by another, in terms of food properties or personality qualities, is a psychical ingestion of what is personally revered or socially valued. The chronic quest for pleasure indicates a rapacity of appetite, both psychologically and sexually. The process of eating others includes a selection of human parts, which are invested with emotional or symbolic meanings which often ignore the whole person; thus, the integrity of one's personality is "sacrificed" even as it is synthesized to a particular role function demanded by consumers.

From sexual cannibalism, it is possible that American males, both heterosexual and homosexual, now reinforce a trend towards symbolic cannibalism. This trend arouses intensified conflict between heterosexual and homosexual males. It also serves as a particularly destructive mechanism between homosexual males.

In *The Manufacture of Madness,* Thomas S. Szasz believes that modern man has moved beyond the confining rituals of mere physical killing and eating of animal or human sacrifices. He considers the possibility that one man can possess and consume another man's soul, symbolically:

> . . . Our ancestors were, and we remain, existential or spiritual cannibals. As a rule, we live off the meaning others give their lives, validating our humanity by invalidating theirs.[52]

Because man is a social animal, the conditions of (male) group membership serve to define expected behaviors and one's sense of identity in relation to one's group. Masculinity is always conditional. "To remain a member of a group, man must often attack and sacrifice nonmembers."[53] Additionally, each man variously defines internal enemies within his group. The element of intragroup competition inspires one man to validate or strengthen his group membership, proportionately to the potential invalidation or weakening of others' group membership:

> Typically, we confirm our loyalty to our group by asserting the disloyalty of others (in or outside the group) to it; we thus purchase membership in the community by excluding others from it. . . . Because of this, the scapegoat is the indispensable victim of non-cannibalistic societies.[54]

Szasz points to the meaning behind the homosexual male's "selection out" of his male totem kinship, from the larger brotherhood of communicants to male power. The heterosexual male confirms his own loyalty to heterosexual group membership, by perpetrating various reasons why homosexuals are disloyal to the emblems (totem) of the masculine group. The homosexual scapegoat is thus declared an invalid male member; he may be sacrificed. Through such invalidation, the heterosexual male can continue—without conscious guilt—to devour the homosexual sacrificial meal in honor of masculine totemism. As Szasz notes, "The cannibal incorporates his victim to give himself virtue; we expel ours to give ourselves innocence."[55]

Perhaps it is not too extreme to consider that the totem of each male is himself, in correspondence with those various emblems of the masculine ideal—which are usually phallic. The homosexual overtly worships the masculine ideal; the heterosexual camouflages his desire for phallic contact with his emblems (phallic) and subjects (male), and deals with his anxieties about such desires, as best he can.

That heterosexual males cannot (or will not) articulate their deification of self-as-phallus, does not prevent their subliminal predeliction to do so.

Millett notices that novelist Henry Miller serves as high priest within the masculinity cult, and refers to his psychic erection of the penis and testicles to arouse the imagination of his readers:

> In the "Land of Fuck" the "spermatozoon reigns supreme." God is the "summation of all the spermatozoa." Miller himself is divine: "My name? Why just call me God." Actually, he's even a bit more than this—"something beyond God Almighty. . . . *I am a man.* That seems to me sufficient." Probably, but just in case, it is safer to develop a theology and know one's catechism: "Before me always the image of the body, our triune god of penis and testicles. On the right,

God the Father; on the left and hanging a little lower, God the Son; and between and above them, the Holy Ghost. I can never forget that this holy trinity is man-made."[56]

The shrine for Miller's worship of his penis is obviously the vagina. Yet, it is never worthy to bear the greatness of his glory. Inadvertently, homosexuals move closer to Miller's reality principle of males—the heterosexual's true object of worship. Thus, homosexuals fellate the male penis—as well as consume its emblematic significance—while heterosexuals remain in conflict with their impulses and prohibitions.

Modern psychology and religion note that heterosexual males suffer a disassociation from themselves, which is perhaps inevitable given the dishonesty and violence of their world and self-view. The modern heterosexual male continues to cannibalize, existentially, women, racial minorities, and homosexual men. He mythically describes and ritualistically reinforces his membership in the heterosexual male group, in order to establish political power over those outside of his clan. Such myths are merely imaginary meanings designed to organize and protect the solidarity of his in-group.

The homosexual male can easily employ similar rituals, adopt similar mythologies, and cannibalize the essence of others' personalities—because both heterosexual and homosexual males share kinship within the phallic totem clan. As the heterosexual can disassociate his emotional and intellectual self from his physical capacity, so the homosexual can experience disassociation from his potentially whole integrity.

The homosexual who yields to the larger heterosexual deification of self, through a symbolic veneration of phallic attitudes, activities and images, gambles with the probability that loss of such phallic elements will diminish his life. The homosexual's temptation to frame his sense of self or others through penile considerations, creates a fragmentation of personality, internally, and a disassociation of self from others, externally. Personality validation depends on total assimilation of one person by another.

Currently, when men internalize each other's masculinity characteristics, they assimilate social fictions, rather than personal realities. Thus, both heterosexual and homosexual males are faced with a primary ethical choice to actualize the reality of their lives:

Partial incorporation or total incorporation; eating a penis and eating a body. Partial incorporation is eating of a representative (symbolic) part, which is only partially (symbolically) eaten; as possession is mitigated (symbolic) eating. The part partially eaten remains a separate part, undigested; the original ownership is not obliterated; it is a part "borrowed," i.e., stolen.[57]

For males, the partial cannibalism of masculine elements contains the imitative element—the borrowed emblems which men feed upon. The ideal is to share one another in mutual totality.

The heterosexual male who symbolically or ethically forces others to swallow his penis, never achieves the unifying symbiotic relief for, and stimulation of, his identity needs. Such a man remains nothing more than a collection of phallic emblems and impulses.

The homosexual male who symbolically or ethically swallows a penis, and then senses that something less than his concept of personal wholeness is being swallowed, remains unincorporated with another. Such a man participates (plays a role) with another, but he does not fuse or incorporate with another.

Both heterosexual and homosexual males face the ethical choice between the fictitious and the real, between partial incorporation or total incorporation of the whole self into another's wholeness. For a man to accept less than total integration in a person-to-person relationship, argues for his being swallowed up. He existentially disappears. He reappears in repetitious circumstances which demand his fragmentation into phallic rituals of masculinity confirmation. Such rituals are often habitual simulations of a deeper desire to perpetuate one's sense of whole fulfillment, in relationship with another.

Plato speaks of partial and whole fulfillment, in the *Symposium*, when he states that "love is desire for the perpetual possession of the good."[58] Then he remarks that love prompts one into an unspoken longing to melt into the loved one, an echo of the incorporation aspect of consuming the whole (body), rather than symbolically partially consuming the part (penis), noted by Brown.

If integration into wholeness appears to be the organic rhythm and design of the self alone—or the self with another—then disintegration of self, in turn, fragments others into perpetual separation. The homosexual male-as-phallus thus *endlessly repeats* "techniques" of longing, pleasure and desire. The *substance* of his action is the *imagined worth* of masculinity as commodity or currency. Sexual currency converts people into products to be consumed, insatiably, in honor of the cult of masculinity. Concentration upon emblematic portions—consumption of phallic attributes—then eradicates the potentially whole meal which could unify one's psychic integrity with another's personal wholeness.

The homosexual hungers for what he annihilates. Love-as-wholeness dies through endless repetitions of facsimiles of love—as sex. The self dies slowly as the homosexual allows himself to be cannibalistically torn apart, in sexual encounter after sexual encounter. The self becomes a repetitious sacrifice offered up to replace the idolatry of the penis-as-All.

Brown refers to the cruelties intrinsic within the sacrifice of one's identity as ". . . self-sacrifice, self-slaughter, self-annihilation."[59] The homosexual thus figuratively consumes himself in his hunger for personal affirmation. The sense of emptiness which too often follows repetitious sexual cannibalism, permeates the technique of sexual suicide.

When I describe the tendency for homosexual males to commit gradual sexual suicide, my theory includes the actual self-inflicted death act, but is not restricted to it. The metaphor of suicide accompanies many personal actions or self-attitudes. One can socially jeopardize, ostracize or sanction oneself through extreme self-assertion or self-withdrawal. One can also achieve respect or aid from others through the risk of oneself in an heroically suicidal manner.

Suicide squads on football teams initiate the extreme hitting and establishing of direction for team members to follow. To commit political or corporate suicide is to take an unpopular stand against general opposition, either because of commitment to one's ideals or because of a risky (but often admired) gamble within the average framework of male competition.

Alcoholism and drug usage can offer men relief through gradual withdrawal of self from social contexts which threaten or thwart their sense of autonomy or success. Some men engage in repeated flirtation with dangerous circumstances which carry an implicit death potential.

Other men socially jeopardize their memberships within various social groups—church, business, fraternity, recreational, friendships, family or one-to-one relationships—by espousing the unpopular view, the socially disruptive position or the esteem-annihilating assertion of self, either verbally or behaviorally. Whatever form such symbolic suicides might take, its function generates a gamble with defeat, in relation to masculinity principles and style.

Willy Loman's suicide in Arthur Miller's play, *Death of a Salesman,* is paradigmatic of the suicidal rationale for the average American male. Loman has lost the ability "to be well liked," by business associates; he has lost the respect of his sons; he has failed as a husband-provider; he is friendless, emasculated and paralyzed by circumstance. Loman is defeated as a saleman, because he can no longer sell himself. He kills himself for the insurance benefits to his family; through death-as-sacrifice, he hopes to regain their esteem and his own sense of self-worth.

Playwright Lillian Hellman's *The Children's Hour,* treats suicide from the woman's point of view, as a retreat from dealing with one woman's recognition of her own lesbian tendencies, and as a sacrifice for her heterosexual friend's damaged reputation and potential for a happily married (normal) life. Martha thus shoots herself; her friend Karen is shocked into a recognition of the depth and honesty of Martha's love for her. The sacrificial element is present in Martha's self-destruction, as it is in Willy Loman's. Yet both characters—for different reasons—share a failure in achievement within the social definitions for success in role . . . as a woman, and as a man.

The suicidal impetus is metaphorically present in various activities or self-concepts. Sexual suicide can also permeate life-styles which homosexual males design to cope with a life defined for them by heterosexuals. Sexual suicide also includes negative strategies the homosexual male adopts to cope with definitions given to him by other homosexuals.

I wish to approach sexual suicide as a progression of sexual acts which tend to maintain the homosexual's feeling of anonymity, alienation and anxiety—within himself as well as in his relationship to others. Serialized sexual suicide works to reinforce the homosexual's conception of himself as primarily a phallic object. He gradually recognizes his personhood is reduced and consumed by those men to whom he turns for positive reinforcement of his humanity.

I do not argue against serial sexual encounters; I do not propose monogamy as the only viable alternative for positive homosexuality. I do contend that the male homosexual progressively annihilates his potential wholeness, when he perpetually offers himself, sacrificially, to another worshipper of his penis.

Such a man *becomes* his penis, which he trades for another's penis, in a ritualized act of compounded sexual suicide. Since *somebody*-as-penis, can be *anybody*-as-penis, such serialized mutual exchange contains elements of anonymity and alientation, which eradicate each man's body-mind-spirit integrity. The person ceases to exist; the phallic function becomes the primary consideration.

Such ritualized sexual suicide can occur in the anonymous safety of the toilet. It can happen within the familiar circumstance of an extended lover relationship. The location of, or one's familiarity with, one's sexual other, are unimportant as to why sexual suicide occurs.

The roots of sexual suicide probe deeply into the contemporary quality of the American male's social and psychological content and techniques for living. These often destructive roots connect the isolated homosexual male to his own sexual in-group. Such connection is frequently and creatively denied on emotional, intellectual or social levels. Connection is as frequently accepted in accommodation to rigidifying sexual role behaviors and self-denying rituals practiced in bars, toilets, bath houses or other homosexual meeting places.

The solitary male homosexual, as any other person in America, experiences a concern with fortification of his whole identity; he wishes to achieve more positive relationships with other homosexuals. Recognition of symptoms, elements and trends within the process of sexual suicide, could perhaps help the homosexual male to sever such roots which support his progressive annihilation.

Being a male in America statistically proves to be dangerous for the individual man—whether he is heterosexual *or* homosexual. Herb Goldberg comments in *The Hazards of Being Male:*

> Up to the age of twenty-four the male rate of suicide is over three times as high as the female's. Over the age of sixty-five, the rate is almost five times as high for the male. Men have a twelve times higher ratio of success to failure in suicide attempts in comparison to women.[60]

The divorced male commits suicide three to one, compared with the divorced female. Bachelors commit suicide on a four to one ratio, as compared with unmarried women.

The homosexual male also belongs in these statistics, but no one is sure to what proportion. Michael Schofield believes the prevalence of homosexual suicides is underestimated. Homosexual motives for suicide are often kept from the coroner by embarrassed family or friends.[61] One cannot say, however, that homosexuality *per se* is the primary cause for any homosexual male suicide, any more than one can attribute suicide by a black or a Jew, to racial or religious causes.

The Homosexual male does belong within the general framework of American maleness—both in life, as well as in physical death by choice. Goldberg summarizes the heterosexual male dilemma, as he calls for a renewal of heterosexual self-understanding. His words apply to homosexual males as well:

> Emotionally repressed, out of touch with his body, alienated and isolated from other men, terrorized by the fear of failure, afraid to ask for help, thrown out at a moment's notice on the occupational junkpile. . . . Perhaps . . . the male has become an artist in the creation of many hidden ways of killing himself.[62]

And perhaps the "artistry" involves degrees of excessiveness in alcohol, work, hobbies, high risk activities, as well as sexuality.

Goldberg points to another deficiency in a man's life, which might contribute to a higher suicide rate among heterosexual males. ". . . The lack of buddyship is also an important factor in the significantly higher male suicide rate and the significantly higher rate of death of divorced males. . . ."[63] He connects buddyship to spontaneity, mutual nourishment, love and a free-wheeling, no-strings-attached form of mutual commitment. The threats to real buddyship are social innuendos about latent homosexuality, or women who attempt to undermine the buddyship because of jealousy: "You're always kissing his ass," "Why don't you go to bed with him?" "You spend more time with him than you do with me!"[64]

Thus, the kiss of death to male heterosexual closeness is aimed at implying a homosexual interest, because it rivals male-female relationships. However, Goldberg constructively presents a case for male-to-male emotional involvement as a stress reliever for general masculinity expectations, which include remoteness, defensiveness and aggression as techniques containing a suicidal potential.

In *Sun and Steel*, author-cinematographer-artist Yukio Mishima artfully discusses his romantic impulse towards death. Mishima believed that perfection of the body and its functions prepares a man for a tragic death. A man's form and function become united tragically, but heroically. Mishima's cult of the hero romanticizes the idea of physical ultra-masculinity: ". . . The cult of the hero is . . . the basic principle of the body . . . and is intimately involved with the contrast between the robustness of the body and the destruction that is death."[65]

Mishima argues that because one's body deteriorates and fades, one should accept the ancient Greek entreaty to live beautifully and die beautifully—but through violent or self-inflicted means. Thus, Mishima laments that too many men do not objectify masculinity to the intensity he believes necessary:

> In ordinary life, society maintains a careful surveillance to ensure that men shall have no part in beauty; physical beauty in the male, when considered as an "object" in itself . . . is despised. . . .[66]

Mishima argues for an annihilation of the self in relation to one's heroic cult members. By this means the individual would share the suffering of one's group, and become lost in the objectification of one another's masculine appearance: ". . . For the body to reach that level at which the divine might be glimpsed, a dissolution of the individual was necessary."[67] In 1970, Mishima committed hara-kiri, partially in protest against the Japanese government's "emasculation" of itself through agreement to limiting military treaties.

The element of sexual suicide within Mishima's philosophy is common to heterosexual and homosexual males who "artistically" attempt to regulate life-in-death. Emphasizing style, such men view the male body as a beautiful *object*. With it, they attempt to create techniques which camouflage the tragedy of its ultimate failure. Italian film director Luchino Visconti explored this suicidal component within fixation on the male body as beautiful object in his interpretation of the Thomas Mann novel, *Death in Venice*.

The aging artist, Aschenbach, becomes obsessed with a beautiful boy whom he watches daily at play at a turn of the century resort. "Ultimately the dying Aschenbach sees the lad as a projection of his own desolate longings for ideal beauty and friendship."[68] Visconti attempts to show the universal problem of integrating ". . . the life of the mind to that of the body. . . ."[69] He captures the poignancy of desire for one's beautiful "object," as well as one's dissolution into failure and personal destruction ". . . in the scene in which the hapless old man garishly paints his face and dyes his hair in a pathetic attempt to close the age gap between himself and the boy whom he idolizes."[70]

Thus, men often dissolve themselves into male groups of like minds, to share their suffering in moment to-moment worship and celebration of masculine perfection. Separately or together, such celebration is centered upon a visibly fading object; the beauty of the male as phallic ideal. Within the process of such celebration is perhaps what Freud considered as the ability of the ego to kill itself, when it is able to treat itself as an object. The dissolution of the self, as noted by Mishima and Mann, perhaps mirrors Freud's belief that "in suicide the ego is overwhelmed by the object. . . ."[71]

Thus, when the homosexual views himself proportionately to his phallic function (as do many heterosexuals), his ego—his self-concept—becomes immersed in phallic considerations. Other homosexuals join him to form a heroic masculinity cult. Together, they objectify their body type, genital size, masculine style and sexual performance. They dissect each other into phallic components. Inadvertently, they fragment themselves into phallic functions which depend on forms—normative stylizations of heroic masculinity.

Functional dependency on such forms then becomes what Ernst Breisach calls "contingencies," in his *Introduction to Modern Existentialism*. The concept of contingency for each man includes:

> . . . The awareness of "being-thrown-into-this world. . . ." Around him is a puzzling, often terrifying world. Similarly life ends with an event beyond man's control, death.[72]

The existentialist thinker considers contingency to death, as necessary to make us wonder about our life's meaning. A sense of contingency helps us intensify our life experiences, as it prompts us to realize the value within each moment's development of our authenticity.

Accompanying our sense of contingency, is our sense of anxiety. For the existentialist, self-defeating anxiety occurs from the feeling that one is unable to conform. Such anxiety creates an unauthentic existence: "Its disturbing implication is the call for strict conformity to the habits of thought and action exhibited by man's society, since it is presumed that they constitute the most perfect way of adjustment."[73] However, self-actualizing anxiety can authenticate our existence when it helps to guide our emerging awareness that who we are eventually includes who we will not be. Thus, we can focus the motives of our lives "to become oneself" rather than to achieve "improved conformity."[74]

Popularized psychology, assertiveness training and other self-help formulae are uncomfortable with anxiety. The messages are: we are anxious because we are maladjusted; our needs remain ungratified because we have not mastered successful techniques of adjustment to our society. Anxiety is then linked to lack of personal success. It is defined as inability to conform. Modern psychology too often reinterprets existential contingencies into success techniques available for shaping the self (or others) into comfortable feelings of happy well-being. Modern psychology uses anxiety to inauthenticate, rather than to authenticate the individual's life.

Anxiety could urge us to become ourselves, to exist in wholeness, simultaneously, with others. Yet the popular structures of self analysis use anxiety to coerce individuals into similar patterns of thought and behavior. Such similar norms narrate prescriptive monologues often designed by white, heterosexual male power groups. These monologues are then socially imposed upon all individuals to define, control and delineate the arbitrary differences between personally and socially "good" or "bad" behavior. The result is that such behaviors are usually habitual imitations of socially given ideal selves, which are fraught with rigidity, punishment and a sense of the synthetic:

> Normal human behavior, then is not natural, but rather habitual behavior that over a period of time has become typical in a particular society.[75]

Homosexuals tend to adjust their lives anxiously. They are told by a heterosexual majority that they are atypical . . . abnormal. Religious monologues narrate spiritual death; legal monologues narrate punishment; social customs narrate censure and expulsion of the homosexual. To ignore this collection of disdain for homosexuality, requires the homosexual male to have strong motivation and skill in defining his own norms for his own life.

Within the collective heterosexual monologue, as well as within the collective homosexual models for ethical behavior, exist fractured images of ideal selves for the homosexual to imitate. The temptation to imitate, also contains a reactionary impulse within the homosexual, to commit symbolic suicide by acting out what James Hillman calls a "model of dismemberment."[76] The result of this impulse achieves for the personality what Fromm terms "automaton conformity":

. . . The individual ceases to be himself; he adopts entirely the kind of personality offered to him by cultural patterns; and he therefore becomes exactly as all others are and as they expect him to be. The discrepancy between "I" and the world disappears and with it the conscious fear of aloneness and powerlessness.[77]

For the homosexual, such attempts to conform to heterosexual standards of behavior merely create the self-in-hiding. He strives to duplicate socially authenticated images of masculinity. Yet, the homosexual who cannot tolerate assimilation into images of social expectation, may anxiously vascillate between the homosexual and heterosexual milieux, as he feigns the requirements for both. The homosexual who accommodates to either territory of masculinity as defined by others, only achieves a gradual—but eventually overwhelming—sense of dismemberment within his own personality, as well as in his community with others.

Dismemberment creates severance; the homosexual senses loneliness, even as he seeks to alleviate his fear of being alone. Dismemberment creates delay; the homosexual vascillates between imitations of others' expectations, even as he attempts to integrate himself as a whole person in fulfillment of his life potential. As the homosexual attempts to ameliorate "the discrepancy between 'I' and the world," his own uniqueness "disappears." In a wish for instant transformation, suicidal annihilation of the self only releases the homosexual into the very delay of dismemberment he wishes to escape. While a reunion with self (or with another) is the motive for his wish for personal transformation, the homosexual's technique for achieving it is frequently only sexual.

The quick lay, the furtive act of fellatio, the perpetual search for variety in sexual partners, all appear to contain the promise of personal transformation. Often, such brief or superficial contacts merely limit or stall the homosexual's potential progression towards personal completeness and finality.

Genital union then becomes habituated attempts to achieve personal reunion of a self dismembered from other homosexuals by adherence to synthetic rituals of intimacy. Such genital union remains only momentary in order for the ambivalent homosexual to cope psychically with his dismemberment from heterosexual images of approved behavior. Reunion is difficult to achieve within an individual who changes his self-concept to suit the expediency of imagined necessity.

Expediency, the ethic of Fromm's automaton conformist, then trains the sexually suicidal homosexual to engage in daily death reheasals. Each time he dismembers himself through internalization of heterosexual abuse, myth and judgment, the homosexual absorbs the psychological poison of the social lie, and debilitates his life with pseudo-truth. Each time he rehearses the emotional content of heterosexual monologues, he turns the weapon of such intent upon himself, or else points his inner-hatred outward to other homosexuals in acts of psychic murder. While the homosexual may thus gain revenge on others, for a life taken from his own control—such revenge on heterosexual or homosexual alike, will not unify his self-concept.

Even in love, the ambivalent homosexual rehearses his preparation for psychic death. He tends to identify with those he seeks to use. The marketing requirement within human consumption requires a variety of products to quiet the demands of emotional hungers. The insatiability of appetite is sharpened by choice. The homosexual as consumer is trained not to expect feelings to endure or relationships to last. Thus, attempts to reunify himself through unity with another, carry the corrosive probability that feelings must die if the homosexual is to tolerate life as it is. This final rehearsal for personal defeat requires the homosexual to unconsciously capitulate to moral dismemberment within the ethical structures of sexual marketing, sexual cannibalism and sexual suicide.

All men—whether heterosexual or homosexual—face the emptiness of rehearsals for a life that denies them ownership of their own potential. Yet the homosexual, especially, must design his own techniques for saying no to the negative—the deleterious monologues which limit and confine the homosexual's emotional, intellectual, physical and social world in which he must live. The homosexual must agree within himself to reunify his own sense of brokenness from the many parts of his personal dream to which he still has access. The homosexual is accessible to himself. To choose against the many choices thrust in his way to self-access, is the beginning of internal agreement. No to the negative becomes yes to self-reunion, or any possible union with others.

Union and reunion imply dialogues which mutually share knowledge of who one is, with knowledge of who others might be. Within the risk of dialogue exists the challenge of truth. In truth is the essence of one's freedom to exist.

The homosexual need not search for techniques of living within the monologues of self-helping therapies, formulae or new terminologies for the old mythologies of conformity. Nonconformity—the beginning of dialogue—begins with the word "no." To describe this beginning point in each homosexual's life, perhaps James Hillman articulates *with* each homosexual, rather than *for* him, as he makes his own choice for living in *Suicide and the Soul:*

> *Until we can say no to life, we have not really said yes to it,* but have only been carried along by its collective stream. . . . The individual standing against this current . . . requires courage. And courage has since classic times been linked with suicide arguments: it takes courage to choose the ordeal of life, and it takes courage to enter the unknown by one's own decision. Some choose life because they are afraid of death and others choose death because they are afraid of life. . . .
>
> The courage to be—as it is modishly called—means not just choosing life out there. The real choice is choosing oneself, one's individual truth. . . .[78]   [emphasis in original]

6/DIALOGUES: The Second Series Exits from the Men's Room of Sexual Habit

Beggars show you their wounds to make you feel sorry for them.[1]—Yukio Mishima, *Thirst for Love*

In the erotic realm, homosexual males usually establish fixed sexual responses without conscious choice. The homosexual's involuntary thoughts, feelings and behaviors are repeated until they crystallize into fairly permanent and voluntary modes. Generally, these orientational modes are acquired, rather than individually created. When acquired, such modes are less than erotic—they become mechanical responses conditional to one's environment. When self-generated, one's orientational modes retain a sensuous and dynamically creative openness, as well as an erotic freedom to be spontaneously human, rather than mechanically imitative.

For many homosexuals, their emerging consciousness of themselves first learns how to operate erotically through available heterosexual forms. Each homosexual must adapt these forms to his own necessary reinterpretation. Whatever his translation might be, he tends intellectually to copy male-female formulae of erotic exchange.

Additionally, the homosexual's erotic framework includes predominantly sexual response patterns which heterosexuals attribute to expectations for homosexual identity. The homosexual develops a mental set that what he does sexually is somehow second rate, extreme, dirty and not to be valued.

Finally, the homosexual's emerging consciousness also acquires erotic customs which exclusively characterize the

170

homosexual milieu—the fabled "gay world." These attitudes, values and expectations are so strongly associated with homosexuality, that their usage borders on fixation. The want ad section of any gay publication repeats the narrow focus on certain sexual phenomena, selected as favorite erotic specialities. If a homosexual is horny, hot and hung, into full body massage or jock strap exhibitionism, likes full-bottom spanking, naked combat, enemas or leather and rubber bondage, he can serve one of the sexual predilictions to which some homosexual men become attached. Then his full range of erotic possibility is superceded by monomanic sexual technique and orgasmic gadgetry.

Whatever the focus on his sexual subject, any man learns how, when and where to have sexual intercourse. The "why" of sexuality derives from historical-religious dictations for man to replenish the population, according to Divine plan or patriarchal folkways which regulate property distribution. Quasi-moral monologues concerning the purpose of sex have been challenged by recent attitudes toward birth control, abortion, feminist rights and the sex-as-pleasure concept. The "what" of sexuality now includes a plethora of techniques, erotic guidebooks, erotic hardware and experiments for obtaining more mileage from the penis.

Combinations of sexual mores are established by heterosexuals for themselves—and for homosexuals. These mores are modified by homosexuals for each other; the homosexual male learns how to have sex with men, where erotic public territories are and when to appropriately comply to sexual opportunities. If he considers the "why" of homosexually erotic encounters, he discovers he has no commonly valued set of ethics to guide his behavior in his male-to-male relationships. And the "what" of homosexual accoutrements—from cock rings, vibrators and water sports, to video cameras, three-ways or amyl nitrate—only habituate his sexual customs away from love, into repeated stagings of cosmetically inspired eroticism.

If the homosexual depends on sexual *habits,* which in turn, trap him in repetitious pursuit of the habit-object, such habits do offer a degree of emotional relief. However, among possible human sexual behaviors, homosexuality receives the most severe moral and social condemnation and control. This treatment escalates the homosexual male's anxiety and guilt, his sense of wrongness over his sexual divergence. At this point, the often inadvertent development of sexual habits provide emotional relief for the homosexual in quite curious ways.

Sexual habits can relieve the homosexual's uncertainty about how to behave sexually with men. Habits provide a comfortably familiar code of conduct; a specific sexual ritual seemingly guarantees a semblance of possible communication via erotic etiquette. Since habits do not require deep intellectual scrutiny, the homosexual feels he is reducing his psycho-sexual confusion or distress.

Habits also tend to reinforce the American value for doing things, in order to establish our sense of being someone. As the homosexual busily runs the gamut of possible erotic formulae, his sexual partner(s) provides the necessary feedback to the modern, haunting question, "How am I doing?"

Sexual habits safely guide the homosexual in automatic responses which require little risk, creativity or growth. He need only repeat himself in comfortably familiar performances, and rate himself—or others—as good, bad or mediocre. While these performances are visible, they are often disconnected from the deeper ranges of human emotion or desire.

However, the homosexual's submission to sexual habits reinforces the very dogmatism of sexual ethics, from which he wishes to be free. Ethics are systematized standards of conduct. They are attached to complementary sets of moral principles. Presently, such moral ethics are equated with our ability to conform to our group's standards of value. Subsequently, our successful adjustment to such sexual rules, requires an overt obedience to the "good" and an apparent avoidance of the "bad."

These standards of good and bad, or right and wrong, are instilled in children, modified by adolescents and rigidified by adults. To infract any acceptable standards of ethical morality implies that we are excessively passionate, morally indiscreet or neurotic. What we do, is attached to what we should feel; ethical infractions make us feel remorseful, anxious or sinfully guilty. We are trained that if we suffer enough for ethical failure, we can forgive ourselves or expect others to forgive us. A moral homeostasis is regained. Yet, dogmatic systems for sexual conduct do not conveniently apply to each person's unique personality.

The homosexual infracts society's sexual ethic the first time he goes to bed with a man (or even thinks about it). Neither abstinence, mindless sexual repetition or rationalization successfully assuages the guilt which far too many homosexuals feel in their male-to-male contacts. To deal with dogmatic systems of sexual behavior expected by heterosexual society, the homosexual constructs a system of sexual habits which is as rigid as the moral authoritarianism against which he reacts. The homosexual's reliance on habit seems to free him from dogmatic constraint. Any such relief is usually marginal and momentary.

Thus, the homosexual seeks relief in self abandonment to promiscuity. Having sex with many men does not require him to identify his personal ethical standards as a homosexual person. The homosexual can find relief to dogmatic sexual expectations by narrowing, or fixing, his sexual behaviors until he only repeats one or several mechanical expressions. This alternative sometimes emerges as the homosexual's chronic response to the general social opinion that moral ethics exclude a variety of sexual behaviors. By fixing several exclusive sexual activities, the homosexual avoids feeling morally out of control. As he limits his sexual behavior, he can even diminish his own fear of being homosexual.

This control of anxiety is often the homosexual's response to a feeling of inner emptiness, a sense that something is essentially wrong (in this case, his socially forbidden sexuality). Thus, a development of homosexual dogmatics can create a simulated sense of ethical goodness—the homosexual rigidly adheres to habits which safely define erotic dimensions. Such rules then provide a good-bad scale with which the homosexual pretends to relieve his anxiety over breaking heterosexual rules for male sexuality. One dogmatic system is merely exchanged for another.

At this point, sexual habits serve to block possible spontaneous erotic exchanges between homosexual males. Two major psychological reactions follow in any reactionary homoerotic ethical system, or even in the apparent absence of one: the homosexual might use his sexual partner as a monitor-parent; and the homosexual might develop dependency on another man to gain a feeling of self-worth.

The current rise of sado-masochism (power of one over another), bondage and discipline, passive Greek and active French, as well as other sexual-technical roles, all imply a tacit obedience of one homosexual to another, much as occurs in a child-parent relationship. The child must be "good" to win approval from the parent. Concomitantly, a habituation to sexual role technique can make one homosexual dependent on another in order to act out a sexual fascination, fantasy or physical exercise. Each must dominate or submit to his ideal figure (parent-child) to experience power, self-worth or completion as a person.

This erotic dependency allows the homosexual to avoid anxiety by safely fulfilling the superficial requirements of a sexual activity, rather than a gradually maturing sense of his independence as a whole identity. Many homosexuals thus remain emotional children, performing for their male "parent" in order to feel "good"—in bed.

The pseudo-relief achieved in dogmatic sexual responses subsequently leads the homosexual into three major identity traps which restrict him from achieving more broadly meaningful relationships with men. Each identity trap lacks a creative basis. Each does not inspire courage to risk the self more freely and responsibly as one's own man—rather than another's.

The first identity trap is the homosexual's reliance on repeating the familiar, and therefore secure. Sexual habits do not require him to develop his self-consciousness or his confidence in himself as an autonomous person with the power of choice. He merely needs to function in blind service to others, loaning out his penis-abilities much as an auto mechanic or a prostitute trades their skills. Each time the homosexual serves another, he increasingly delays his own growth potential. He extends his passive approach to self-awareness. He regulates his erotic imagination with superficial attention to sexual performances.

Many homosexuals do experience a type of self-consciousness, but it is often a self-preoccupation with doubt and worry—he pays too much attention to erotic feed-back as an appraisal of his sexual skill. This is not a growth in self-consciousness which gives him deepening awareness of how to enlarge his capacity to love himself and others. He blocks affirmation of himself by chronically repeating similar erotic patterns with different men. Thus, he avoids the risk of vulnerability to change—which is always unfamiliar, and sometimes disconcerting. Ultimately, the homosexual has difficulty completely loving someone, because he relinquishes his power consciously to value himself—rather than what someone else can do for him, to him, or both.

The homosexual's retreat into the familiarity of sexual habits develops a second psychological trap which characterizes the operation of his blind service to others. He learns to manipulate parts of a sexual relationship, without creating a sense of wholeness to what he does. He is not whole himself. He fragments his identity into appropriate secret roles, sexual specialties and emotionally narrow response patterns.

His erotic stimuli may range from large penises, well-formed buttocks, uncircumcised racial minorities, defined biceps or hairless chests, to romantic visions of the ideal lover into whose role he attempts to manipulate the man he meets. In his manipulative response pattern, the homosexual requires a special feature which, like a triggering mechanism, seems to bring him relief for his habituated erotic desire.

This attachment to parts of people, or the special features of a sexual context, abbreviates the broad range of identity factors which both the homosexual and his partner might possess. Concurrently, the homosexual diminishes his own confidence to grow inclusively, rather than exclusively, and thus he fails to affirm his human qualities which might have no immediate value in the sexual market.

If the homosexual manipulates parts of socio-sexual contexts, he cannot effectively integrate his body with his intellect and emotions. He has difficulty in differentiating himself from the power of his erotic habits. He fears the emotional risk of deliberately moving beyond dependency on sexual technique, into the psychological independence of the mature person. Doubting his power and ability, he comfortably preoccupies himself with reinforcing minor successes at flirtation, tentative beginnings of love relationships, scoring with many anonymous strangers in chance sexual encounters, or refining his prowess in sexual experimentation.

He remains without definite erotic goals—unless "love" exists for him as a romantic ideal. The difficulty in attaining love by the means repeated in the homosexual's habitual actions, makes the promise of it so much more enticing. His faith in elusive love gives the homosexual enough gratification to continue his habitual manipulation of people, events and erotic equipment. Unfortunately, he learns to tolerate this fragmented search for a substantial meaning to his life and he enters a third psychological trap in sexual habits: the surfeiting of his emotions.

In this trap, the homosexual experiences the warmth of physical contact, the excitement of erotic sharing and the completion of orgasmic fulfillment. He is overwhelmed by an elevation of his senses. Sex fills him with the feeling of being able to feel. Yet, when emotions are chronically heightened, often they become dulled. They convey inaccurate messages to one's consciousness, or else minimal ones, compared to the untapped range of feeling which many homosexuals have no opportunity to communicate freely with casual partners.

What feelings the homosexual does share are usually attached to erotic activities. These contexts quickly satiate emotional expression, leaving both partners convinced that they have achieved all there is to achieve in erotic exchange. They withdraw to search for additional circumstances which promise to stimulate their need to feel stimulated.

Eventually there appears a weariness in much homosexual interaction. The promise of sex arouses emotional anticipation, but it also fosters boredom with the familiarity of promiscuous cycles. And yet many homosexuals confuse the restlessness of their dissatisfaction with such a routine, with the excitement of another erotic engagement with a stranger. Hope blinds a man to the difference.

Despite the homosexual's trained emphasis on his body as the primary aspect of his personality, ironically he functions as a disembodied man. He relinquishes his power to choose in favor of his power to perform. He disincorporates into often inconsistent and opposing elements of himself. Sexual function, emotional fever or fantasy attainments become more important than the homosexual's necessity to stand alone, evaluate and continually recreate the erotic dimensions within his whole personality. This is personality integration. The embodied man chooses to create himself erotically. He designs his own personality context which others may accept, reject or contribute to in their own way. His design considers commitment, care, integrity, vulnerability and love.

Such erotic creativity holds no guarantees. It originates from each man—alone. While the homosexual's independent autonomy can foster mutuality, it cannot be derived from those with whom we only have sex. Our erotic creativity is not lonely. It contains our capacity to include and enrich others, as they witness or experience us. Towards this view, hopefully, each homosexual will engage with other men in the creative dynamic of love. Anything less remains a debilitating imitation of erotic freedom. Or the false security of confinement in the narrow cell of sexual habit.

1. As a homosexual, how can I escape the tyranny of my penis?

The tyranny of my penis is the government of myself by which a single part of me has been invested with absolute power. My genitals make arbitrary demands, and I vascillate between will and caprice in service to them. If I seek to extend my sexual power over others, I perform an act of encroachment. Either I tyrannize another with my genital power, or I submit to another's sexual domination of my will. Rarely, then, am I able to experience a feeling of true integration with another man, a mutual sharing, an authentic democracy of erotic union.

The operation of my penile tyranny is often ruthless, mindless and without passion. It has its own appetite which—like some animal I am fearfully fascinated by—I feed occasionally to keep its distress or demands from turning inward upon me. I forage obediently for some erotic morsel to feed its insatiable demands.

I notice as I search for my erotic outlets, that they are generally other penises, intent on satisfaction of their own urgings—to find me. And as I undress before each stranger, I watch the insistence of their government rise to match my own. I know that the tyranny of the penis is intent merely on its own operations, quite apart from the whole of me. As we mutually masturbate, which is all that tyrants effectually require of each other, I am touched by the absence of sentiment. Passions are muted and brittle; there is little mutual regard.

I merely watch my penis function and wait for the moment that its sometimes feverish appetite is glutted. Then I withdraw, emptied of desire or imagination—or even pride. I have served my master so well, and gained little praise or stature from the effort.

I would rather inspire myself to revolution against my erotic tyrant, and equate my penis with my deeper human capacities to which it is only instrumental. Then, placing my penis beside—or within—another man, I would mutually and dynamically attach my integrity to his. As an invitation or an offering, our whole selves would be shared in common. Anything less would be a sham of dominance, because I would not wish to know or care whom I conquered. Or else it would be the sham of submission, because I am already a slave to erotic power.

My wholeness is so much more than a rising or falling of a penis to circumstance or luck. My mind, my body and my emotions unite in wit, choice, affection, honesty and care to celebrate who I am with the increasing knowledge of another. This freedom to be affectionately whole unblocks the frustration of pretense which passes for love each time only my penis meets another.

Misrepresentation in my sexual encounters with men springs from the false enthusiasm of my sexual desire. My penis busily fulfills the letter of my brief sexual contracts which read like edicts, or treaties—in which human essentials are forfeited, and I am lost to myself. Despite the simulated freedom of my orgasm, I know I must return again to the tyranny of my discontent.

I would rather strike a truce with men I meet, lifting my heart upon my penis into the unknown interior of one man's sensitivity to another man. My self unity I would lay beside him, like a brother, candidly, without reservation or design. Face to face, we would dissolve layer upon layer of the mystery we hold in one another. Without secret, I would penetrate him as I would myself—unconditionally—to erect the trust that what I do sincerely represents who I am. Anything else is a tyranny of one over the other. Or part of me, chronically defeating all of me.

2. *As a male homosexual, how can I integrate my sexual practices with self- and other-love?*

American males generally are not taught how to love themselves; they are conditioned to persuade others to love them. In male-female relationships, men mechanically idolize women with many of the patronizing Victorian attitudes which elevate, but isolate, the role of women as wife-mother-romantic figure. Eventually, men erotically bargain with women to forfeit their autonomy, submit to and admire male supremacy and thus trade the romantic ideal for more pressing masculine needs. In effect, men train women to relinquish their given role as romantic idol, and to idolize those men who displace them.

This erotic arrogance of men could pass for self-love. Instead, it indicates a frustrated need many American males have to express their emotions in a society which inhibits such freedom. Many men only know themselves through self-controlled performance. They value what they do and obtain, rather than what they emotionally demonstrate. As they compete, men learn to over-compensate, camouflage or hate the failures they imagine (or are told) they are. They are emotionally distant from themselves.

Male egoism is not self-love. It is an objective self-view which includes the viewpoint of others. If men are socially encouraged not to display self-affection, women conveniently indulge men's need to be loved. Ironically, men have difficulty with loving those they have made subordinately different from themselves. Thus, what often passes as love between men and women, is the man's need to be fostered by a woman because she makes him feel less worthless than his competitive society continually tempts him to believe he is. The paradox here is that men find ego-relief from the women they consider to be inferior to them.

As a homosexual male, I, too, have learned not to love myself. Few men help to foster my emotional identity. Heterosexuals fear or hate me. Homosexuals often hide their sense of failure in random sex, and thus we both rely on each other's momentary proof that we are personally worth something to someone (or anyone). Sex becomes our transient cure for self-doubts. We dose ourselves with it to correct the symptoms of our emptiness. Men exist for me to make me feel loved, because I suspect I do not love myself.

I recognize that I have not learned to love myself enough to love others. I will always remain separated from men, if I continue to be separated from the me my sexuality implies. I must first teach myself that I do not require other men to supplement what is really my imaginary sense of fragmentation. I am all I have. Each aspect of me unites to form my freedom from dependence on others' necessary esteem. My self-love requires that I recognize my idolatry of other men, by which I bargain them into idolizing me. If my sexual practices disregard my entire being, I merely stroke my ego and morbidly stave off the fear of feeling worthless because I continue to act as if I am worthless.

If self-love is my necessary re-engagement of my body, mind and feeling which society has fractured in my character, then other-love becomes a true engagement—in which I love another as I love myself. What I offer a man is more than a summary of my being, or even my doing. I extend myself in perpetual growth of all of my unique faculties as a human being, enlarging others as I enlarge myself—lovingly. The logic of love constructs a framework for mutual regard. It elevates lonely and discouraged people, even as it lends humility to the insecure proud. Sex has no such logic, apart from love.

3. *Why do I so often fail to create and maintain a committed relationship with another man?*

Most of the criteria of human commitments seem to imply an obligation to control the future. We confide or place ourselves in trust to someone else. In a sense, we transfer part of our self control into another's realm of control. Thus, we rely on each other to cause our future to happen. One major criterion of such a commitment is *time;* other criteria are *action, belief* and *commonality*.

Curiously, I can fail to create a commitment to another homosexual if I rush time. I hurriedly act—usually sexually—in the belief that sex will erase our possible differences in taste, interest, character, sensitivity or life goals. But the apparent commonality in my sexual exchanges is misleading. Differences in ambitions, opinions, talents, values or attitudes quickly blur with over-concentration on the orgasm. Sex is not the most reliable time structure for two men to conceive as a portent for their future.

I seem frustrated in maintaining a commitment to my homosexual lovers, because I am tempted to control future-time. Emotionally, I wish to contradict my socially trained view of time as a contextual deterrent to human commitment: this logic of time excites restless curiosity, limits duration and lends boredom to the meaning of repeated events.

Yet, my emotions and imagination are not so conveniently measured out by the current rationales for time's logic. For example, some believe that brief affairs are less valuable than long term commitments. Others will not expect a homosexual relationship to last, because men are innately promiscuous. Some claim it is unrealistic to expect to live with one person for a lifetime; the changes in personal growth eventually create entirely new people.

In my search for personal commitment to another man, I am tempted to value my attention to time, rather than the richness of my human contacts with another. Undoubtedly, even lengthy commitments can grow stale without my conscious efforts to give creatively what I am becoming, as though each moment together is special and may never last. Forever, is an infinitely remote ideal by which we entertain and torture ourselves. Nothing is available to us, except what each moment contains as it infinitely reveals itself to us.

While time might become one deterrent to my full commitment to another man, so common social beliefs also provide a context for my frustration. Society frowns on two men living together beyond the "marriageable age" or the "reasonable" convenience of economy or friendship. Male lovers are tempted to leave each other to save appearances, or to assuage their homosexual guilt. It is sometimes easier to dissolve a homosexual relationship than to suffer from potential social sanction.

In addition, the psychological context of my commitment to another man burdens me with subtle adjustments to myself; I must accommodate to a man—who is so similar to me. Perhaps I desire to escape the extra rigors of self scrutiny which our closeness requires. After all, I am socialized to live with women, intimately—not men.

Yet, it seems reasonable to believe that two men can achieve the trust, the tenderness and the same capacities for endurance as do men with women. If my society does not prepare me to expect such, I can!

To design my future will require my *patience* with time and events. Each of my daily actions in work, physical recreation, emotional growth and intellectual exploration contribute to my gradual development alone—with or without a lover. I only control the inevitable unfolding of my own life, and no one else's.

I do not want a man to be bound by my intellectual demands or emotional expectations that we "live up" to each other. Rather, I wish to trust that we will share a common goal, a mutual destiny which invisibly ties us in affection and regard. Our life's direction can then become like two travelers who have mutually agreed to journey by one destiny. We consult our own resources to enhance the means each of us selects to achieve our agreement. We inspire each other forward. We choose our own path, often observing the details of our travel within ourselves. And in each moment we meet, we share a complete resolution of our agreement together.

Each of us does not begin again with some new life, should separation occur. We merely continue to live our life alone—with someone else—completely, in each moment through which we move freely towards truth.

4. As a homosexual, how should I avoid attachments of my personality to "erotic territories"?

Erotic territories are fields of emotional interest which we play out in geographical locations. Certain behavioral patterns develop in relation to these territories. These generally require us to conform in fairly persistent psychological attachment to rituals; these often substitute for our own unique interests or desires.

Erotic territories for the homosexual male are generally parks, steam baths, rest rooms, bars or bedrooms—anywhere men congregate publicly to display their erotic interests. The homosexual's behavior and attitudes gradually conform to territorial rituals. Feelings of anxiety, desire, aggression or ambivalence often overwhelm the homosexual's particular personality.

He is necessarily more than territorial rituals imply he should be. He often feels less than what he could be.

As a homosexual, I obviously wish to meet and participate with others like me, so I go where they are. I do what they do, or else I withdraw from these public territories to the neutral safety of my home. Erotic territories are never neutral. They are charged with sexual possibility, erotic display and psychological rejection.

I can easily absorb the ethos of an erotic territory and then behave in contradiction to my own expressions, values and ambitions for my life. While I participate in the superficial rituals of social encounter with other homosexuals, I notice I develop a peculiar vernacular, a guarded style and a mechanical efficiency by which I deal with them. I suppose my very presence in erotic territories implies that I am sexually ready, even when I'm not always; that I am self-gaining rather than other-caring; and that I am probably a one night stand, too promiscuous to develop into more than a sexual adventure or I wouldn't be where I am.

It is difficult to disavow these possible misconceptions about myself, when the required pace of rituals in erotic territories is so fast. It is also difficult for me to preconceive anything different about those men I meet.

Despite the confusion of interests which occur in erotic territories, it is so very easy to become attached to them. They all represent fields of sexual fantasy in which I can actually participate; inevitably, *I* become an erotic territory to someone else.

Territorial expectations then camouflage my inner essence. I am cloaked by men's assumptions that I exist as a sexual object. Narrow social rituals for erotic encounter screen me from saying what I really feel—my doubts, my expectations, and the more enriching ambitions I have for my own identity. I tend towards the silence of anonymity, the acceptance that I could be anyone—that I am willing to serve my sexual purpose, rather than explore the multiple richness of my identity—and share it. Thus, the full terrain of my personality remains unknown. Few penetrate the surface of the identity I present. They view my details, touch my exterior and overlook my range of human qualities which territorial attachments never call forth.

I must recognize that I am my own erotic territory. If I derive my erotic fulfillment from being what others want me to be, I am no different than a sexual beggar who scavanges what he can, moment by moment, in the depleted fields of erotic possibility. If I beg, no one can fulfill my larger instinct for a richer life. I will become dependent on the occasional sex which anonymous men might be willing to give me. My passions will continue to hunger.

To be my own erotic territory means that I must energetically widen the borders of my knowledge of myself—as well as others. I am not defined by the furtiveness of parks and toilets, nor the brittle glitter of a discotheque. These encompass me in the dark privacy of a sexual cycle in which I always remain the supplicant—begging notice from men with whom I conspire to keep me hidden from them—or myself.

5. Is a sexual ethic possible for the male homosexual?

It is *impossible* for a written or traditional system of values to be "true" for any one person. If I rely on others for answers to moral questions of what is the greatest "good" or "evil," I reduce my personal creation of my own life. I ask for a formula to which I can conform. These theoretical rules which I attempt to imitate do not necessarily contain "truth" for me.

My parents, religion, philosophy, law and social tradition have described appropriate actions for my social situations. As a child, and now as an adult, I continue to deny my own creativity and conform to others' ethical standards for behavior—especially the sexual one. Such general sexual ethics often contradict my own passionate interest and sexual subjects. I am "unethical" if I sexually love another man. I must recognize that common ethical standards are partially dead to me. This does not mean that I cannot construct my own.

My living ethics, then, require that I decide for myself why I choose what I do, in every situation I encounter. Living ethics are thus shaped dynamically between myself and others, in all the events of our lives. It is easy to capitulate, as a homosexual, to the overwhelming quandry which heterosexual expectations create for me. I can submit to rigid value attachments to my sexual behaviors, and then experience guilt, duplicity, or even neurotic despair. Or I could choose to enter the easy circumstantial liberty of behavior without ethical regard which my outlaw homosexual status permits me.

Certainly, as a homosexual, I have personal ethical resources available to me. I can resist conforming to the safe authoritarianism of heterosexual ethics, as well as to the nonconforming mindlessness of certain homosexual rituals. There is no truth for me in either extreme.

My first consideration for my personal system of ethics, is to dare *to invent my own choices*. Ultimately, my choices must be my own, if I am to achieve responsibility for my own life. Secondly, I must *decide to act,* to overcome my fear of decisions which imply my homosexuality. Here, I must finally meet the challenge of accepting my own uniqueness, despite the greater ease in hiding my sexual orientation. I must decide if I like myself as a homosexual person. Thirdly, I must *select avenues of self fulfillment,* by which I enable myself to grow forward into life, rather than merely allowing life to happen to me.

In these considerations, I recognize that my only ethical evil is my separation of myself from what I actually am and could become. Even my sexual situations then become only "good" or "bad," according to the honesty of my whole involvement in them. Only I can evaluate the motives of my actions—whether they be sexual ones or not. Only I can compare myself now, against who I wish to become.

And it is I alone, who can now choose to integrate myself alive. In self evaluation, I am my own judge. I fix my own value, according to the evidence of my life.

PART IV/The Closet

7/The Homosexual Ghetto: Dachau Becomes a State of Mind

Although "straight" society may be affronted at
the thought, homosexual art is by no means without
insights into heterosexual life, out of whose milieu it
grows and whose notions it must, perforce, imitate
and repeat, even parody.[1]

Kate Millett,
Sexual Politics

The artist is . . . "a dancer whose movements are
broken by the constraint of his cell. That which
finds no expression in his steps and the limited
swing of his arms, comes in exhaustion from his
lips, or else he has to scratch the unlived lines of his
body into the walls with his wounded fingers."[2]

Rainer Maria Rilke,
Letters to a Young Poet
Cited by Norman O. Brown, in
Life against Death

The homosexual in contemporary America exists in a sexually
fascist society. Heterosexual males philosophically demand extreme social regulation of homosexual males. At times, they
impose physical suppression or symbolic confinement of
homosexuals, much as Hitler's Nazism required of Jews. As the
purity of Germanic Aryanism required expulsion of contaminat-
ing Jewry, so heterosexuality remains intact as long as "deviant"
homosexuality is not allowed social legitimacy. Thus, curious
parallels occur between the historical traits of Jews which resulted from their confinement by Gentile majorities, and those
homosexual behaviors developing from confinement by
heterosexual design.

187

In *The Manufacture of Madness,* Thomas Szasz equates an earlier dread of Jews as heretics with that of contemporary fears of homosexuality in our secular society. As heretics, historic Jews were frequently forced to practice their "illicit" religion in secret. So, homosexuals largely resort to secret consortia of same-sex behaviors. As Jews were considered not human because they were not Christians, homosexuals are deemed abnormal because they are not heterosexual. Homosexuals now serve as secular scapegoats, in parallel to Jewish mistreatment by Gentile religious and social interests.[3]

The homosexual as sexual scapegoat suffers personally, as well as collectively. To comprehend the style, intensity and manifestation of the homosexual's suffering, one must first follow the behavioral progress of the solitary homosexual male who discovers who he is, as others tell him he must be.

Like the Jew, the homosexual's personal understanding and growth as an individual are enclosed: first within himself, and then within social-symbolic collectives containing the intense dynamics of the ghetto, the concentration camp and the prison. It is imperative that the homosexual understand the various stages of social institutions through which he must pass. These are prepared for him deliberately or inadvertently, by his society. He must adapt to them constructively or destructively.

To understand himself, the homosexual has the Jew available for comparison. That such a comparison may be extreme to both homosexual and Jew, does not invalidate it in the Gentile heterosexual mentality. Homosexuals and Jews are more causally linked within the dynamic of majority prejudice than are homosexuals and blacks.[4] Thus, the heresy implication is more directly related to sex than to race.

Current discrimination against homosexuality links a quasi-religious stance to social judgment. On a bill-board en route to Los Angeles from Long Beach, one reads: "Drought! God Says Something Queer Is Going On." In a white Christian newspaper published in Arkansas, the *Torch,* an editorial states, "It is becoming increasingly clear to many Americans that homosexuals can no longer be tolerated and that efforts should be made to make it a capital crime punishable by death." (By gassing).[5] Using religion, law and science to condemn homosexuals, propagandists' arguments reiterate German pronouncements against the "Jewish problem" of the 1930's.

Within this social context, the individual homosexual who

recognizes that he is oriented sexually to other men is socially encouraged to feel uniquely despised and predominantly alone. He initially isolates himself with his knowledge. Society demands this. The homosexual then continues to hide his personality "flaw." His successful camouflage maintains the isolation of his identity; it prepares him to assume the voluntary ghetto of separation as a state of mind. In *Homosexuality and Psychological Functioning,* Mark Freedman believes this voluntary ghetto serves as a safety reaction to social sanctions against homosexuality:

> . . . The pressures against homosexuality have caused the behavior to go underground, and individuals who engage in this behavior in Western society have, by and large, taken on the mask of heterosexuality in their everyday dealings with the outside world, much as many Jews—the Marranos—disguised themselves as Christians during the Spanish Inquisition.[6]

Coupled with this voluntary confinement, overt aggression and implicit violence within American legal, religious and social tradition, provide the homosexual with his compulsory ghetto. As Freedman describes the pervasive and intense heterosexual attitudes against homosexuality, he concludes, "It is amazing how quickly most people will write off an individual when they discover his homosexual orientation, regardless of his intellectual or social assets."[7] The homosexual is thus institutionalized, through reluctant choice or by social decree.

George Weinberg outlines the stages of self-institution which are available to all of us. In *Society and the Healthy Homosexual,* Weinberg lists these stages as social messages which frame "normal" development for a male as being, ". . . Childhood, going to school, graduating, getting married, becoming a parent, making a sum of money, dying, leaving the money to his children, and finally being forgotten."[8] The institutional stages of development for the male homosexual often set him apart from these majority aspirations and accomplishments. Such separation begins his haunting sense of personal failure. The minority member begins to construct his symbolic or social ghetto.

The self-recognized homosexual is not acculturated for his alienated homosexual identity: no child is prepared for such self-recognition. The general male population, whether eventually heterosexual or homosexual, overwhelmingly and unconsciously *receives* the structure and content for various types and degrees of institutionalized life. There is little else available for an individual to choose against such controlled social processes.

Yet, the messages received by homosexuals are generally illusory, offering few accurate or positive resources for his unique identity development. He is a member of an invisible collective, mockingly visualized first by heterosexuals, and experienced later by homosexuals as they variously encounter each other. The newly aware homosexual senses his discordance; life becomes a burden.

As the Jew in a world history among Gentiles, so the homosexual often feels hampered, excluded or merely tolerated by heterosexuals. His inner temperament may become brooding, apathetic or melancholy. No homosexual who initially discovers his sexual minority identity, greets it with joy, comprehension, satisfaction or relief. Isolation shapes his character and the nature of his social life.

As with Jews, homosexual survival traits of mobility and adaptability develop psychically and actually. The homosexual learns to specialize behaviors in order to integrate with heterosexuals, with varying degrees of success. He recognizes that his social status is precarious. His selfconsciousness is defined for him as deviant, by virtue of sexual-social rules maintained by the heterosexual majority. Application of this heterosexual power against the stigmatized homosexual then *escalates* his sense of confinement in his identity and lifestyle. His self-institutionalism becomes more or less intensified. The homosexual either labels himself, or accepts society's stigma.

The themes and biases within self-institutionalism by the homosexual, are constructed from conflicting misinformation. One's identity should develop as one experiences it; for a homosexual, *society imputes his identity, instantaneously*. The homosexual is then encouraged to deny and divide himself into appearances of normality. He becomes essentially enclosed within his secret life, preserving it from external threats and judgments. *The homosexual feels selected and removed* from access to the freedom to be what the majority defines as socially valuable.

As in the selection and removal of Jews to concentration camps, the impact of self-selection and disavowal varies from homosexual to homosexual. The personal intensity of necessary isolation, because of fear of social reprisal, then creates a concomitant ghetto of selfconsciousness. This ghetto attitude can metamorphose into a more severe concentration camp mentality. The homosexual receives his stigma, as a Jew received his number. He is marked as a collective member with negated identity. He does not understand why he was selected. His first reaction to initiation or admission to the homosexual "concentration camp" is one of shock.

Bruno Bettelheim writes of his own initiation to Jewish concentration camps in *The Informed Heart:* "Whether and how much the initial shock was experienced as severe trauma depended on the individual personality."[9] Viktor Frankl recalls his internment as a Jew in *Man's Search for Meaning:* "Under certain conditions shock may even precede the prisoner's formal admission to the camp."[10] So, Howard Brown compares the homosexual's selection in *Familiar Faces, Hidden Lives:*

> Homosexual men discover their sexual nature in a variety of ways and at a wide range of ages. Some have been happily married for years when they find, abruptly or gradually, that their sexual relations with women leave them unsatisfied and that it is men they crave. Others engage in homosexual acts for years before realizing—or admitting to themselves—that they are homosexual. . . .
>
> In both cases, the realization generally comes as a shock. And an overwhelming feeling of loneliness is invariably part of that shock.[11]

Sexual identity predominantly relies on social labels which select and categorize people according to their overt sexual behaviors. Covert sexual orientations may "pass" as a phase, a potentiality, an expediency or a socially rationalized interest in admired (and approved) masculinity traits. Understanding of the "meaning" to an individual's overt sexual behavior, as well as his covert orientation, interest or desire, appears to rely on simplistically inadequate social labels of Heterosexual, Bisexual or Homosexual.

Yet, the sexual identity of the homosexual—as well as the heterosexual—begins unconsciously at some point in time and place. It also includes a later conscious recognition of one's homosexual orientation, which can either be denied, sublimated, replaced or accepted.

Adjustments are made either positively or negatively, because American society demands that sexual identity be linked with behaviors appropriate to masculine or feminine gender traits. Any sexual activity must then convincingly reinforce either one gender identity proscription or the other. Since homosexuals disconcertingly appear to blur the connection between gender and sexual behavior (men only have intercourse with women), they threaten the heterosexual male investment in specific gender divisions which enclose and control both females and males.

Heterosexuals, in turn, do not provide the homosexual male adequate preparation for an accurate understanding of his sexual identity, because sexual ambiguities render competitive opponents more impotent. Heterosexuals do offer sexual myths, labels, and sanctions which heighten ambiguity, fear, and guilt—then, the homosexual misconceives himself.

Social monologues thus attempt to define and control diverse sexual behaviors. More often, they compound misunderstanding of all sexual behaviors, due to moralistically inspired power motives. Alfred Kinsey clarifies contemporary bias in social definitions and moral imperatives attached to sexuality:

> Viewed objectively, human sexual behavior, in spite of its diversity, is more easily comprehended than most people, even scientists, have previously realized. The six types of sexual activity, masturbation, spontaneous nocturnal emissions, petting, heterosexual intercourse, homosexual contacts, and animal contacts . . . all prove to originate in the relatively simple mechanisms which provide for erotic response when there are sufficient physical or psychic stimuli. . . .[12]

Since one's sexual identity can include masturbation and fantasy objects, as well as sexual activity with either males or females, the emerging homosexual consciousness is merely a part of an available continuum of sexual interest, fantasy, and activity. This sexual continuum defies simple and final categorization of the self as Heterosexual, Homosexual, or Somewhere Between both of these socially defined—and mutually exclusive—orientations or behaviors.

While society attempts to locate sexual identity through expeditious label or category, individual male sexual behaviors can relocate on a changing continuum of behaviors or orientations. According to Kinsey, only an estimated four percent of American males primarily locate at the exclusively homosexual end of the available sexual range. Such a sexual continuum seems to defeat the purpose of socially categorizing and labeling sexual behavior, unless society can successfully convince its members to assign moral, ethical or status value to sexual behavior.

Again, the competitive dynamic between majority and minority sexual behaviors prejudices essential issues. To define and isolate a role according to a sexual behavior is one mode of behavioral control. To attach value to sexual behavior is another. Thus, the homosexual definition only confines possible personality range.

Attachment to a negatively valued role fractures the emerging homosexual's consciousness; he cannot adequately clarify his own sexual role when rigid role expectations and values are socially attached to this sexual phenomenon. Already, society is prepared to distort, demean and defeat his identity. Kinsey addresses the homosexual's plight; what the homosexual does not comprehend about himself, society claims it does:

> There is little evidence of the existence of such a thing as innate perversity, even among those individuals whose sexual activities society has been least inclined to accept. There is an abundance of evidence that most human sexual activities would become comprehensible to most individuals, if they could know the background of each individual's behavior.[13]

In lieu of comprehensive evidence of such background, the emerging homosexual consciousness is unprepared for the shock of recognition—at some point in time or place—that he is in the sexual foreground of heterosexual fears and expectations. He appears to fit the description of sexual deviant. John Reid poignantly records his moment of homosexual recognition in his vivid autobiography, *The Best Little Boy in the World*. As Reid's father passed through the den where the author was watching the television, he overheard his father say to a friend, " 'I've read that, too; but ten percent just couldn't be right. There couldn't be that many people with homosexual tendencies. . . .' "[14] As any adolescent experiencing the vague expansions of an erotic identity, Reid's included a difficult added dimension:

> . . . I sat there with my head aimed at the TV—but my face on fire with recognition. I *knew*, I'm not sure how, but I *knew* I was in that 10 percent. So *that's* the word for hating dancing school, for not playing baseball, for admiring Chip's athletic prowess, for the phony feelings, and lonely feelings, I sometimes felt.
>
> It was hazy and vague, aged eleven . . . I was being jolted into thinking a little, into becoming aware of myself. I no longer just looked at the picture of the Golden Gloves boxer in the magazine and liked it—I started to wonder *why* I liked it. And whether I was supposed to like it. And if not, whether I would stop liking it.[15]
>
> [emphasis in original]

Frankl noticed that confined Jews' shock over their selection, changed to a conscious speculation about their future. A configuration of psychic phenomena resulted; initially, they engaged in illusions of reprieve. They believed that they would be saved from their fate. They objected to being treated like criminals; they resented their loss of status. For the homosexual struggling with his secret identity, there is the temptation to "pass" in significant situations by denying one's homosexuality through careful imitation of heterosexual behaviors. Such a person creates illusions of reprieve from total self-commitment to who or what he is not supposed to be.

The self-recognized homosexual does not reveal himself to family members, and thus creates a wall of silence and surreptitiousness between himself and his family, which intensifies the homosexual's feelings of social estrangement. Jewish concentration camp victims also withdrew from any form of contact with their families. They could then avoid the accusations of friends and family members that it was somehow their fault that they were incarcerated in camps. To avoid the guilt or accusation of being at fault, the homosexual must appear to be heterosexual, while he furtively seeks sexual relief through anonymous encounters with male pickups or casual sexual partners. Single homosexuals often find they can sexually perform with both women and men. They sometimes marry women in order to act out a socially rewarded aspect of instutitionalized personal development; they become husbands and fathers. The camouflage of marriage allows them to continue contriving homosexual encounters, in order to achieve the emotional release they desperately require. Real or spurious, such forms of "bisexuality" offer many men one more illusion of reprieve.

John Reid began a systematic construction of his own illusionary identity. He created conscious modes of self-denial, by committing himself to heterosexual mores; he hoped others would not recognize what he feared to recognize about himself. Reid thus *re-described* himself. He became an overachiever in "normal" adolescent activities. He studied ardently. He carefully avoided stereotypical homosexual behaviors. He faked his way through high school as a "double agent": he dated girls. He confined himself within a pressurized context of simultaneous identities.

Wilhelm Reich speaks of this conflict between repressed self and social expectation as being rooted in the conflict between sexual prohibition and sexual impulse—typical of most American adolescents. To abstain from what society sexually forbids, adolescents must repress their sexual excitation. What they strive for, they then learn to fear.

Reich indicates a dilemma which Reid attempted to resolve by simulating heterosexual expectations and repressing his own homosexual desires. Reich warns of pathological results from such sexual self-confinement:

> Sexual excitation without gratification cannot be tolerated for long. There are only two solutions: suppression of the excitation or gratification. The first regularly leads to psychic and physical disturbances; the second to conflicts with today's society.[16]

In *Identity: Youth and Crisis,* Erik Erickson suggests another form of compensation for the sexual dilemma described by Reich: it also resembles the structure and dynamic within Reid's over compensations—for what Erickson terms a "surrendered identity."[17] The conflict in "the best little boy in the world's" double (agent) life, was tentatively resolved by a masochistic denial of himself to others. He was sexually aroused by other males. To remain undiscovered, he inflicted social judgments on himself for his deviation from normal heterosexuality. Reid's natural impulses collided with social messages concerning appropriate desires and behaviors. He could not gratify both extremes. The homosexual's shock of recognition is almost always psychically traumatic.

Reid's descriptions of his illusions might be termed an identity collision and fragmentation. Frankl, too, noticed that the Jews' loss of illusions resulted in diversely conflicting mental sets. They developed a grim sense of humor, curiosity, depression and thoughts of suicide.[18] These victims' abnormal reactions to their abnormal confinement, was actually normal behavior.

Bettelheim does not consider it too remarkable that interned Jews would turn their aggressions against themselves, as a logical means of coping with felt extremes. So, Brown also notices that ". . . Contemplation of suicide is typical of many homosexuals who discovered their sexual identity. . . ."[19]

The loss of illusion can take other forms of mental set, which also diminish the homosexual's sense of identity. Frankl and Bettelheim noticed that Jews engaged in psychological regression to infantile levels of dreams and wish-fulfillments. Strain and anxiety forced Jewish prisoners to resort to fantasy to deny their utter dejection.

So the isolated homosexual consciousness resorts to dreams and fantasies to reduce the stress and anxiety in his social vilification. If he happens to be geographically isolated from other homosexuals, he must rely on media content for information about himself. This is usually partial, negative, or exaggerated. Or if he is able to engage in periodic sexual encounters with men, he frequently does so in secrecy, keeping his isolated identity intact. His sexual encounters merely serve as reference points for his future "ideal" man. By rationalizing his withheld commitment to any man, he guarantees that each encounter will fail to fulfill his ideal.

These symbolic or actual forms of sexual information continue to help the defensive homosexual sublimate or hide the imagined meaning of his sexuality, from himself and others. Even the homosexual who has sex with his wife or female friends, can fantasize such women are men. Objects of sexual fantasy, even dreams of being heterosexual, then offer relief to self-imposed fear, punishment or denial of the homosexual's negative and partial identity given by society.

Perhaps dreams and fantasies feed the hunger of the emotionally famished homosexual, much as Frankl's confined Jew experienced ". . . The soul-destroying mental conflict and clashes of will power which a famished man experiences."[20] Hungering for human affirmation, the homosexual receives little emotional nourishment from his society or himself.

He can adopt a type of fatalism and believe that he is worthy of his suffering, as did confined Jews. He can also believe that all men must conform to society's models, and thus make self-diminishing efforts to assimilate into heterosexual models of behavior. Or, he can imagine that his suffering results from a personal deficiency, when he actually suffers because of his social classification into a homosexual group. Then he will resemble those Jews described by Bettelheim who felt freed from their guilt and responsibility simply because they were victims. Such imaginary freedom then becomes license for sexual hedonism and personal victimization of fellow homosexuals.

Both Bettelheim and Frankl acknowledge that the process of their dehumanization was difficult for the Jews to understand. So, the homosexual who discovers his sexual proclivity for other males, does not fully comprehend his sense of anxious and solitary existence.

Attempting to "pass" in order to remain inconspicuous and alive, the Jews' existence descended to an animal level as they relaxed the struggle to save their self respect. They became one of the masses, in order to achieve types of inner integration or sense to their existence as oppressed people. In "passing," the Jews responded to a violent weakening of their identity, by attempting ". . . To 'regain' strength by becoming part of the tyranny and thus enjoy its power."[21]

For the homosexual, such passing is an attempt to join the heterosexual majority through *stigma conversion*. The homosexual disappears into identification with heterosexual appearances; in joining his oppressors, the homosexual hopes to maintain his survival. Yet, the Jewish loss of personal autonomy happened in time, through a gradual disintegration of the personality, worn down by anxiety. As the Jew, the homosexual then patiently endures a gradual process of mistreatment. Within this process, some believe that perhaps their stigma will redeem them—as a logically merciful reward for such suffering. Yet, time erodes the homosexual's personality—as it did the Jew's—because he does not choose to act within a decision-making process which will ultimately create a stable ego. He does not consciously resist capitulation to his enemy.

Mark Freedman remarks that the homosexual who limits his self-awareness to crisis concerns over his sexual identity, often unconsciously chooses forms of functioning which are enclosure reactions. Some homosexuals may accept society's stereotype of the homosexual, and engage in role fulfillments of exaggerated minority traits. "The facets of this stereotype which they accept, and act on, are, for men, effeminacy, superficiality, promiscuity, and maliciousness. . . ."[22] The more pragmatic homosexual may achieve effective personality integration of his sexual identity, despite the dangers and obstacles within heterosexual society. "Such a person is simultaneously a part of society and an outsider abiding there. He disguises his sexual identity . . . wearing the mask of heterosexuality. . . ."[23] Another homosexual may choose to function in creative opposition to negative social pressures. This man confronts his stigma. So, for these homosexuals, their ". . . Talents foster the creativity, but it is the societal pressures that determine the form their creations take."[24] Thus, degrees of passing—by accepting or denying one's homosexuality—help form the structure and content of the homosexual's unconscious psychological functioning. Stigma conversion, stigma redemption and stigma confrontation provide the impetus within such forms of passing.

While Freedman focuses on the qualities of creative survival available to homosexuals, such functiong is usually only reactive to those active homosexual roles distributed and maintained by the heterosexual majority. Each of Freedman's three role reactions tends to attach each homosexual to degrees of psychological and physical anonymity, in contrast to public images of heterosexual masculinity. Such "closeting" is always compulsive. It is imposed upon the homosexual from without, or it is spontaneously created by the homosexual from within. Whether other-imposed or voluntarily generated, the closet contains a style, dynamic, structure and resolution based on techniques of survival. Such techniques helped confined Jewry similarly to adapt to their social requirements. Survival skills are inadvertently crafted for homosexuals by heterosexuals reacting to their power threats: social ostracism, incarceration or symbolic enclosure are heterosexual reactions. The homosexual creatively responds by converting heterosexual enclosure techniques into skills which communicate his will to be.

Hugh Duncan notices that these social stimulus-response relationships possibly describe a pathology in social communication. Such pathologies occur in extreme social environments. In a person's will to be, Duncan implies in *Symbols and Society,* that such ". . . Expression depends on communicative forms which can arise only in relations between the self and others."[25] Thus, extreme environments thwart free communicative exchange.

The prisoner and his guard are pathologically related. The man who works at a monotonous job feels boredom—he is easily fatigued. Noise polluting an environment can develop damaging emotional and physical disorders in people. A prisoner held too long in solitary confinement becomes disoriented and passive. So, the enclosed homosexual—sensing a limitation in his communication of social autonomy—can develop reactive manifestations. These are pathological accommodations to environmental forms of social enclosure. Thus, one's role expression and environment are intimately linked.

One form of social enclosure for homosexuals is structured as a militaristic drama of defense. Heterosexuals depict homosexuals as embodiments of criminal principles within the social order. Heterosexual males who strongly identify with socially pathological images of masculinity then view homosexual males as traitors to these male norms. To defend social order, i.e., masculinity, heterosexuals pathologically spy upon, hunt down, entrap, arrest, confine, ridicule and eradicate the homosexual through social pogroms of varying intensity. Yet, as Duncan emphasizes, such "Defense is an admission of weakness, for in saying that we have to defend our principles, we admit them to be in danger."[26] As an actor in the heterosexual drama of defense, each homosexual fights back as best he can: through law, social appeal, minority collectives or the enclosure of personal anonymity.

The homosexual recognizes that he is described as the heterosexual male's enemy. Why this is so is perhaps unresolvable, but at least it is symbolically comprehensible. Kate Millett offers one illustration of why such violent polarities occur between both male groups:

> The hostility which the swish provokes from a crowd of college boys and toughs, their taunts, their desire to strike down, their mindless rage, is . . . the uneasy response of insecure virility erupting into violence to cover its own terror of a possible "false self". . . .[27]

Fear of one's potential homosexual interest by heterosexual males can inspire an irrational self-hatred which must then be projected onto selected others. In accommodation to, or withdrawal from such stigma, the homosexual deserts to his closet of anonymity. This shelters him from violence to his masculinely false self, even as possible violence atones for or covers any false sense of masculinity in the heterosexual.

In effect, the homosexual as victim appears as a socially dramatic expiation for the heterosexual who doubts his own virility. Unfortunately, the accommodational or withdrawal techniques used by homosexuals to secrete or protect themselves strongly resemble pathological traits expressed in other institutions of enclosure. Historical motives, social structures, human dynamics and psychological manifestations springing from the ghetto, the concentration camp or prison directly describe pathologies of the homosexual's confinement.

Initially, confinement generates "normal" accommodation to an oppressively abnormal environmental existence. Confinement induces a desire—sometimes a strategy—for escape. Whether voluntary or imposed, an enclosed life creates simultaneously constructive and destructive survival modes. Of necessity, the homosexual can elevate these modes to ingenious art; at the least, he can perfect mechanical contrivances in order to expedite immediate relief. At whatever level of complexity the homosexual chooses for his internal and external modes of survival, his intellectual and emotional dynamic can be communicated only through available social structures and motives.

Additionally, the homosexual's personality variables must also interact with those of the homosexual subculture. This double social interaction contributes to, or defeats the homosexual's internal stability of identity—as he vitally responds to his stigmatized attachment to a low-status minority group. Personally interacting within heterosexual or homosexual social structures, the homosexual enters with his own style and dynamic. Social motives and structures also provide a potential stability of commitment to heterosexual people, or to those within the alleged homosexual milieu which stands ready to absorb him into its collective mores. For the homosexual, this milieu is symbolic and actual from two points of view: from either the heterosexual prefabrication of its existence, or from the homosexual fabrication of its various essences.

Invariably, most social motives and structures which are available to the homosexual as communication pathways, tend to be opposed to him, rather than open to him. For instance, the emerging homosexual consciousness initially confronts the danger of viewing himself as a fabricated person. His existence is symbolically acted out in roles designed by heterosexually dominated social dramas. What he witnesses is social messages communicating ideals necessary to heterosexual social order. As Duncan notes, any such "ideal" social order depends on linking personal identity-in-action, to a specific arena or stage. Thus, social actors play roles required of, and then modified by their environment or scene:

> In this linkage, social conditions are said to call for roles in keeping with the stage, and the stage in turn, is depicted as in keeping with the role. Thus, we hear of politicians who are "prisoners of the situation," movie stars who are "forced" to live up to the public image. . . .[28]

In keeping with his roles, the homosexual stage is an environmental set of social enclosures. Heterosexuals link roles to environment for homosexuals: deviant, psychotic and criminal perpetually link homosexuals to rest rooms, schoolgrounds, mental institutions and jail. So the homosexual is aware of his public image prepared for him by society, well before he discovers his sexual orientation towards men. He is already a prisoner in socially designed situations; intellectual and emotional confinement will merely fill out his ascribed role. Such scenic determinism forces the homosexual to rigidly repeat social rehearsals until he learns his place. He is told that his whole repertoire of emerging behaviors, attitudes and desires must be characteristically homosexual.

As such a character actor, the homosexual also discovers that scenic determinism requires secrecy, isolation and efforts to imitate heterosexual roles. Perfection of these protects the homosexual. Yet, scenic determinism also requires that the homosexual must successfully imitate homosexual roles. Perfection of these protects the heterosexual. Thus, the homosexual is always typecast. His social scripts are thematically redundant. Any factual or personally creative awareness of his human identity is superceded by the heterosexual's imagination. Restraint of homosexuals by stigma, isolation and social coercion helps to control imagined threats to heterosexual society. Shame, fear and misunderstanding of one's homosexual consciousness help to condition the homosexual to isolate himself for protection from inner anxieties as well as external aggression. The homosexual effectively learns to control his identity potential. He rehearses self-denial; he remains cooperatively invisible, in acquiescence to heterosexual expectations.

Heterosexual male culture provides sexual scripts to most minority groups; they sexually victimize whoever threatens their socio-sexual authority. Women who threaten men are raped, beaten or subordinated psychologically, socially or economically. Women are attached to traditional stages of bedroom, nursery and kitchen. Their roles are defined by these environments. Identification with such role environments carries certain rewards, which women are trained to value and believe in. It is no accident in logic that homosexual males are traditionally affiliated with women, in the dominant-subordinant mentality of heterosexual males. Homosexuals are convinced to accept a psychic status level of women. Homosexuals are sexually engineered to function within environments where they may perform their pedestrian roles. Such roles are often symbolically limiting.

Thus, symbolic arts provide American society with metaphorical heroes to elevate, as well as victims to abuse. In this sense, certain public dramas created by various authorities continually work to re-establish heterosexual male communication of social power, control and coherence.

The symbolic public dramas in art, law, religion, politics, the media, etc. condition all to accept necessary social definitions. Authorized beliefs and behaviors which reinforce male social authority, persuade all to imitate selected and favored social definitions as their own. Unauthorized versions (homosexual, racial, female, religious . . .) of social definitions are subject to heterosexual white male attack. In most of these public dramas, the homosexual receives his active roles; initially, he is presented, and subsequently reacts as, symbolic victim.

Secondarily, the homosexual is victimized in actual social experiences in which he is detected or recognized by heterosexuals. In both cases, the homosexual entertains his audience's need for him to perform as victim. This scapegoating maintains the appearance of control within the social order.

The man who is just emerging in consciousness of himself as homosexual, then confronts three basic socio-symbolic messages which are consistently communicated into society: the homosexual as a tragic, comic and radical figure. The overwhelming consistency of these messages makes it difficult for the self-discovering homosexual to argue against them. No homosexual is prepared by American society to expect a logical validation of his unique identity. He *is* prepared to accept these fictional images and negative roles, by which all society views him. In effect, the homosexual is only free to choose his own confinement, dramatically rehearse his minor scripts and remain linked to the rituals of scenic determinism. He has few major social supports for other alternatives.

On the one hand, should the homosexual play out his identity as a tragic figure, he must expect to function as a sexual abstraction, rather than an erotic person. He must expect happiness, security and status to elude him. He should believe that his life will be superficial, fraught with purposeless pursuits of pleasure and concluded in lonely regret.

On the other hand, if the homosexual opts to play a comic role, he must caricature himself as a feminized male. He should be flighty, fickle and passively dependent. He must humorously ratify the correctness of masculinity, by displaying "erroneous" feminine traits of exaggerated effusiveness, limp-wristed mincing and lisping enunciation—always the hallmark of the homosexual.

Should he reject either or both the tragic and comic roles, the homosexual's remaining alternative is the radical image. He must then threaten the integrity of the American family ritual. He should expect castigation as a seducer of children. He must adapt to intolerance and brutality from society—he must not expect better treatment since he challenges moral decency by tempting social members to embrace emotional or sexual anarchy. The homosexual as radical, can only expect what he is told he deserves: control through confinement.

These tragic, comic and radical roles are traditionally prefabricated for the emerging homosexual consciousness. What else does the homosexual have to compare himself against, as a positive model for his identity clarification? Society offers him nothing else because he has no value-investment for heterosexual males, unless they can exploit homosexuals through economics, medicine, labor, law, the media or religion. As crime indirectly provides a livelihood for noncriminals, so homosexuality economically benefits heterosexual males. Emotionally, heterosexuals use homosexuality as a contrasting validation of their manufactured masculinity. But, the real homosexual who must also confront his fabricated homosexuality does not recognize himself. The disparities between homosexual fact and heterosexual fiction are too complex and myriad.

The fractured expectations within the interned Jews' environments were often too confusing to be logically or consistently internalized. So the homosexual is provided many separate or opposing elements for his expected behaviors. These contradict his sense of inner integrity. The result is an adaptive inferiority complex.

Bettelheim stresses that Jews were encouraged to interiorize their captors' aggressions and thus victimize themselves—and each other. To destroy their sense of autonomy, Jewish prisoners were systematically reduced to ". . . masochistic, passive-dependent, and childlike attitudes which were 'safe' because they kept the prisoner out of conflict with the SS."[29] As tyrannical parental threat-figures, the SS encouraged childish attitudes and behaviors among Jews.

While heterosexuals similarly threaten the self-recognized and then suppressed homosexual identity, other homosexuals can also arouse anxiety in such a man. To avoid conflict, the homosexual develops masochistic and passive-dependent traits which seem to adjust and reconcile his internal differences with others. So, John Reid entered Yale as a safely anonymous homosexual, met a vocally avowed homosexual and grew to hate him:

> Jon was particularly threatening to me because along with exposing himself as a homosexual, he had taken it upon himself to expose everyone else. He talked constantly of "closet cases" and "closet queens." He believed in liberating the world. He thought it was sick and hypocritical to hide one's true sexual preferences. . . .
>
> I dumped on Jon Martin at every opportunity. I was an Uncle Tom, a peroxide-blond Jew with a nose job and blue-tinted contacts who persecuted other Jews to keep the Nazis off his back. . . .
>
> Here I was centering my being on the cosmic feelings I had and the burdens I bore, here I was carefully cultivating all traces of normality and masculinity—and here was Jon Martin spitting on the temple, laughing at closet queens, ridiculing my entire value system.[30]

Many homosexuals childishly think they are safe in their play-acting imitations of heterosexual appearances. They construct inner personality consistency attached to a value system they think is their own. Thus, "passing" reinforces the attachment of the homosexual's rigid roles to his demanding environments. Fear is usually the dynamic impulse in this dramatic deception. And soliloquy is often the dramatic convention used to maintain a necessary inner sense of equilibrium by the homosexual.

Reid used the dramatic technique of soliloquy to achieve his emotional survival as an anonymous homosexual. Soliloquy, as a language device, creates a rationale for one's social role. It seemingly resolves conflict and offers stability of identity. All people talk to themselves, holding inner conversations—or soliloquies—much as did Reid.

In *Symbols and Society,* Hugh Duncan believes that the "Soliloquy is often an expression of conflict among 'outer' roles an individual struggles to confront, and, hopefully, to resolve contradictions and incongruities."[31] The homosexual thus fears that others will think or discover what he thinks, or denies, about himself. He must remain covered. For how long, depends upon multiple threat factors: attitudes of others, intensity of circumstances or imagined losses.

Conflicts between the homosexual's possible self and society's impossible expectations for anonymity, arouse his anxiety. With little heterosexual reinforcement—and possible exploitation from other homosexuals—"The individual struggles to develop an ego strong enough to resolve these conflicts."[32] Thus, soliloquy offers the homosexual a symbolic rationale—a logical cover—for him to "pass" anonymously through time and space. The homosexual actor can thus remain hidden in motion through both a heterosexual, as well as homosexual audience. Each monologue of enforced soliloquy isolates the homosexual from all others. Each defeats the spontaneous growth of the homosexual's organic identity:

> The final audience whose response is necessary to our sense of order drives us to say in the anguished cries of soliloquy what we cannot say in open dialogue.[33]

Additionally, soliloquy enhances a complex of well regulated inferiority. The homosexual encourages himself to become lost in the anonymity of self-denial and self-effacement. So incarcerated Jews achieved similar self-preservation within social defeat, by logically rationalizing their submissive behavior to themselves, much as the homosexual does in his symbolic soliloquy:

> Just like sheep that crowd timidly into the center of the herd, each of us tried to get into the middle of our formations. That gave one a better chance of avoiding the blows of the guards. . . . It was . . . an attempt to save one's own skin that one literally tried to submerge into the crowd . . . in conformity with one of the camp's most imperative laws of self-preservation: do not be conspicuous.[34]

Unfortunately, chronic dependency on secret soliloquy delays self-actualizing dialogues with others—whether one is heterosexual or homosexual. While soliloquy helps the homosexual to deny his minority membership, and thus gives him identity protection and reduction of anxiety, it also hinders the homosexual's stability of commitment to anyone. It also limits his internal stability of identity, by maintaining the homosexual's passivity or withdrawal.

So, the soliloquy as cover story connects the homosexual to his role, much as an actor is in character while in a dramatic presentation. Passing as a dramatic technique of survival becomes the homosexual's art of self-denial. It also denies other homosexuals with whom one has potentially negative and dangerous social identification.

Delay and denial contain degrees of guilt, rationalized by

pragmatic expediency. As the homosexual acts heterosexually in space, he delays authentic self understanding and personal expression in time. Passing then creates a static state of being; the homosexual exists in between space and time. R.O.D. Benson describes this inconspicuous existence as always a marginal one:

> I accept my homosexuality and do not consider myself either sick or depraved. However, society prevents me from expressing this mode of behavior freely. Society is monolithic. People are too bigoted and it is virtually impossible to change public opinion. Therefore, I will continue to exist as all minorities are forced to do. I will live in the interstices and crevices of society. I will be realistic . . . There is only one successful way that a homosexual can play the game: simulate and dissimulate.[35]

Gordon Allport also comments on minority members who attempt to pass as having created for themselves, an inwardly regressive personality, or an involuted identity. In *The Nature of Prejudice*, Allport states:

> People who deny their group membership may, by conviction, be "assimilationists" and regard it as desirable for all distinctive minorities to lose their identities as fast as they can. But often, too, the member who denies his allegiance suffers considerable conflict. He may feel like a traitor to his kind.[36]

If a marginal existence is one which perpetually involutes one's identity, then the homosexual's conflict over betrayal of himself or others is rarely resolved. As a man hesitates against acknowledgment of his homosexual identity, this self-as-actor diminishes or confines himself. His internal time passes through external time; his internal space passes through external space—rigidly self-contained. The homosexual's identity potential remains compressed and insulated by his rehearsals of characterizations within dramatic structures of illusion.

In *Beyond the Chains of Illusion,* Erich Fromm notices that both Karl Marx and Sigmund Freud shared the concept that most of what we think about ourselves—is based on illusion. Fromm interprets Marx to have ". . . Believed that our individual thoughts are patterned after the ideas any given society develops, and that these ideas are determined by the particular structure and mode of functioning of the society."[37] Fromm also notes that a minority member's precarious social status makes that person insecure. Such a person becomes eager to accept majority cliches which gain him acceptance and security. These "masks of illusion" which the homosexual wears to pass, are adoptions of status personas for public (even personal) approval.

The dramatic structures of illusion which the homosexual creates, with time, tend to affect the natural growth of his personality. He becomes preoccupied with stultifying rearrangements of disguise. What once may have been creative adaptation to environmental requirements, can become chronic duplicity to achieve approval. Marx notices the importance of time as a measurement of manifest personal change within a man: "He is a product of history, transforming himself during his history. He becomes what he potentially is."[38]

Yet, if the passing homosexual attempts to separate his unique nature from socially negative manifestations of his nature, he merely imitates and retains a style of heterosexuality. As he holds to the masks of heterosexual appearances, he simultaneously alienates himself from deepening awareness of who he is, or could be. In time, the mask sticks and the homosexual actor cannot enlarge the limitations of his role.

Anyone's efforts to integrate personal time and space within the larger social framework, is a normal strategy for systematizing one's self-meaning. All people must do this to confirm their sense of existence in their socially shared symbolic universe. For the homosexual's use of time and space, this process is described by Carol Warren, in *Identity and Community in the Gay World,* as an exchange of contexts for one's personal biography. The homosexual gradually learns the history of his sexual group and slowly socializes himself into it. He becomes a validated member through a systematic exchange of symbolic information.

However, Warren also believes that the symbolic "gay world" legitimizes the homosexual's identity within his larger social universe. Following this reasoning, the homosexual's gay time and gay events integrate him into general world history.[39] Despite Warren's honest attempts to devise a metaphysics for homosexuality, her "gay world" really underscores the homosexual's alienation or degree of illegitimacy in relation to homosexuals.

A homosexual "world" or community may offer some comfort and clarity to its members' sense of identity, but it does not offer general social legitimacy. As a Jew or black—"in community"—does not have his own racial identity legitimized within the larger social universe, so the homosexual's world does not legitimize him in the opinion of heterosexuals.

If "passing" delays time, then the homosexual's "biography"

becomes redundant. It fraudulently occupies space as a preoccupied replaying of the self as others require him to be. Passing is then a staging of identity. So, as the conventions of the stage require the audience's willing suspension of disbelief in regard to time and location, the homosexual requires himself to do the same. He thus capitulates to his heterosexual audience's control.

Many homosexuals often praise passing as heterosexual as a highly skilled dramatic art of survival. Without analyzing its results, they elevate successful anonymity to heroic proportions. In *Out of the Closets,* Laud Humphreys focuses on the homosexual's multiple identities as though they were successful auditions performed by professional craftsmen:

> From the time a homosexually oriented person first becomes aware that he or she is different, or "queer," in a very basic way from others, he or she begins to develop acting skills. . . . testing a repertoire of identities. . . .
> The art of passing is an acting art, and most homosexuals have an edge over others that varies with the number of years they have practiced. . . . Those who create new styles must be able to "sense" when the time is ripe for them.[40]

While expeditious timing serves an actor, it hardly means that artificial selfconsciousness is commendable as a mere punishment avoidance.

What Humphreys attempts to do is to ennoble the art of passing as a form of personal militancy against a rigid heterosexual value system. He romanticizes the homosexual's calculated deceptions as potential forms of social revolution. That the homosexual's very need to pass, does argue against such socio-sexual restrictions, does not nullify the damaging results of resorting to such ploys. The homosexual's consciously doubled time and space cannot integrate his inner and outer world as he awaits some future socio-sexual utopia hinted at by Humphreys.

Gordon Allport notices this circularity in his studies of neurotically habitual behavior as ". . . A tendency on the part of an organism to persist in a particular behavior even though the original reason for engaging in the response is no longer present."[41]

If one's biological survival behaviors, as well as social behaviors, can become attached to interests, values and styles within past or present contexts—then habitual behavior can arrest the future development of one's personality range. The healthy personality should develop ego autonomy only as it actively confronts each experience, without the need for subterfuge in neurotically circular behavioral responses.

So the homosexual's personality which merely passes as a set of skills or appearances, is a simultaneously secret and public person who only rotates between appropriate roles. Yet, can the homosexual know when to stop acting, or even whether he is able to stop? There is an implied identity trap in Humphreys' praise of passing skills practiced to perfection. The homosexual, in effect, institutionalizes himself within the remote and repetitious confinements he finds so burdensome; this is the oppression of his closet.

The remoteness of a closeted existence is basically the distance between the homosexual's personal and public identity. While the closet may control the homosexual's sense of security, he is also susceptible to a more subtle form of remote control: the technique of population control through isolation employed by various social managers.

The homosexual who recognizes that his sexuality isolates him, has learned to fear a general self revelation to others. He lives as a prisoner of fear within the metaphor of his internal ghetto, his psychological concentration camp—his denigrated sexual identity. His fear is the first aspect of heterosexual remote control which effectively paralyzes and removes him in time and space.

Additionally, the very size and complexity of the heterosexual value system in which the homosexual male lives also contributes to his sense of being overwhelmed. The structure of American social traditions, with a high premium on heterosexual masculinity standards against which the male homosexual must measure himself, affords him no valued position within it. To compensate, the homosexual can justify his anonymity by soliloquizing his powerlessness to change himself, to combat a stronger heterosexual majority, or even to influence individuals directly for personal redress. Psychologically and socially, the homosexual is encouraged to keep his distance.

Thus, the homosexual's necessary survival distance from his heterosexual managers, as happened with confined Jews who avoided the SS, often makes him more dependent on his managers. This apparent contradiction rests on illusion. The more powerless the homosexual is taught to believe he is, the more powerful and correct the heterosexual managers appear to be.

If many homosexuals believe the many demoralizing statements made about them, it is because they cannot forthrightly test their own realities against those described realities manufactured for them as social identities. The carefully maintained physical and psychological distance of Jews from Nazis tempted the Jews to believe that the Nazis were correct in the extremes of their concentration camp management. The more pervasive the Nazis' imaginary power was over the Jews, "The greater the threat, the greater the need to deny it. . . ."[42] And so the Jews believed in the virtue and power of their superior managers, in order to gain physical and psychological relief.

The hidden homosexual will go to many extremes to fashion modes of visible distance from homosexuality, even as Jews attempted to imitate the SS by altering their prison uniforms to resemble those of their guards. They wished to identify in appearance, goals and values with the SS, much as homosexuals attempt to imitate or ameliorate with heterosexual society. In addition to maintaining visible distance from their alien self, homosexuals also experience a distance in time; they often cannot share time as "complete" persons with heterosexuals. They cannot externally be their internal selves with family, friends, co-workers or in areas shared with the heterosexual public. Homosexuals even wonder if they are really themselves when they participate with other homosexuals—since time and space are as dichotomized as their personality.

When homosexuals become habituated to outward conformity to various social remote controls, they face the loss of inner control. Such control must spring from more direct and spontaneous personal relationships than many homosexuals feel able to achieve. As Bettelheim warns, "The more a person conforms to society's standards on a shallow level of convenience or fear, the less he internalizes its mores. . . ."[43] Again, the hidden homosexual experiences internal discrepancy from external social expectations. He feels adrift.

Authoritarian societies tend to have high degrees of prejudice in order to justify control of imagined threats by minority deviations from the majority's norms. When there is an imagined loss or disruption of these general social structures or values—known as anomie—Allport notices that prejudice can then provide a pseudo-validity for external control of any threatening minority groups. Thus, Hitler accused Jews of responsibility for German anomie, which was more a result of war fatigue and economic depression. He proceeded to confine the entire German society. He was justified by the simplistic logic of cause and effect transference; who caused German social distress—the Jews.

There is general agreement that America is highly homophobic, or fearfully prejudiced against minority sexual behaviors. Such homophobia justifies mistreatment of homosexuals, even as it sexually encloses the entire American society. That homosexuals feel that they have already lost control of their individuality by fiat, thus prepares them to accept control or confinement by others. They acquiesce to separation, and capitulate to silence and anonymity. This process of cooperation with heterosexual managers, is similar to Jews who allowed their own mistreatment because they did not have psychological preparations for defense against the logic of prejudice.

An interesting correlation to the homosexual's loss of control to heterosexual managers, is that of loss of control through cooperation with other homosexuals. This can be unconscious, or deliberate, self-modification because the more experienced homosexual fears heterosexual reprisals. Homosexual friendships sometimes depend on strict regulation of appearance and behavior—which passes as heterosexual, and thus protects the homosexual group from any flamboyance on the part of the newly emerging homosexual.

So, in confined Jewish groups, Jewish friendships were extremely fragile. The newly confined Jews were encouraged to isolate themselves for the benefit of the more "skillful" prisoners. Veterans divided from newcomers. Thus, *esprit de corps* did not spontaneously develop as a threat to Nazi authoritarianism.

If remote control provides the systematic technique for creating depersonalizing distance in time and space, then image selection and repetition acts as a continual content in such personality control. Most of the institutions in America—the family, the school, the peer group, the performing and visual arts, the media, the law, the military, medicine and religion—have been accused of inspiring impersonality in their members. However, these institutions continue to serve as mediators of one's culture.

The messages conveyed through these institutions appear to have a familiar interrelationship of uniformity. The reliability of repeated similarities offers a specious warmth and friendliness— even trust—to the images within these messages. If one feels inner doubt or weakness, there is the temptation to look outside of the self for more positive images of success, happiness and value. Thus, we imitate, rather than originate much of what we think and feel. While negative images or informational messages are also available, people tend to avoid these, rather than analyze them.

So, institutional messages remain similar in their intention— they select and repeat variations of one basic theme. All must conform, adjust and submit to these monitored appearances of variety, choice and personalized uniqueness. All institutions reward such behavioral modification.

In effect, the institutional image makers, taste shapers and information sources are able to manage most individuals. Any conflicts between one's personal and social worlds seem resolved because one needs only conveniently to allow institutionally designed comforts, distractions and desires to define one's personality as others wish it to be, rather than as what one might choose it to be. Thus, the most pervasive institutions in America which now supercede the many more humanly realistic groups, are those of mass media. Media messages are the most remote, the most domineering and frequently the most inaccurate. So, media apparently serve heterosexuals and homosexuals as the most formidable controlling devices in homosexual identity awareness.

In America, homosexuals first receive information about themselves through symbolic art. Symbolic art forms create distance between the homosexual's own reality and heterosexual representations of that stigmatized homosexual reality. The purpose of informational alienation and containment of the homosexual identity, is to solidify the heterosexual majority's power by contrast.

To achieve this, heterosexuals consistently and selectively fabricate denigrating homosexual images and thematic situations. If homosexual role models are continually transformed into stereotypes, each man's emerging homosexual consciousness is educated to feel uncomfortably detached from himself. The method used to establish the process of homosexual detachment from social communication, is again that of remote control. Instruments of control are the available forms of mass media.

Electronic media, printed material, the performing arts and film now exist as selectively manufactured social systems. These systems convey images and attitudes which allegedly express through parody, contrast or verisimilitude—the actual social systems in which we live. Melvin De Fleur suspects that now mass communications probably form synthetic social systems in themselves. Accumulated social data are artificially converted into behavioral abstractions of real persons in situations.

These situational plot contexts depict people as symbolic components. Unique personal realities are thus leveled, standardized and duplicated in mass communication, until audiences learn not to notice any division between fact and fiction, or the specific and general. Any audience of real people is tempted to imitate these representational data models and, in effect, fictionalize themselves. As De Fleur notes in *Theories of Mass Communication,* while our personality emerges from our given social symbols, if these symbols are repeated too frequently, then both the self and society tend to be abstracted.[44]

For the emerging homosexual consciousness, media forms usually distort more than they define. Media forms select parts of personalities, situations and conflict resolutions to represent social realities that are attached to values. While media select "meaningful" realities, many creative "authorities" argue against their dubious veracity, contrived realism and comforting fiction with a message. Still, the message for the homosexual is always partial, pointed and comfortless: there is nothing personally or socially valuable portrayed about his life.

Carl Jung believes that any such expressed group phenomena cannot represent the unique man. Fiction—illusion and delusion—frequently is organic to any mass communication of symbolic truths. Jung's belief implies a potential hazard for the male homosexual who receives information about himself through most social representations of the homosexual identity. It is difficult for the homosexual to recognize the accuracy of assumptions about himself, if he believes he has objective facts against which to compare himself. These facts usually argue for majority prejudice against minorities.

As the homosexual discovers himself, he has few personal or social resources to challenge others' critical creations of the homosexual stereotype. As Jung warns in *The Undiscovered Self,* such a man then becomes vulnerable to social control because media systematically confuse distinctions between the real and the ideal:

. . . All sorts of attempts are being made to level out glaring social contrasts by appealing to people's idealism, enthusiasm and ethical conscience; but, characteristically, one forgets to apply the necessary self-criticism, to answer the question: *Who* is making the idealistic demand?[45]

However, the idealistic demands to level glaring social contrasts are not always necessarily made by media creators. If anyone, it is the spectating person with access to media who poses the criticism.

In a *Time* MAGAZINE essay, "Blacks on TV: A Disturbing Image," Lance Morrow notices that blacks now have high visibility on television, but low image appeal. Spectators see blacks continuing to entertain or threaten white audiences as pimps, hustlers and humorously devious manipulators. Blacks caught in their perpetual domestic chaos show little interest in ideals; they are preoccupied with momentary material or personal gratification—often childishly. White messages created with black images reinforce what whites wish to believe about blacks. Unfortunately, black viewers also absorb their social "reality" from such television fantasies.[46]

Along with racial minorities, homosexuals are currently more visible in electronic media. *Newsweek* Magazine estimates that homosexuality apparently emerged from the prime time "closet" about five years ago. However, Ginny Vida, media director for the National Gay Task Force, claims this emergence from invisibility initially abused the homosexual image. Early portrayals of homosexuals as sick, murderous, child molesters or comically effeminate, merely increased a more sophisticated misrepresentation of homosexuals as individual (or normal) people:

> Television's overlords have hardly declared a moratorium on limpwristed portrayals of homosexuals, arguing that many do indeed seem to act that way. Nor is the medium displaying any inclination to shy away from the subject's more sordid aspects.[47]

As with blacks, heterosexual messages about homosexuals usually depict what heterosexuals stereotypically want to believe homosexuals appear as, engage in, or value. Homosexuals, in turn, only see their role as tragic, comic or socially radical.

A recent survey of television movies summarizes traditional messages available to homosexual viewers about their social "reality." *The Moneychangers* featured a homosexual assault by prison inmates. *Alexander: The Other Side of Dawn,* depicted the tragedy of young male hustlers whose salvation rested in a return to heterosexuality. *That Certain Summer* chronicaled the sorrow of a divorced homosexual father whose heterosexual son discovers his father's love relationship with another male homosexual. The film concludes as the father weeps over the loss of his son's affection and respect.

As with television, newspaper and magazine articles purport an objective presentation of social events; yet, they effectively and continually reinforce negative images of homosexuality. The National Gay Task Force *Action Report* responds to the distortion factor in such reportage:

> We are all hurt when the news media refer to crimes of criminals as "homosexual" even though the sexual orientation of the persons involved is irrelevant. Reports about a "homosexual hijacker" or a "homosexual murder(er)" tend to fix in the public mind a wholly unjustified link between homosexuality and criminality.[48]

Again, the linkage of role with stage can scenically determine the homosexual identity. When the homosexual as audience hears and views his own symbolic abstractions, his identity options diminish.

Such role monitoring also occurs in plays; homosexual motifs of tragedy, comedy and radicalism limit homosexual characters to pathetic or dangerous people, whether the play is written by a homosexual or heterosexual. For instance, LeRoi Jones' play, *The Toilet,* depicts a group of boys tragically victimizing an adolescent homosexual in a school rest room. He is beaten by the boy to whom he had privately revealed his homosexual capacity. The young "heterosexual" aggressor later returns alone to comfort his victim and thus attach himself psycho-sexually—in secret—to the beaten boy's stigmatic scapegoating.

In *The Ritz,* Terrence McNally offers a comic spoof of mistaken identity (homosexual vs. heterosexual). The pursuit of the heterosexual-as-homosexual occurs in the context of a gay steam bath. Tired stereotypes of homosexual foppery and sexual fantasy are juxtaposed against bumbling heterosexual machismo and virile reality. *The Ritz* satirizes itself as a shallow exposure of the follies of homosexual steam bath mores. It compounds homosexual ridicule—ridiculously.

In the much more accurate *Fortune and Men's Eyes,* John Herbert dramatizes a heterosexual adolescent's introduction to homosexual abuse in a prison context. His beleaguered (heterosexual) innocence drives him to contemplate emotional relief through assuming the role of (homo)sexual predator. Homosexuality is depicted as the brutal tool of revenge, survival or control of weaker prey.

As with dramatists, heterosexual and homosexual writers of nonfictional studies of homosexual identity continue overwhelmingly to emphasize theatricalized homosexual themes. Individual homosexual personalities are filtered through collectively presented sexual phenomena. Identity characteristics, life styles, social folkways, value orientations and favored goals are permeated with dominating sexual overtones. Identity appears to be motivated, shaped and confirmed by chronic attention to one's appearance, sexual prowess and social fluidity.

In concert, writers of printed fiction primarily communicate the homosexual's life to be sexy, sad and transient. Such fiction is frequently apologetic. It is complicated with pretenses aroused by fear of discovery. It is closet or ghetto literature into which the public may peek for titillation, while the homosexual sees his existence as sexually dominated and basically futile. The emerging homosexual consciousness thus derives a fantasized and superficial treatment of his complex dilemma.

For example, in *The Front Runner* by Patricia Nell Warren, an older homosexual track coach is separated from his younger runner lover by a heterosexual revenge murder. The grieving coach raises his dead lover's "son," gained by artifically inseminating a cooperative lesbian friend with the murdered youth's semen—apparently stored against an emergency need to perpetuate their love. The message is: the remaining homosexual male's life continues to have meaning by perpetuating his lover's memory in a simulated heterosexual "marriage." In *The Fancy Dancer,* Warren elevates a Roman Catholic priest from the moral difficulties of sexual fidelity to one man by making him a "universal" lover as he spiritually ministers to all mankind. The message is: homosexuality diffused into everyone as a worthy cause, is homosexuality without the entanglements of commitment to anyone.

In contrast to Warren, John Rechy avoids homosexual romanticism in favor of (homo)sexual athletics. His *City of Night,* as many of his novels, depicts the homosexual as transient hustler. Sex is commerce, or even a weapon, which is used against male heterosexual oppression of homosexuals. Rechy creates discrete emotional distance between his ambivalently homosexual characters. Thus, they can freely exchange their genitals as currency or ammunition, in order to trade or steal their ticket to freedom from the compromising entanglements of emotional love between men.

Similarly, Gordon Merrick's male homosexual characters are uncomfortable with emotional involvement. His characters tend towards two extremes: the homosexual who can have intercourse with women, and thus prove himself free from the homosexual stereotype or stigma; and the homosexual who affects femininity i.e., devotion, androgynous appearance, lisping terms of endearment, in order to appeal to his more masculine lover.

Merrick, as with many writers on homosexuality, creates a series of mini-climaxes to elevate conflict between orgasms. The homosexual mentality appears redundantly to concentrate on the magical erection. Merrick's character dimensions are first measured by penis size. Their concerns revolve around the choice of social liabilities and personal rewards in revealing their homosexual identity. To remain closeted, or not to remain closeted, add dramatic tension to Merrick's works.

These various media forms all rely on symbolic language constructions to circumscribe the homosexual identity. The Nazis used language in a similar manner to humiliate and isolate Jewish prisoners. SS guards symbolically attached Jews to the anal sphere; calling them "shits" and "assholes," the guards ridiculed the Jews into regressive levels of pre-toilet training. Jewish prisoners were debased from self respecting adults to obedient children—first symbolically, and then psycho-socially. So, homosexuals who are managed by heterosexual information and artistic propaganda about themselves, regress into silence and anonymity to avoid such "blows of the guards."

While Frankl viewed the Jewish reaction as a natural avoidance technique for self-preservation, heterosexual critics frequently blame homosexual behavior for conforming to those repressive or dependent patterns which heterosexuals deliberately construct for homosexuals. In *Homosexuality: Disease or Way of Life?* language logic reveals a heterosexual paternalism in psychiatry as it monitors proper behavioral values. So, author/psychiatrist Edmund Bergler plays the parent when he contends that homosexuality is not biologically determined, nor is it a result of situational bad fortune. He contends that homosexuality is neurotic, childlike syndromes of unresolved conflicts. "It is an unfavorable *unconscious* solution of a conflict that faces every child."[49] In Bergler's and other psychiatrists' concentration camp psychology homosexuals are offered socially justified injustice, whether they think they need it or not. Such sexually fascist logic symbolically creates Dachau as a state of mind well before such facilities actually existed as reasonable solutions to the Jewish "problem."

The homosexual's problematic position in the heterosexual majority's system of logic resembles that described by Erich Fromm. He reminds us that the "law of identity" in Aristotelian logic is generally still accepted as correct by American society:

> Aristotle states it: "It is impossible for the same thing at the same time to belong and not to belong to the same thing in the same respect. . . ."[50]

It is apparent why the homosexual male contradicts the "logical" conception of what he is in the heterosexual male's thought patterns. If a man is homosexual, he cannot be many other things, i.e., normal, moral, legal, heterosexual, male, etc. The homosexual "logically" does not belong in the larger social symbolic universe. He exists in the excluded middle; here he internally filters such social language logic and converts it into negative identity manifestations.

As the homosexual engages with the symbolic requirements of his society, he also finds himself disengaged from the real aspects of his nature. The consequences of symbolic language constructions can be termed as filters of experience, which isolate the homosexual as a symbolic captive. His internal symbolic space then diminishes proportionately to his external symbolic world. He denies himself or is filtered from others. He is symbolically circumscribed. Language is thus used intellectually to control and enclose the phenomenon of homosexuality.

Various filters of experience shape the homosexual's inner identity, even while they create a symbolic universe, in which the emerging homosexual consciouness must function—with heterosexuals and homosexuals alike. Such filters can be literal or figurative, situational or theoretical; but they are always negative.

Passing dramatically is one major filter of actual social experience. Passing encourages the homosexual to select ideas, beliefs, emotions and behaviors which will not ostracize or isolate him from others. However, passing inevitably achieves what it seeks to prevent.

An equally important filter of experience which is socially provided for the homosexual consciousness, is that of metaphorical language. First, stigmatic tags, such as "queer," "fruit," and "fairy," stereotypical behavior patterns, often associated with effeminacy, and stigmatic mythologies, such as homosexuals must be child molesting, murderous perverts all symbolically frame a constrictive persona upon the homosexual.

Secondly, such stigmatized language provides the homosexual with distorted information about himself because it filters reality by mixing fact with fiction. Social illusions then become self-delusions. The irrationality of such heterosexual language constructions of homosexual phenomena, screens the homosexual from realizing the rationality of his own identity. Assuming that language provides a credible social description of his asocial existence, the homosexual then encounters a third linguistic filter of experience; (Aristotelian) logic is created from generally held patterns of facts and fictions.

While the language of symbol, myth and logic serves as intellectual control of an individual, the language of taboo is socially constructed to filter or block emotionally aroused thoughts and behaviors. Fromm notices the arbitrary nature of this most extreme reality filter, as well as the span of its duration. In order to control human impulse, Fromm notes a delusionary emphasis in this language filter which:

> . . . Does not *permit* certain feelings to reach consciousness and tends to expel them from this realm if they have reached it. It is made up by the social taboos which declare certain ideas and feelings to be improper, forbidden, dangerous. . . .[51] [emphasis in original]

Since homosexuality is the most emotionally charged social taboo in America, the emerging homosexual consciousness learns that all social and linguistic structures offer him degrees of inclusion or exclusion, acceptance or rejection, reality and illusion. Linguistic structures even help to reinforce any contradictions felt in his simultaneous identities-in-passing: the homosexual must both be present and not be present in his sense of time and space.

It is as though the emerging homosexual awareness enters a conspiracy with society—against himself; heterosexuals require that all males ratify forms of secrecy, simulation and self-denial to integrate their shared homosexual taboo into social reality.

Heterosexual males then achieve their masculinity accreditation through maintenance of the homosexual taboo, by displaying their separation and distance from it. Only the homosexual male can truly discredit himself in this process. The cooperative homosexual must divide into a double identity; he must externally display distance from his internal impulse, to avoid his social discreditation.

So the Jews often behaved as though their confinement had no connection with their "real" lives outside the prison camps, and thus they did not recognize that the subtle process of their identity collision with Nazi enforcement, resulted in their identity fragmentation.

The emerging homosexual awareness now occurs atomistically in American society. Portions of the homosexual's real self identity collide with elements of ideal social expectations. The emerging homosexual then becomes enclosed within an artificial sphere of enforced personal and social congruence. The real and the ideal become indistinguishable. By this means, the homosexual can become the stereotype he attempts to resist.

The collision of a homosexual's atomistic thinking, in conflict with "atoms" of social identity, can often help to delineate borderlines and clarify forces working within and without any man's growing sense of identity. Yet, the homosexual's self-awareness is intensely threatened by atomistic thoughts contrasted against social ideals.

To diminish this conflict between self and his society, the homosexual may resort at any time to the phenomenon of "totalism"[52] as a protective relief measure. Totalism is similar to an all or nothing orientation to circumstances. It seems logical, and certainly advantageous.

Fear, misunderstanding and anxiety cause many homosexuals totally to rearrange internal self images, thus allowing potentially destructive social identity elements to dominate their personalities. Emphasis of positive (although uniquely personal) elements can be excluded or suppressed—totally.

Currently, most American males attempt to totally rearrange their personality "atoms" to avoid conflict with socially provided—and rewarded—images of success. Various masculinity complexes are offered as patterns to personally imitate. They always emphasize a necessary totalism involved in such personal reconstruction of each man into a uniform maleness.

Thus, the American white heterosexual middle class male now

tends to be the general ". . . provider of an identity of consumers. . . ."[53] Unfortunately, this identity provision is too often accepted at face value by male homosexuals who totally relinquish their identities to such heterosexual (sometimes homosexual) social models. As in Erickson's "surrendered identity," these men can comfortably imitate or compete in social contexts which seem to confirm the eclectic, but safely similar middle class images of identity.

Yet, Wilson Key warns in *Media Sexploitation* that such consumption of appearances as a search for personality integration merely becomes an unending process of self absorption. Each man learns to consume a manufactured otherness,[54] and then wonders why he feels disassociated from what he sees himself becoming.

Interestingly, such atomistic media images which are manufactured primarily for heterosexual male consumption, are totally regrouped to exclude the homosexual male. If the homosexual male child and adolescent are socialized as allegedly equal "phallic-ambulatory males,"[55] they eventually threaten the credibility of the heterosexual's masculine images. Homosexual males tend to reveal the artificial aspects to the heterosexual's "territoriality of identity,"[56] which rests on fairly constant systems of masculine images and ritualistic behaviors. Then the "territorial imperative" is merely an arbitrary attachment to any social design which signifies masculinity, which in this case also symbolizes power, virility, dominance or other self-serving insignia.

If the heterosexual male majority, in effect, conceives itself into existence, it is what Erickson terms a "pseudospecies . . . which is 'naturally' superior to others. . . ."[57] The heterosexual claim to natural superiority must also project an even more blatant pseudo-identity onto homosexual males, in order to discredit their claim to participation in the heterosexual pseudospecies' superiority.

This identity discreditation can then result in identity instability for the homosexual male. He is moved to two extremes. He can join the heterosexual pseudospecies by displaying (as "passing") social-appropriate masculinity images which require total rearrangement of his own authentic personality elements. Or, the homosexual can accept the pseudo-identity of discredited homosexuality, which also allows for totally rearranged identity elements to dominate his personality.

The very totalism within the heterosexual male ideology of sexual politics provides a formidable barrier to the homosexual male. The dynamic within this ideology seeks to ameliorate conflicts or erotic interest. The male majority seeks identity confirmation through opposite-sex behavioral display; the male minority seeks confirmation through same-sex behavioral interest. Thus, Erickson notes that conflict in interest does not resolve itself through mere recognition and acceptance of ideological borderlines, or even uniquely personal forces within each identity's development. The heterosexual male pseudospecies totally projects its sexual anxiety onto homosexuals (as well as each other), and border warfare erupts:

> Where they do not desire, they find it hard to empathize, especially where empathy makes it necessary to see the other in oneself and oneself in another, and where therefore the horror of diffused delineations is apt to kill both joy in otherness and sympathy for sameness. It also stands to reason that where dominant identities depend on being dominant it is hard to grant real equality to the dominated.[58]

This social totalism (totalitarianism), as a form of personal confinement, is the uniform dynamic within most social institutions. Along the lines of pervasive environments, Marshall McLuhan postulates in *The Medium is the Massage* that electronic circuitry now serves as a more powerful extension of our central nervous systems. McLuhan rhapsodizes that "Ours is a brand-new world of allatonceness. 'Time' has ceased, 'space' has vanished. We now live in a *global* village . . . a simultaneous happening."[59] In addition to McLuhan's concept that all live in cosmic togetherness, he believes that "media work as environments. . . ."[60] and that media ". . . are so inclusive in their personal, political, economic, aesthetic, psychological, moral, ethical and social consequences that they leave no part of us untouched, unaffected, unaltered."[61]

McLuhan stresses that with this loss of privacy we are now freed from private guilt. The implication is that former systems of classification and discrimination have been proven archaic by the immediacy and community of media. Thus, "The whole concept of enclosure as a means of constraint and as a means of classifying doesn't work as well in our electronic world."[62]

Yet, McLuhan's enthusiastic theories do not appear to apply to the homosexual—or other minority groups, for that matter.

Media classification and constraint through stereotypical distortions still confine the homosexual quite thoroughly—perhaps better than ever.

If media represent, or even create environments, then perhaps McLuhan is correct in at least one respect: "the medium is the massage." Or, as Wilson Key states in *Subliminal Seduction,* modern media now constitute a language within a language, which manipulates us both consciously and unconsciously. From McLuhan's reassuring praise of a simultaneous "global village," Key more critically describes American culture as one enormous, subliminal "massage parlor."[63]

Key believes media manipulate our perceptions through mass suggestion. Since we consciously perceive in mental "sets" or clusters, these groupings of what we see, hear or experience comprise our reality in conjunction with our learned social traditions. Another dimension to our reality is our subliminal or unconscious mental sets.

These subliminal perceptions are highly susceptible to social manipulation because they are often beyond our conscious control. Such sets (or value groupings) are similar to Erickson's "atomistic images" of identity; they also can be totally rearranged to cope with value threats. They can even be trained to imitate value manifestations which carry social rewards.

People notice ideas with which they already agree. Yet, media content along with other American social institutions, remains impersonal and remote in its edited versions of reality. As Key states, this information—the issues, events and images of personality—usually is not the "real" thing, but is convincingly presented as "real."[64] Then our models for behavior continue to be based on stereotypes, or packaged social sets of reality perceptions and reactions. Through these representations of reality, Key believes the media function to maintain the prejudices of various audiences. Attitudes, opinions and beliefs remain static, rather than subject to change or personal expansion.[65]

The major image that heterosexual managers of remote control rely upon to organize and saturate our social reality, is a chronic presentation of what Key calls the "archetypal symbolic family":[66]

The symbolic family archetype is today present in politics, business corporations, military and civil organizations, and virtually any closely integrated group with a collective security need. . . .

In the neighborhood, at home, fraternally, at work, in sports . . . even in religious groups. These family archetypes surround each of our lives almost everywhere we look. . . .[67]

Heterosexuals project the homosexual as a primary threat to the integrity of the archetypal heterosexual family, the value of sexual reproduction and the moral protection of children. It is as though homosexuals' main interest is sabotage of the human species. So the SS imagined Jews to be actively conspiring against the Hitler state.

For most citizens, the symbolic family defines, structures and controls their self concept. Manufactured images of political leader (father), spiritual leader (mother) and subordinates (children) create levels of power based on sex roles. These images tell all of us how to behave, purchase, labor, interact, value or desire. When these remote archetypal family images of stereotyped realities are generated through the media, we contrast them against ourselves or our various and real life situations. The result is our eventual disappearance into an archetypal conglomerate containing few variations to meet the individual's personality needs. The emphasis within the archetypal family is on the self as the part of a unit; each member is enjoined to fulfill a carefully prescribed role in a power hierarchy.

Howard Brown believes a conspiracy of silence against the homosexual provides a sensed remoteness, an ignorance of relationship with historical or contemporary homosexuals that perpetuates the homosexual's feeling of being out of time . . . or place. Brown indicts the contrived silence of paternalistic managers of the archetypal family structure:

Compounding the fearful loneliness that accompanies discovery is the general absence of role models. . . . People become, in large part, what they perceive they can become—a perception that depends on their knowledge of what others like them have become. And homosexuals have been a people almost totally without a history. Moreover, the fragments of history that do exist are still largely kept from the view of the general public.[68]

Thus, social value sets concerning positive homosexual models are filtered from both homosexuals and heterosexuals. In their place are substituted traditionally denigrating images and myths, as well as silence. Without access to the knowledge of his community of identity, which is symbolically transmitted through time and event, the homosexual continues to remain atomized and ambiguous, victimized and controlled.

While the physical and emotional extremities of the Jews in Nazi concentration camp or social ghetto are not identical to those of homosexuals in America, a consistent parallel of human dynamics within the relationship of oppressor and oppressed does link the Jewish and homosexual phenomena:

> At that stage of imagination where we deal almost solely in stereotypes, few of us are able to conceive of homosexuals as oppressed. What, then, if we define oppression and move to a logical level of analysis? I suggest a definition that applies to the condition of Jews in Hitler's Germany, blacks in South Africa (or wherever whites possess greater power), American Indians, or peasants and women in almost every time and place: *oppression obtains when those holding authority systematically impose burdens and penalties upon relatively powerless segments of a society.*[69] [emphasis in original]

For both the historical Jew and the contemporary homosexual, confinement of autonomy is first achieved symbolically and then actually. These two factors are always monitored by more powerful others. Either heterosexuals aggressively control the metaphors of homosexuality—and thus the homosexual—or the homosexual controls himself through acquiescent confirmation of his metaphors. Recognition of this illusion-reality dynamic, permits the homosexual to ask himself two essential questions: How long do I wish to remain contained? How shall I choose to be free?

The emerging homosexual consciousness will face any emergence from his closeted identity as a dangerous, frustrating and continual process. Such a homosexual risks employment jeopardy, alienation from heterosexual friends and family, ridicule, rejection by more secretive homosexual acquaintances and even physical harm. Risks force the homosexual to adjust identity to accommodate to each new person he meets, each new context he experiences.

Yet, rewards can be gained by risking emergence from his secrecy: greater self-esteem, personal freedom of expression, stronger bonding with other sexual minority members and a more healthily integrated life with both homosexual and heterosexual people. The social framework of illusion and reality in anyone's life does not preclude the responsibility of choice for one's existence.

Time is one such reality by which Benson believes a homosexual may convert an active intellectual acceptance of himself, into a more supportive emotional self-acceptance. Time can be utilized to do ". . . two things: strengthen his inner world; create an outer world which is sympathetic to his desire to live his own life."[70] The homosexual must teach himself to believe in and to accept his own sense of self respect. He must actively pursue his own behaviors and values which strengthen, rather than diminish his ego identity. He must create a logical and factual defense about the "rightness" of his sexual identity.

Time makes available an active development of an ethical philosophy, which contains specific principles by which to live. The homosexual's external world can be strengthened by searching for allies within social institutions, which are sympathetic to authenticating his own life. As Erich Fromm argues, every man must mobilize his own human experience in order to engage himself with others. Such active engagements deny the necessity for a closeted life.

To Benson's exhortation to the homosexual to use time to strengthen his internal and external world, Fromm adds the necessary reality of action in space—apart from any provisional social containment:

> . . . *I* need to be *I* . . . I need to be myself . . . my own authentic, unique self. . . . As long as I have not established my own identity, as long as I have not fully emerged from the womb, from the family, from the ties of race and nation . . . I have not fully become an individual, a free man. . . .[71]   [emphasis in original]

In time, the emerging homosexual consciousness must pass his way—physically, emotionally and intellectually—from the closet, the ghetto or the concentration camp of his imagination into partial identification and commitment to some available homosexual collective. Only collectively can homosexuals gain some relief from voluntary or heterosexually imposed confusion and confinement. Collectively, homosexuals can learn to re-establish identity free from fear, coercion, stigma and deception.

Chronic attempts to engage in secret "passages" only risk division of one's inner identity. Perpetual passages merely prolong the homosexual's achievement of personality integration, through which he gains his sense of wholeness and worth—without artificial shams. Yet, passsages include risks. The final risk is the last passage: devising personal supports to "come out" of identity simulation or assimilation.

Coming out of hidden identity requires a perpetual process of self-confirmation through all the time in one's life, in whatever location one might be. The only available time is now. Each of us can only choose the moment for our own existence. The past is remembered, the future is anticipated, but the reality of our existence is caught in each moment we choose, autonomously.

Bettelheim stresses the necessity of Jewish prisoners to have made autonomous choices, even when the destructive extremities of their confinement seemed totally beyond their ability to avoid capitulation:

> . . . To survive as a man not a walking corpse, as a debased and degraded but still human being, one had first and foremost to remain informed and aware of what made up one's personal point of no return, the point beyond which one would never, under any circumstances, give in to the oppressor, even if it meant risking and losing one's life. It meant being aware that if one survived at the price of overreaching this point one would be holding on to a life that had lost all its meaning. It would mean surviving—not with a lowered self respect, but without any.[72]

While some imprisoned Jews chose their point of no return, others did not. They lost touch with the essence of their life's meaning.

Contemporary American homosexuals face a similar ethical choice and a dominant reality. Some homosexuals choose their point of no return; others do not. Some choose to protest their treatment in time and space; others pass silently and listen, watch and wait.

Yet, Carl Wittman articulates a poignant cry for all homosexuals, which echoes the Jewish outcry of grief—against injustice and inhumanity. The motives of the contemporary homosexual's indictment then parallel the historical questions shouted by any victim of a malicious majority: Why me? What have I done? The imprisonment of innocence is always extreme. Thus, Wittman focuses on the real human content caught within the metaphors of social constraint, as he writes "Refugees from Amerika: A Gay Manifesto":

> San Francisco is a refugee camp for homosexuals. We have fled here from every part of the nation, and like refugees elsewhere, we came not because it is so great here, but because it was so bad there. By the tens of thousands, we fled small towns where to be ourselves would

endanger our jobs and any hope of a decent life; we have fled from blackmailing cops, from families who disowned or "tolerated" us; we have been drummed out of the armed services, thrown out of schools, fired from jobs, beaten by punks and policemen.

And we have formed a ghetto, out of self-protection. It is a ghetto rather than a free territory because it is still theirs. Straight cops patrol us, straight legislators govern us, straight employers keep us in line, straight money exploits us. We have pretended everything is OK, because we haven't been able to see how to change it—we've been afraid.[73]

8/The Homosexual Ghetto: The *Haute Rigor* of Small Group Survival

> The ghetto shows that what matters most in social life is not so much the "hard" facts of material existence and external forms as the subtle sentiments, the dreams and the ideals of a people.[1]—
> Louis Wirth, *The Ghetto*

> The place to improve the world is first in one's own heart and head and hands, and then work outward from there. Other people can talk about how to expand the destiny of mankind. I just want to talk about how to fix a motorcycle.[2]—Robert M. Pirsig,
> *Zen and the Art of Motorcycle*

The homosexual ghetto functions as a social machine. This machine relies on increasing refinements of socially erotic technique. As it develops towards its ideal organization, this technical ghetto becomes distinguished by organization, integration and efficiency.

Most American social groups now tend to use the machine as their social mode. They standardize their human elements; these groups produce degrees of selfconsciousness as social growth. Any personal doubt, conflict or anxiety "aroused in man by the turbulence of the machine is soothed by the consoling hum of a unified society."[3] Harmonious submission to the mechanics of our social groups, represents a specilization of our selves as social technicians.

In the homosexual ghetto—that specialized environment of erotic diversity—rituals of technique also are standardized. For

229

homosexuals, technique becomes the means for "apprehending reality, of acting on the world, which allows us to neglect all individual differences. all subjectivity."[4] Technique is objective. It neutralizes personal opinion in favor of collective expression. While technique creates a visible bond between men, it also produces subtle forms of alienation.

Those homosexuals who function within such a shared technical framework, do form a brotherhood of perceptions—a shared reality. Yet, this is often a speechless and anonymous fraternity. Such homosexuals "who know the technique of a given operation have no need to address one another in order that the necessary motions be correctly performed at the right moment."[5] This was also the mood of Jewish concentration camp workers; they did not need to know or understand each other. They were only required to understand expected techniques and know in advance what their team members would do. They automatically functioned in the compressed specialties of worth to their Nazi captors.

Likewise, the homosexual male participates in the mechanized operations of his ghetto. He enters it as an isolated or anonymous member of a socio-sexual team, similar to a worker on an assembly-line. Repetition of various specialized social rituals train each homosexual "worker" to adjust to his primary function, which is usually sexual.

Thus, many homosexuals become fixed to their social labors. Any thoughts of personal change or alteration of social patterns, produce anxiety in most men. Any personal opposition to collectively reinforced techniques of the ghetto system appears futile.

The homosexual's chronic participation in various depersonalizing sexual labors tends to enlarge such employment tasks to fill most of his waking hours. His "non-erotic" nine-to-five employment occupies his devotion to market-place requirements; his more-or-less erotic leisure time activities carry a similar task-consciousness—rather than a recreational respite. Erotic expectations form the homosexual's "job-profile" within the ghetto techniques of his social-leisure milieu.

Technique—efficiency, style, contribution and harmony—is tantamount to the homosexual's social survival, much as Bettelheim's concentration camp Jews struggled to achieve within their time allotments:

> . . . Finishing all required tasks in the time allowed asked for great experience and skill in each prisoner; even a few slow or clumsy ones

threw the whole process out of gear. That kind of skill was acquired only after hundreds of performances. . . .[6]

Bettelheim uses technical terminology to describe human cooperation. Those Jews who did not contribute were considered a drag on the group. Their work was often nonsensical labor, which contributed to the Jews' personality disintegration.

So, homosexual ghetto labor is often frivolous and boring activity. The unpredictability of sexual success offers some sentiment of morale, yet the homosexual who finally adapts to his specialized milieu more often senses only personal inertness and a withdrawal from social risks. As the Jew, the homosexual learns to internalize his need of participation in his ghetto, even while personal rewards remain so few.

If the men within the homosexual ghetto operate together only through the technical agencies which organically dominate it, then the ghetto mechanically perpetuates itself. Thus, every minority group creates and maintains the techniques of its own ghetto in order to isolate and protect its members. Such isolation reinforces a group's integrity. It also imposes moral definitions, through which it rewards and punishes according to its code of values.

Isolation can also accommodate one subordinant group to various dominant ones. Here, the need to create a ghetto springs from external forces, rather than internal desire. A dominant social group's fear of being proselytized by suspected heresies held by minority group members creates the issue for separation from that minority. Minority withdrawal is then first circumscribed by psychological attitudes, and secondly by physical fact.

The emerging homosexual consciousness thus enters two avenues to acquaintanceship—or operation—with other homosexuals: the covert ghetto, which includes dinner parties, church groups, counseling seminars or activities within private homes and friendship circles; and the overt ghetto, comprised of public institutions such as bars, parks, steam baths, beaches, gyms, public toilets and restaurants. Within each operational context, the homosexual must resort to degrees of covert or overt techniques of participation. These match his willingness to identify himself as homosexual, or his skill in handling specialized erotic acquaintanceship.

However he enters, the emerging homosexual must gain access to his ghetto through varying stages of self-institutionalization.

These stages are both positive and negative, internal and external. Since the mechanics of the homosexual ghetto exist much as those of any ghetto group, the homosexual's first stage of entrance is by that of identification and attachment.

The self-identified homosexual somehow, at sometime, recognizes the social stigma of his sexual orientation. Other homosexuals offer possible stability and social sanction to those meanings that the homosexual attaches to his sexual experiences and minority world view. They suggest to the individual male, a program for his homosexual maleness. They also offer reinforcement or understanding to homosexuals who socially succeed or fail. They provide clarification to homosexuals who have doubts concerning what it means to be such a man, given the competing definitions and values of heterosexual maleness.

Homosexuals then share their definitions of reality and pay allegiance to these, according to their personal attachment to the techniques of their sexual roles. These roles are basically adaptations to situations or experiences of the ghetto participant. In this environment, there is little idealization of expectations concerning the self or others. Rather, emphasis is on specialty.

The ideal man one hopes to be (or find) is attached to an imaginary role imitation, selected and perfected in one's erotic exchanges with others. These ideal roles emphasize those monodimensional images of masculinity which inflate a faltering ego to heroic proportions. Such selected images—which often conform to those presented by media, sports, entertainment or advertising—form ego-visible systems relying on erotic technique. These socially available male model builders promote a social structure and value content which each man can internalize as an automatic program for his own self concept.

Within the demands of his ghetto, the homosexual additionally learns to become a sexual specialist. Without the ghetto, he learns masculine techniques of social integration, in which passing as heterosexual continues to reinforce his performance towards the ultra-masculine.

In addition to identification and attachment, the second stage of self-institutionalization relies on the homosexual's self-perception conjoining with group conception. This avenue into the ghetto incorporates three levels of awareness: the *formal,* the *informal* and the *technical* levels. Within these three levels of thought and behavior, the individual homosexual gains access to knowledge of himself and others—as homosexual. These levels of communication structures control individual and collective values, intensity of social interaction and collective approval or disapproval of homosexual group members.

The formal learning level of the homosexual's activities is generally conveyed as a system of right-wrong precepts. At this level, one's formal emotions automatically apply pressure to conform rigidly to one's contextual situations. Formal emotions tend to rule out toleration for alternative thoughts and behaviors.

Informal learning occurs through models generally accepted as valuable for imitation. Informal awareness allows high degrees of personal or collective patterning because the informal includes activities or mannerisms which, once learned, become automatic responses to everyday life. Informal emotions, such as anxiety, spontaneity or ecstasy, are not aroused unless one deviates from informal norms. Even informal arousal of emotion (as with the more formal emotions) tends to make one aware that permission must be granted for any infractions of permissable expression.

As with formal and informal learning, technical learning becomes a strategic device for managing collective thoughts and behaviors. Such technical awareness, however, always occurs at the highest level of consciousness. The technical requires deliberate suppression of feeling, since emotions often interfere with efficient performance.

Institutional patterns of social operation, by their very dynamic and structural relationship, tend to limit personal or collective change. The formal, informal and technical aspects of group dynamics provide a continuity of homosexual traditions from within the ghetto, even as these same forces provide competitive or imitative models to the outside heterosexual majority.

The outer dynamic of prejudice operates upon the homosexual ghetto to make it distinct, separate and communal. The inner dynamic of shared secrecy and stigma, operates within the homosexual ghetto to create the tension between trust and danger. This contributes to the homosexual male's sense of restless atomization, his state of apparent flux.

The tempo of ghetto techniques is generally intense. The erotic combustion of the homosexual social machine elevates each homosexual's hyperattention to synthesize himself into harmony with pervasive ghetto techniques.

The third level of self-institutionalization within the homosexual ghetto, is finally the degree of commitment each man makes to it. As the homosexual internalizes available ghetto controls—

erotic opportunities, jargonese, rituals and values—he often limits himself from his larger human potential. He is on the periphery of two worlds—heterosexual and homosexual. Louis Wirth notices a similar marginal position of the ghetto Jew, who observed the larger world from his subcultural vantage:

> He never lived fully in either world, and was torn between the impulse to remain in the intimate circle of his own kind, where he found security, and where he had some sort of status, and the conflicting impulse to escape into the life outside. . . .[7]

So, the homosexual develops a selfconsciousness and a social aggressiveness which alternate in emphasis between both his homosexual and heterosexual contexts. Inner struggles to hide, oscillate with external conflicts about self-revelation. To deny his ghetto, is to urge the homosexual to leave the familiar and escape into anonymity. To remain ghetto-bound is to make possible a homosexual fanaticism, bigotry and identity ignorance which plunge the individual man into a potential impotency of constraint.

This constraint is intensified by increasing technical success in the homosexual's adherence to rituals which form the dynamics of the homosexual ghetto machine. Sexual-technical success depends initially on the homosexual's age, appearance, style and social facility. Ultimately, success depends on his ability to attract and/or keep multiple sexual partners for periods of time.

Degrees of technical success then encourage the homosexual to greater commitment to his ghetto. His identity, or social potency, is validated within this sexual milieu. Validation is dependent upon commitment to the ghetto, either covertly or overtly. The only difference between the homosexual male and the heterosexual male's submersion into the mechanics of his self-institutionalization, is that the heterosexual male usually is not required to be covert in his social-sexual rituals.

Human motives, too, form a dynamic feature within any ghetto population. Such motives are inspired by a sensed personal and collective isolation, which then shapes the character and intensity of the homosexual's social life. From this initial sense of one's identity isolation, any person attempts to confirm himself socially, rather than solitarily. As Gail and Snell Putney have determined, each phase of any human need is primarily a social desire, rather than a biological drive. In *The Adjusted American,* they conclude that each person needs an accurate and viable self-image; each then seeks verification of that self-image through its continuing expansion in association with others. Finally, each person desires confirmation of his identity through action.[8]

Consequently, the human motive to know the self in relation to others activates the homosexual. He first faces heterosexual pressure to assume a collective responsibility for his homosexual deviance. The homosexual's self-knowledge begins with guilt. His identity is primarily represented and thus restricted by heterosexual definitions—those formal and informal ideas and attitudes which appear to be rational and efficient techniques of social confinement. Secondarily, the individual homosexual receives reinforcement in any erotic values and behaviors which help technically to regulate the homosexual milieu.

In effect, both aspects of heterosexual representation and homosexual reinforcement conflict with the need of the emerging homosexual identity to expand randomly, spontaneously and without rigid limitation. Any verification of the homosexual's self-image then relies on what become ritualized efforts to defeat his feelings of isolation. Unfortunately, he is described in ways which often enclose his identity into a closed system of socially valuable (predictable) behaviors. Here, the homosexual is effectively denied free access to others. Access to himself continues to be channeled through erotic rituals which positively or negatively satisfy the narrow expectations of both heterosexual and homosexual groups.

While the Putneys depict such adjustment as a form of social confinement, Philip Slater emphasizes this attention given to identity modification as a conscious pursuit of approval. Slater warns that it is delusionary to believe that when we assert our individuality, our responses can be considered autonomous or spontaneous.

In *The Pursuit of Loneliness*, Slater considers people to be too selfconsciously aware of others in competitive America. He thinks that most people ". . . accommodate to others . . . to look good, impress people, protect themselves from shame and guilt, and avoid confronting people directly."[9] So, each person vascillates between assertion and withdrawal as the basic rhythm in the socialization of an identity. To be alone, perhaps allows the possibility to be an individual; to be together almost insures that a person is tempted to compromise his identity.

In creating a viable self-image, the homosexual is particularly eager to confirm himself in social action with other homosexuals. To alleviate his loneliness, the homosexual attempts to abandon isolation for commitment to others. Yet, self-image, social action and commitment to others are always conditional and tenuous.

The homosexual's attempt to connect with other homosexuals, carries a sense of desperation, as well defensiveness against exploitation. Often, self- and other-expectations appear impossibly demanding. In order to trust others, the homosexual tests (and is tested by) those he meets. Fantasy, fear and emotional isolation form difficult standards for trust-confirmation. Obviously, many fail the conditions of such tests.

In his extended isolation, the homosexual (as might heterosexuals) fantasizes someone who will be everything he wants or needs in a love subject. Then, as Suzanne Gordon emphasizes in *Lonely in America,* "With actual confrontation . . . comes the possibility of disappointment if that person doesn't coincide with the fantasy. This only increases the panic of loneliness . . . or . . . total withdrawal from others."[10] Whether one is heterosexual or homosexual, in America, to be lonely is to imply personal failure. Conversely, social success often creates a perpetually desperate drive for human confirmation by a variety of people.

Success, for the homosexual, implies multiple social contacts, which includes the skill to achieve and/or sustain primarily sexual relationships. Fear of sexual failure thus dominates the homosexual's ghetto interaction. Fear motivates him to develop techniques of persuasion, by which he bargains for others' favors. He becomes involved with relationships that force him also to focus upon techniques of maintenance.

Failure to maintain sexual potency, erotic appeal or social fluency, isolates the homosexual within a collective atmosphere of cynicism. Trust is shattered so often, that one becomes emotionally brittle as an emotional defense. By disbelieving the innocence of another's motives, the homosexual creates a buffer against self-recrimination for his own imagined faults. Thus, the homosexual can rationalize his fear of failing to maintain himself, as a deficiency of technique.

R. D. Laing comments that such men in groups who tend to assign themselves (or each other) the technical functions, roles, rights, obligations, patterns and strata germane to their group, actually create a social machine which then they attempt to control. Unfortunately, the very inertia of the group system controls them. In *The Politics of Experience,* Laing states:

Once people can be induced to experience a situation in a similar way, they can be expected to behave in similar ways. Induce people all to want the same thing, hate the same thing, feel the same threat, then their behavior is already captive-you have acquired your consumers or your cannon-fodder.[11]

So, the homosexual experiences himself less as a person, and more as a defense mechanism functioning strategically in relation to other male defense mechanisms. He bargains less for a personal confirmation of himself and others, and more as a fantasy machine distinguished by erotic success.

While fantasy can be creative, more often it is destructively demanding and emotionally alienating. Too many of one's fantasy elements are imposed on others, rather than shared. If one's fantasy merely enlarges the distance between human possibility and the rhetoric of idealism, one does not create imaginatively in response to others. Rather, one only secretly conspires to gain ready-made demands from strangers.

The homosexual then, as Slater notes of most Americans, cynically surveys his opportunities within his ghetto rituals, and reacts with systematic selfconsciousness. His techniques of success maintenance require that he chronically produce desirable effects on others. Any homosexual who functions as such an instrument within his social mechanism, encounters others and withdraws from them with a falsified sense of individualism.

If the homosexual cannot continually produce the effect he wants, in order to overcome his loneliness, he can elevate his loneliness into a style of martyrdom. In other words, he can blame others for that independence he claimed he wanted anyway. Thus, social failure is rationalized into personal success.

As various human motives help to express the dynamic within the homosexual ghetto, human forces also modify and perpetuate its social system. These forces rely on the intensity of one's sense of threat as a homosexual. They also form patterns shaped by the homosexual's personal adaptability to heterosexual behaviors and attitudes towards him, or as displayed towards members of his homosexual group.

As with the institutionalization of a Jew's identity within his ghetto phenomenon, so the homosexual's identity passes through similar stages of development. The first human force shaping both Jewish and homosexual social systems is that of heresy dread.

Thomas Szasz argues that there is a strong relationship between Jews and homosexuals, because both have traditionally undermined the beliefs and values of dominant groups: "As the

238 / Which Way Out of the Men's Room?

man with Jewish religion was considered not fully human, because he was not Christian—so the homosexual is considered not fully human because he is not heterosexual.''[12]

The homosexual now replaces the Jew as historical scapegoat. The homosexual is the dreaded heretic, carrying the ''communicable disease'' of dissent from sexual averages. He is then the modern and necessary archetypal outsider. He provides the dominant target for emotional prejudice. In this role, he offers heterosexuals the social catharsis needed for their own sexual guilt and fears.

In attitudes and logic, if not extremities in treatment, American homosexuals encounter in post-World War II society much of what Jews experienced in Europe and America before World War II. Louis Crompton, however, believes that even historical extremities afforded Jewish victims match those of homosexuals. He contends that ''genocide'' best describes the historical record of homosexual ostracization, mutilation and systematic extermination.[13] Then, the homosexual ghetto phenomena occur much as they did for Jews within their urban areas of enforced withdrawal or separation. The more extreme confinement phenomena of Jewish concentration camps, or general prison life, are also duplicated in certain homosexuals' lives.

To understand how the homosexual's identity is institutionalized—or how any identity based on stigmatized membership in a group is regulated—one must first recognize the dispute between imputed identity and self-generated identity. Then, one must acknowledge that human nature is technically separate from manifestations of social behavior. Ultimately, one is led to consider that perhaps the ideal Jewish identity, as well as the ideal homosexual identity emerges as an identity reaction to personally antagonistic social expectations.

If we wish to comprehend how the homosexual element figures into a man's personality development, the Jewish example of identity in sustained crisis offers the best pattern against which to compare the contemporary homosexual. By placing those human forces which shaped the Jewish experience, against those human forces which affect the homosexual, a dialectical awareness occurs which partially explains the violence in logic to the homosexual-heterosexual partition. Such examination is a rational attempt to approach the irrational. For the homosexual, the borderline of madness must move closer as he reviews the dialectics of his history.

In this vein, Erich Fromm notices that human forces perpetuate or modify each person's behavior. However, Fromm believes that it is essential ". . . to penetrate through the surface of past or present behavior and to understand the *forces* which created the pattern of past behavior."[14] Historically, the metaphorical bond between Jew and homosexual is that of archetypal outsider. Both were heretics and strangers, who represented what their social majority dreaded as challenging, different, peculiar, contagious and taboo. Both were needed by their majority to validate majority beliefs and practices, as well as frighten back majority members' own lusts, desires and penchants for the "evils" they ascribed to others.

By the social force of heresy dread, both Jewish and homosexual identities sprang from an isolation which shaped the latitude and mystique of available social life. So, isolation in ghetto structures provides a human force which affects the homosexual, because he functions with others who have been excluded from the majority society. Emotionally and traditionally, the ghetto's mechanisms shape the homosexual's sense of identity.

As with historical Jews, the contemporary homosexual ghetto first provides a cosmopolitan atmosphere which is intellectually stimulating, and often *avant garde* in nature. Transmission of ideas and expression of life values tend to generalize throughout these local cultural areas. Cultural hallmarks often focus on material acquisition.

The homosexual male is as susceptible as the heterosexual in his desire for status employment, display of goods, the status insignia of houses, cars, boats, clothing, furniture, hobbies, travel and friendship types. There is a tendency for these males to level people, activities and things as interchangeable elements within a recreationally ethical life structure. Personal life values are not self-created, but are rather superficially recreated—imitatively and chronically—to restore a cosmetic self in successful duplication of transitory trends or styles.

Many homosexual males are single; their relationships with other men are frequently experimental and tenuous. Like Jews, these homosexuals emphasize mobility and adaptability as survival skills, although for different motives. Because homosexual males concentrate on specializing—whether in loving, cooking, decorating, entertaining, collecting or buying—the homosexual ghetto reflects a highly technical orientation towards pursuit of leisure activities, achievement display and sexuality.

Personally, the single (sometimes the "married") homosexual often bears an extreme burden to provide many critical satisfactions to an other-directed homosexual consumer group. He must be lover, friend, confidant, entertainer, sex object, house mate, wit and ornament. Being a full-time homosexual can be exhausting. Thus, the survival skills of mobility and adaptibility require great expenditures of time and energy. Tiger considers such involvement in male groups as residual behaviors of primitive hunting tasks. More accurately, Brenton terms such masculinity survival tasks as hustling.

This mobility and technically shifting orientation to life often prevents any ethical system from being much more than tentative or situational. Any formal ideologies for homosexual groups only imitate those of heterosexual society; they remain fraught with competitiveness, hypocrisy, shallowness and anxiety. Informal values often habituate the homosexual into a specialized and patterned existence. He is conditioned to define his life through elements of sexual awareness and codified behavioral displays. The transmission of these homosexual "specialties" from one man to another, generally creates a pseudo-stability to mutually shared principles of conduct.

In addition to an *avant garde* cosmopolitan atmosphere, available urban institutions also shape the homosexual ghetto's manifest forms and functions. Whether in business, church, social league, resorts or politics, institutionalized "gayness" parodies a sex as profit ethic. It is the essence of the homosexual's stigmatic isolation. Within such gay institutions, homosexuals attach an economic standard to their psycho-sexual ethics. This attachment is similar to what David Riesman claims that Jews now do in marketing their personality as they compete for success.[15]

In *Individualism Reconsidered,* Riesman states that Jews traditionally created an ethical position based on their belief that they had something of particular value to Gentiles. Their Jewish social program would benefit the social majority, once it was recognized for its unique contribution.[16] Yet, these Jews were ultimately dominated by Gentile systems of social theory and practice.

So, homosexuals' self-declared uniqueness becomes swallowed by the more pervasive heterosexual market mentality. Jews who are now required to "show their stuff"[17] or overmatch Gentile expectations for success, are equaled by overt homosexuals who ply their special skills and attributes within urban institutions. Homosexuals thus frequently appear to excel in those areas which are specially reserved for them: social service, design, the arts, and business for pleasure—whether it be alcohol, travel or eroticism.

Along the line of urban institutions, historical Jews achieved a mystical attachment to each other within the lore and ritual of their shared isolation in assembly houses or synagogues. Homosexuals, too, assemble together; their public bar life unites sociability with a quasi-worship of phallic symbols of appearance, social skill and erotic potential. Jewish dance houses, public baths and guest-houses as public facilities, provided Jews with formalized self and group consciousness.

For homosexuals, discotheques, steam baths, resorts and restaurants function as avenues of encounter which encourage degrees of anonymous surrender to covert sexual technique. The primary purpose of these institutional encounters is to provide a frequent accessibility to erotic possibility. Thus, the homosexual's selfconsciousness, as well as the context of his group dynamic, reduces to confinement within technique. The ability to arouse one's erotic desire, or successfully to fulfill others' ideal male fantasies remain contingent emphases in the homosexual's technical awareness.

While Jewish ghettos had their boards of guardians which were basically philanthropic and protective in purpose, so homosexual ghettos contain local and national groups which provide counseling, information, political expertise or social liaison with heterosexual society. B'nai Brith, The Anti-Defamation League and the American Jewish Committee offer physical and emotional relief for Jewish victims of prejudice. Homosexual organizations, such as Gay Activists Alliance, Gay Liberation Front and the National Gay Task Force, publicly instigate identity clarification for both homosexual and heterosexual.

Inadvertently, many homosexual organizations serve to validate even stronger delineations between the two sexual polarities they decry. Their goal is to legitimize the homosexual orientation, as well as to elevate contemporary consciousness concerning homosexual problems and issues. Their mode is to link homosexuals to the future by publicizing their historical past. Their rationale is that homosexuals have traditionally created unique contributions to all societies. An extreme of this rationale is the homosexual activists' claim for the existence of gay "culture," which inevitably leads to competitive separatism, similar to those complaints against Jewish Zionism. Then, as Altman suggests, such separatism might even reinforce homosexual alienation from the larger society. It would tend to over-specialize only a few of the vast range of human possibilities available to any homosexual.[18]

It is apparent, then, that many urban institutions which describe and reinforce homosexual information, ritual and tradition, can frequently generate a life style of confinement for homosexuals. The pressure dynamic in such technique-inspired restrictions can also arouse emotional distress when the homosexual must manifest (or fails to manifest) institutionalized social expectations. Intense activity restricted to "one's own kind," as well as restriction from the heterosexual other, often provides an emotional pressure cooker in which the homosexual stews.

Abraham Myerson, writing on "The 'Nervouseness' of the Jew," notices that enforced intimacy often resulted in Jews seeking emotional relief only from other Jews. So, the human force of in-breeding further isolated the Jew, even as it seemed to protect him:

> The ghetto life was not only unwholesome physically, but unwholesome mentally, emotionally, and spiritually. Living in constant dread of massacre, exposed to ridicule, degradation, and more sinister disaster, the race developed an apprehensiveness and acquired a lower threshold for fear stimuli. This kept up by the drawing in toward an over-intimate family life.[19]

The closed, inbred homosexual group, like the Jews, then encourages marriage only among its members—in this case, male-to-male. The distress factor of confinement in homosexual ghetto life is softened by what might be termed the creation of surrogate families. This human force is similar to that of other confined groups which are isolated from their natural nuclear and extended family support groups. Thus, homosexuals use each other in a loosely affiliated and dramatically stylized structure of familial relationships.

What is often antagonistic description, or emasculated terminology for "family" members within homosexual socialization, reveals much more than a psychological idiosyncrasy or mere camp sarcasm. Homosexual males who refer to each other as "girls" or "sisters," ridicule what heterosexual males consider the male homosexual to be. Positively, homosexuals confirm their bond of alienation and shared understanding of their femininely imputed worth in these family networks. Older homosexual males—"aunties" or "mothers"—assume or receive the roles of mature and protective guides, much as a nurturing source within the homosexual social structure. Negatively, such terms can also reveal an age, a self-concept, or an appearance which no longer has much sexual value in the competitive market.

In *Children in Trouble,* Howard James observes that correctional institutions for girls frequently evolve these homosexually played family roles. Assumed roles are based on traditionally learned passivity and aggression which are generally tagged as feminine or masculine. Adolescent females, confined away from their male peers and natural families, then imitate these gender dichotomies stressed in the larger society:

> . . . Girls developed "phantom families" with one playing the mother, another the father, while others were children, aunts, uncles, and cousins. Many have been rejected by their own families.[20]

Kathyryn Burkhart notices a similar "family" structure among incarcerated adult women. In *Women in Prison,* Burkhart believes confined women face their emotional deprivation and unnatural isolation by modeling their confined world after the more familiar ones outside the prison. Separated from real families, these women adapt to their confinement by creating a fantasy world with a logical connection to reality. Imprisoned women have no men available to them. They manufacture the roles necessary to their emotional nourishment:

> This is an affectionate world of families—people we relate to as though they were our mothers or fathers, children and sisters or brothers. . . .
> Women don't necessarily set out to build families. Rather, they wander into relationships and adopt those friendships which have meaning to them. The friendships are much like friendships we have on the outside—where, for instance, you guide and counsel a friend as though he or she were your own child.[21]

Thus, the prison world is a blend of fantasy and reality which offers prisoners "constructed" comfort and support. For the homosexual, surrogate families and repetitious "intra-marriage" lend a loose type of social support, though often for only short periods of time.

Betrayal, competition, aging, boredom or other rationaliza-
tions, are frequent motives for dissolution of homosexual relationships. They provide an intensification of emotional insecurity and eventual instability for the homosexual—which for the
Jew often occurred through his biological and social inbreeding.
However, the Jew had actual family commitments and social
constraints to stabalize him. The homosexual is essentially only
sustained by private agreement, rather than a public validation of
his relationships.

While homosexuals are faulted for their promiscuity,
heterosexual society encourages the very behavior it cites as
reprehensible. Heterosexual society initially seeks to prevent
men from becoming homosexual. Yet, it also works to invalidate
stable relationships once a man does become homosexual. Under
this chronic pressure, Martin Hoffman remarks that it becomes
convenient and expedient for one man to engage in sexual acts
with another man and then disengage from the person, as well as
the guilt, fear and self-loathing which that person symbolically
inspires. In *The Gay World,* Hoffman believes society urges the
homosexual to discard the intimacy he seeks, or at least merely to
play at it:

> . . . To commit oneself to a living relationship with another man in
> which, 24 hours a day, one is reminded of one's homosexuality by the
> presence of the other person in one's life . . . requires a greater effort
> in overcoming the social barriers toward homosexual feelings . . . an
> effort that is simply not possible for many homosexuals to make.[22]

Additionally, the homosexual ghetto's characteristics share an
almost universal similarity. The homosexual who travels from
one geographical location to another, finds similar divisions of
private and public space, rituals and folklore which express the
specialties of his milieu. The formal, informal and technical stages
of entrance into the homosexual ghetto, the human motives
expressed within it, as well as institutional forces which modify
and perpetuate the ghetto, await the homosexual wherever he
may be.

So, as with any social institution, the homosexual ghetto also
exists by status divisions and class concepts. These functional
levels guarantee the homosexual certain successes or failures,
depending on his degree of identification with, or commitment to,
real or ideal operations of ghetto society.

The homosexual ghetto is universally stigmatized. It has no

social worth to heterosexuals. The homosexual's personal security within his ghetto varies according to its geographical features. The homosexual's voluntary secrecy, or heterosexual intolerance of sexual deviance, lend atmospheres of safety or threat. Even as the homosexual pursues his social or sexual encounters in parks, rest rooms, bars or streetcorners, he does so through specific rituals, treating and being treated as an other-occupational person.

Apart from sexuality, social contact with other homosexuals is freighted with occupational hazards and rewards. Arrests, beatings, ridicule or rejection can reinforce the homosexual's sense of stigma. However, whether one is successful or not, homosexual interaction does create a sense of *esprit de corps*, because the homosexual knows he is not alone. His stigma relates him to all other homosexuals.

Ghetto class and status consciousness can evolve in more precise ways than heterosexual stigmatization. Regardless of location or types, homosexual ghetto institutions shape each man's behavior towards uniformity and predictability. A sense of security arises for all when each subscribes to a fairly rigid and familiar etiquette. From city to city, the need for the homosexual to be inconspicuous is linked with the desire to be conspicuous to one's own kind.

Conspicuousness must carry a constraint against choosing one's own attitudes or behaviors in any given circumstance. Roles determine rituals, and personal expectations are made concrete through a repertoire of subtle signals which serve as social stock in trade. Thus, entrance and participation in the homosexual ghetto rely on formal, informal and technical socialization patterns and expertise. These "normalize" homosexual behavior and social aspirations.

While such etiquette and ethos continually regenerate the homosexual ghetto, its hierarchical social structure also serves as a dynamic force which modifies and perpetuates the ghetto's stability. Class concepts and status divisions within the more visible homosexual network, help to enforce possible identity goals for each man. Class and status display, too often urge him to accept those value orientations which are embraced by the more vocal, flagrant or distressed homosexual representatives of gay rights and life styles. A major issue here becomes who represents whom, and what values and goals are necessary for a man to hold, in order to be considered a *bona fide* homosexual.

Within any city, there are locally and nationally represented committees, clubs and organizations which claim to stand for the homosexual community. Actually, they generally represent only their own limited memberships, or the private visions of several leaders, rather than the majority of homosexuals who remain hidden in society.

With access to the media, city government and business elements in the homosexual ghetto, these small groups appear to speak for all homosexuals because they maintain a visibility and devise a logic to their representation. Within such groups, publicity often equates with superior status. The illusion of power or authority is often enough for the rank and file homosexual to believe such homosexual spokespersons have it.

These homosexual groups often compete as rivals, due to differing strategies on social education, militancy against heterosexual institutions, or varying philosophies of how to exist as a threatened sexual minority. They generally share a strong emphasis on passing-as-straight. They tend to be sensitive to their conceived image, either as imputed by heterosexuals or devised by themselves in reaction to imputation. Such concern marks the general American preoccupation with achieving effects, by regulating socially acceptable identities.

So, these groups manufacture features of homosexuality as legitimate by-products for heterosexual consumers. They attempt to define the homosexual identity in manners, which will achieve rapprochement with heterosexuals, somewhat like a state of civil comfort. The newly emerging homosexual consciousness thus encounters another "brand" of homosexuality to imitate or avoid.

Similar social frictions, as well as ideological levelings, occurred as Jews designed their concentration camp hierarchies. Bettelheim noticed that new prisoners had to combat weakening of their self-sufficiency or personal resolve by the established members of various subgroups in the Jewish camps. New prisoners complained that, "Old prisoners seemed mainly concerned with the problems of how to live as well as possible inside the camp. Therefore they tried to reorganize their personalities as well as they could to be more acceptable to the SS."[23] Because the SS punished the group for individual infractions, prisoners tended to monitor each other's behavior.

So, homosexuals entering more established homosexual groups carry a threat to harmonizing and valued tradition. The aroused consciousness of their homosexuality—including its stigma—is unknown and unpredictable to the older membership. Falling between extremes of personal radicalism or corporate accommodation to heterosexual tolerance, their influx creates potential hazards to established homosexual hierarchical structures and procedures. Friction occurs, and homosexual groups split or cooperate according to differences or similarities in social and political images tactics and goals.

While these groups represent only a fraction of all homosexuals, they do lend a modifying structure, definition and energy to the individual homosexual's ghetto experience. While their impact is often felt distantly by those persons who are only marginally committed to open group participation, all homosexuals are generalized by these various forms of collective visibility.

Status and class discrimination exist in the homosexual ghetto, for reasons similar to why they existed in Jewish ghettos and prison camps. The homosexual elite's treatment of the radical, poor, or ill-educated homosexual derives from the desire to protect their ideal identity as well as economic and social advantages for themselves. The more subtle motive for such class consciousness and status disputes is then based on the appeal of power.

All homosexuals sense degrees of powerlessness when facing the heterosexual majority. To feel powerful, some homosexuals militate against other homosexual groups, focusing on their negative "specialties" as points of debate. Conservative political groups who want a good press image, stress the "club tie" and dinner speaker approach; they leave the cosmetics and jewelry to the unwashed masses championed by "Third World" homosexuals. Leather bars mock the jock bars. The cocktail-disco set sneers at the toilet queens. The average male homosexual views the drag style of the urban "court" systems with embarrassment. Ideological power struggles ensue. However, such class competition reveals a simple lack of tolerance by wealthier, better educated or more socially successful homosexuals for less "successful" homosexuals. Thus, a related motive for such internecine friction is that of consumption display.

In the homosexual ghetto, physical appearance, age, style, ownership of things, even sexual success, lend a false hierarchy of personal values. The apparent degree of homosexual commitment—the comparison in which one is "more" or "less" homosexual than another—also uses visible display as status divisions.[24] Depending on one's point of view, the monogamous homosexual is more (or less) superior to the male hustler; or, the macho homosexual is more (or less) authentically gay than the drag queen. Such comparisons are purely arbitrary, however bitter.

In contrast, Carol Warren contends that positive social benefits are available to all homosexuals members, because their homosexual stigma tends to reduce conflict within their group, rather than escalate it. Citing Jews and blacks as examples of stigmatized groups, Warren claims that stigmatized people feel they are an elite group, even a martyred elect. This "aristocratizing principle,"[25] according to Warren, arouses a shared sense of equality among its members.

However, while this sense of superiority may bolster the homosexual's imputed status loss through identification with homosexuality, such superiority is assumed by homosexuals rather than offered by heterosexuals. Also, there is no automatic equality by virtue of membership in this low status group. While homosexuals may devise their own specialized class concepts and status divisions, their traits are usually parodies of heterosexual values available to all American citizens. So, any special, or allegedly "aristocratizing" principles intrinsic to this homosexual group, are either unavailable to all homosexuals or undesirable to some. Any homosexual class competition remains a mixture of homosexually and heterosexually valued "specialties."

In addition to class distinctions based on power displays, fear can also motivate homosexual class rivalries. The more closeted or conservative homosexual fears the risks in visibly challenging heterosexuals for civil rights or psychological relief. The younger, or more radical homosexual enthusiast additionally challenges the more cautionary homosexual establishment. Homosexuals then must frequently dispute on two fronts—between themselves and against heterosexuals.

Those homosexuals who have an acknowledged level of high status or upper class—by heterosexual definitions—tend to avoid visible affiliation with homosexual social structures; they tend to remain aloof from ghetto politics. These homosexuals prefer to function within a private sphere of homosexual interaction. Often successfully "passing," these homosexuals attract "clients,"[26] much as certain confined Jews formed exclusive social groups which reinforced each other's superior wisdom in detaching themselves from the more pedestrian Jewish conflicts with the Nazis.

This distant overview of the heterosexual-homosexual conflict, seemingly removes the supercilious homosexual from the jeopardy of status loss by publication of his homosexuality. This self-imputed special status is a particularly false one. Avoiding ghetto associations, or resorting to anonymous sexual encounters in less visible public territories, such men do not necessarily "save face" publicly. Rather, they attempt to gain self-esteem (even status among their clients) by denying the reality of who they are as they seek sexual fulfillment from other men.

Whatever the mode of operation chosen by homosexuals in relation to their ghetto, the resulting status and class divisions offer only marginal benefits to the individual homosexual identity. As Jews acknowledged ". . . that in the camps, not the SS but the prisoner was the prisoner's worst enemy. . . ."[27], so the homosexual tends to dramatize his inauthenticity even as he struggles to establish a self concept consistent with an environment in the extreme.

As the homosexual functions in his private or public territories of confinement, social mores of awareness and behavior perpetuate the ghetto. In contrast with apparent caprice and transiency of his collective life, the continuity of ghetto traditions maintain formal, informal and technical expressions which the homosexual must successfully learn. He becomes conscious of dramatic techniques demanded by his need to stage serial sociodramas. Skill requires perpetual shifts in emphases, according to whether other actors or spectators are homosexual or heterosexual.

Since he has access to both heterosexually and homosexually dominated territories, the homosexual's formal rules and technical displays vary according to the density of a homosexual, or heterosexual population. Predominantly heterosexual public space thus requires more formal modes of behavior. Here, he usually avoids "acting like a homosexual." His informal attitudes and manifestations automatically inspire a dependence on "passing" techniques.

And yet, while in heterosexual space, small groups of homosexuals may stop acting-as-heterosexual and deliberately draw attention to themselves in a type of dramatic role-confrontation with heterosexuals. This invasion of heterosexual territory may be fairly secret or stridently overt. Such "backstage" or "frontstage"[28] choice of behavior depends on mood or circumstance. Then, the "screaming queens" may be thumbing their noses at their straight "guards" or just claiming emotional relief on their own terms.

Yet, any blatantly dramatic challenge of heterosexual territory assumes the level of a technical presentation in a formal environment. Usually, homosexuals consciously choose to depict an exaggeration of their expected identity stereotypes. They carefully flaunt displays of inauthenticity. Flamboyant feelings are controlled and directed, thinly covering the aggression and rage which energize their well choreographed "loss of control." They elevate their heterosexual audience's awareness by technically selecting behaviors designed to shock, disgust and confront.

In whatever manner homosexuals may treat heterosexually dominated public space, their territorial invasion continues to characterize homosexuals as alien to the heterosexual world.[29] Consequently, the ghetto phenomena of isolation are reinforced by homosexuals who define themselves by confrontation. The artificiality and status rivalry of in-group and out-group identities is sharpened. Such walling in and walling out are simultaneous reactions for the homosexual invading heterosexual space.

Should heterosexuals invade the public space of homosexuals—either wittingly, such as a gay bar or beach, or unwittingly in a public rest room—homosexuals observe various offensive and defensive protocol. They may ignore such heterosexual "tourists," tolerate them, accept them or sometimes challenge the heterosexual right to observe or participate in the social rituals and structures of the homosexual enclave.

When in private heterosexual space, homosexuals also tend to observe more formal behavioral patterns. Informal (automatic) characteristics of passing are employed out of consideration for heterosexual hosts, family members or social acquaintances. To alleviate tension, anxiety and threat for all, homosexuals often practice techniques of behavior which reinforce their identity mask and direct sociodramatic interactions. Speech, mannerisms and intellectual content derive primarily from heterosexual scripts and cues; the homosexual knows his antagonist's lines as well as his own.

When in private homosexual contexts, the homosexual continues to rely on specialized techniques as he manifests his identity. Here, Warren believes the homosexual drops his mask in private, "lets down his hair" and becomes himself. Such "gay space" supposedly permits homosexuals their freedom from acting out aspects of themselves.[30] Yet, even in Warren's alleged "gay space," too many homosexuals continue to be actors who remain very conscious of refining their technical behaviors. These techniques reinforce formal and informal codes of ghetto conduct and attitude. Too often, ghetto-appropriate mannerisms and mystique invade the homosexual's private sphere. He is never really free from its impact.

As a result, homosexuals often remain psychologically and emotionally distant from friends and acquaintances, although such distance is camouflaged by degrees of humor and playfulness. There remains a forced artificiality, a mechanical aspect to social interaction with others. The homosexual too successfully absorbs the parameters and expressions of the ghetto machine.

The homosexual can confide in homosexual friends, share his sexual adventures, fears, accomplishments, future projects, or even express elements of cynicism or lack of success in the "gay life" (usually sexual difficulties). Yet, the homosexual avoids testing or straining his friendships by revealing too much of his inner self. He avoids thinking and behaving beyond conventional expectations. Inappropriate expressions of personal distress can arouse feelings of defeat in other homosexuals who obviously contend with similar problems.

Additionally, too much expression of an individual's erotic success can arouse jealousies in those who at least remain secure in the equality of failure or despair. An overdisplay or underdisplay of goods, success or failure with varieties of sexual partners (or lovers), the lack or possession of technical mastery of appropriate homosexual manifestations and unpredictable indiscretions—these are a few among many examples which arouse atmospheres of distrust between homosexuals.

The homosexual, then, is generally controlled by an excessive obedience to his ghetto mores. Whether he is in public or private space, either dominated by heterosexual or homosexual participants, the homosexual uses such spaces as a stage. Elements of drama then structure most homosexual relationships. Here, technique is paramount to social success; this results in mechanical uniformity of behavior, rather than spontaneously creative contributions to the ghetto machine.

While homosexual mores contribute to the persistence of the homosexual ghetto, heterosexual forces also help to perpetuate it. Most significantly, civil and criminal law offer formally definitive barriers for the homosexual identity. Despite popular contention, these laws often have less immediate impact on the majority of homosexuals than do the more informal heterosexual mores which traditionally deal with homosexuality at a person-to-person level. Yet, by their very existence, civil and criminal laws do potentially confine all homosexuals—in psychical and actual manners.

Various state laws seem quixotically at variance with those explicit or implied federal guarantees for all citizens, regardless of their minority membership or individual idiosyncrasies. Constitutionally, the homosexual is offered a form of civil equality with heterosexuals. Against this, municipal or state laws formalize a wide range of proscriptive, rather than descriptive rules and punishments for sexual "misbehavior." Deviating from "due process" and "right to privacy," current sexual laws attempting to regulate private, consensual morality, do so through informal tradition. Current sodomy and solicitation laws often are subject to moralistic and capricious attitudes of prosecutors, attorneys, legislators and juries. These attitudes are attached to the logic of penis in relation to vagina, the primary basis for patriarchal politics.

Thus, when the legal interpretation and application of sexual laws fall upon arrested homosexuals, these formal laws are converted to informal status-degradation ceremonies. "Law" and its legal representatives maintain the status of heterosexual patriarchal power. The structure of this power is based on the fantasy system of the social "family." To ratify and internalize the fantasy system of the family model in society, the patriarchal church and state combine to regulate consensual sexual behavior, in its own image.

Within the social family model, heterosexuals remain the familial "we" and homosexuals the threatening "them." So, contemporary sodomy laws merely phrase formal controls for the perpetuation of the family drama. Such laws are directly related to those prohibiting incest, since incest must be considered "unnatural," because it is injurious to family unity and stability. If homosexual males are members of a general male brotherhood, then for a man to have sex with his "brother" can be termed symbolic incest. In this vein, paternal sexual law creates and applies labels to family model offenders.

Gilbert Cantor states in "The Need for Homosexual Law Reform," that once these sexual offenders are labeled and sanctions are applied to that label, ". . . The social ideal is made clearer by contrast and is made alone to appear desirable."[31] The undesirable homosexual becomes the deviant "they" who cannot be identified with the familial "we." So, the homosexual suffers legalized status degradation. He is less than "family," less than a man, even somewhat subhuman. The family fantasy structure remains potently intact.

As informal sexual mores are coded into formal law, they label, denigrate and confine the homosexual. However, he encounters other informal traditions which provide even more subtle and pervasive identity restraints. In general society, each person's informal awarenesses carry safely automatic responses to society's collective norms. People only have to reasonably imitate or conform to images and patterns which are shared by them.

In contrast, the homosexual arouses extreme anxieties in heterosexuals because he is the model for non-conformity. He threateningly deviates from normative patterns in ways which force the heterosexual to think about him. Rather than intellectualize, most heterosexuals emotionalize the homosexual's non-conformity—the ultimate transgression in a society dedicated to the smooth operation of the social machine.

As a child molester, rapist, perverted, violent and suicidal person, the homosexual encounters variations in prejudice, tolerance or sympathy from heterosexual employers, friends, family, landlords and the social institutions of religion, medicine, law, business and government. Forms of social friction and degrees of hostility arise wherever the homosexual's identity is recognized or revealed. Concomitant friction from informal homosexual traditions within the pressurized ghetto context, also face the homosexual who finds that other homosexuals have developed automatic responses to homosexual norms.

Ultimately, such tenuous social harmony lends an ambivalence to the homosexual's informal social patterns. His technical adaptations to often contradictory expectations of both heterosexual and homosexual collectives, provide a tension within his consciousness. In choosing an affirmation or denial of various collective norms, the homosexual struggles to be himself—resisting or capitulating to existing mores. Thus, his identity achievement is characterized by efforts-in-extreme.

The ultimate extreme of homosexual ghetto life is the inability of many homosexuals to escape the tension of being or not being homosexual. One's identity development is thus a task, a demanding (pre)occupation in which one constantly labors. On the job, the homosexual scrutinizes himself: is he "too homosexual," is he "heterosexual enough"? In his sociability or leisure time with other homosexuals, even those relaxed times assume social patterns which require informal and technical concentration of thought and feeling. Homosexuals are chronically aware that even by what they say, do or represent together, they continually create a pervasive homosexual mystique.

So, Jews remind each other of their unique status. In their activities and conversations there is tacit attendance to issues, understandings and reinforcements which ultimately and indelibly mark them as Jews together. Socially, recreationally— whatever the context—they involve themselves as Jews. Minority members are rarely free from their task identity.

So, the homosexual too, whether in bars, private homes, restaurants, vacation resorts, or merely shopping or skiing with other homosexuals, must work at appropriate expression of somewhat limited "homosexual" passions. These "passions" are events, objects, goals or people which emotionally act upon the homosexual to arouse his devotion or dominate his conscious interest and dedication. Any display of his passion-possession must be controlled by the homosexual. Again, such passion elicits the tension of selfconsciousness for him.

Therefore, the homosexual must carefully balance between appropriate inhibition and exhibition of his passionate involvement. This balance is dictated by social context. While the homosexual's social constellations help to model his thinking and being, indirectly, he tends to focus directly on only several tasks as passions. These are primarily and repetitiously reduced to forms of phallic display. Performance skills, and accumulation of success insignia, often outweigh the importance of less popular pursuits which would better expand the potential wholeness of his personality. As he concentrates on refining his techniques in social leisure pursuits, the homosexual becomes absorbed in ritualized performances. He gravitates towards passions which enhance his phallic image. He strives for social tumescence.

Primary personal passions, regardless of context, too often are circumscribed by the primary element which energizes the social structure of male homosexuality. The homosexual, consciously or unconsciously, trains himself (or is trained) to react as a sexual potential to men at large. The homosexual thus learns the overt and covert techniques in the skill of "cruising."

Cruising requires a readiness for success encounters in all of the homosexual's social-leisure time activities. It provides the burdensome challenge of any homosexual's identity to frame himself within idealistic task commitments, which promise utopian sexual possibilities. Technically, cruising is a system of body language. It is designed to attract attention or communicate erotic interest, understanding or agreement. It is also an imaginative preoccupation with the unknown, but hoped for, which heightens the erotic potential of any social context or activity.

Given the romantic quality in cruising, the homosexual's attention is usually other-directed, but generally unfocused. In cruising, the homosexual looks for the specific idealistic encounter, which must be cooperatively engineered. As the homosexual erotically acts to influence other men into participation in his fantasy actualization, his success requires that someone confirm his action, i.e., physical messages. Lack of actual confirmation still allows the homosexual to be in a state of emotional readiness or erotic arousal.

Ultimately, cruising is a process of daydreaming one's fantasy attachment to other men, within daily events or pedestrian contexts. It creates an emotional intensity, as well as an escalation of one's consciousness of being homosexual. Cruising appears to offer the homosexual a mechanism of potential escape from his social isolation, or his emotional enclosure within the demanding task structures of homosexual sociability.

Yet, cruising too often compresses the homosexual's personality into a narrowly defined set of expressions, or else generally flattened features. The homosexual must either concentrate on developing uniform "effects" as hallmarks of an appropriately male homosexual image, or he must chronically duplicate those formal and informal expectations valued by his social context. Whether specific or general, the homosexual's security derives from conformity to normative behaviors.

Laud Humphreys holds an opposite view of homosexual social conformity. He terms the gay ghetto as geographical areas of cities which are zones of "respectable" and "unrespectable" deviance. He contends that these homosexual districts have an expectedly high tolerance for deviant behavior.[32] Yet, his contention might better suit heterosexual attitudes towards display of homosexual deviance. Heterosexuals also have their own sexually charged enclaves: singles bars, massage parlors, parks and beaches are "zones" for sex in public. These also bear labels of "respectable" and "unrespectable" deviance, depending on how or when heterosexuals choose to establish such norms.

Thus any alleged gay ghettos containing sexually oriented institutions, are less characterized by homosexual or heterosexual tolerance for deviant homosexual behaviors, than they are more aptly marked by an intolerance for irregularities in homosexual mores. Even though the homosexual may symbolize a sexual deviation to most heterosexuals, the homosexual is as regulated by his own minority group's sexual sanctions, as any heterosexual is regulated by his.

The dreams of each homosexual to achieve love and acceptance by men of his orientation are altered or shattered by the hard facts that his ghetto life too smoothly and perpetually contributes to the very alienation from which he seeks relief.

There is no relief in the ghetto. Its various institutions insure that most homosexual participants must continue to specialize themselves as separately competitive and erotically productive agents in the operations of its organization. The homosexual ghetto encourages the belief that the oppression derived from one male group (heterosexual), does not have to occur in a more sympathetic and compatible male group (homosexual).

However, for many men, one form of confinement is merely substituted for another. And the oppressors may be of our own kind, mechanically monitoring our movements inside the walls of efficiency and integration, organizing us to enjoy the techniques of our own imprisonment.

9/The Archetypal Outsider

The rebels revive the desperate laughter and the cynical defiance of the fool as means for demasking the deeds of the serious ones who govern the whole.[1]
Herbert Marcuse,
An Essay on Liberation

. . . The first time you get it in the belly you holler brotherhood. But you can't have your brothers and eat them too. You're alone, pal, all alone.[2]
Budd Schulberg,
What Makes Sammy Run?

The concept of the archetypal outsider depicts a popular American passion for the romantic alien. This is the dangerous stranger who may positively affect society, but is ultimately antithetical to its civilized structure and intention.

The glamor, excitement and romantic vision surrounding the image of the archetypal outsider remains a moving force in literature, film and folklore. It is a particularly idealistic treatment of progressive change and accomplishment within the American value system of self-reliant individualism.

Currently, the cinematic cowboy, heroic outlaw or cop portray romantic confrontations with a physical or moral frontier. However, as traditional frontiers disappear, new ones must be created. Land, sea or air now transpose into money, technical inventions or sex. Or, as with Ayn Rand, one may choose to romanticize man's very egoism as a heroic machine, which acts on the cosmos as frontier,[3] thus providing intergalactic possibilities for the lonely lusts of the heroic imagination. Regardless of context, the traditional archetypal outsider has restlessly stirred imaginations—civilizations—to admire, imitate and fear what he represents.

257

The Wandering Jew as lonely alien, has also been reexamined continually in literature, poetry, drama, autobiographies and oral tradition, in an effort to comprehend the Jewish spirit within confinement contexts in the world at large. In American culture, the Wandering Jew is typified by the romantic alienation of the Western outlaw, who participates and withdraws—or is driven away—from the social groups he serves or threatens.

Jenni Calder emphasizes in *There Must Be a Lone Ranger,* that the mysterious stranger in film, literature and folklore is not necessarily a criminal. Instead, both the mysterious stranger who self-imposes his own exile, and the outcast who elevates himself beyond the law, carry heroic qualities. Both represent unknown powers. Both symbolize forms of anarchy.[4]

The paradigm of the archetypal outsider particularly suits the sociological reality of the homosexual's existence. It also lends a personality form against which the homosexual male can readily compare himself. Even though the ghetto conformity often institutionalizes the homosexual through ritualized behaviors and standardized images, the primary dynamic in the "cruising form" is the romantically heroic quality attached to personal isolation.

The homosexual views men as elements of a sexual frontier. He penetrates this frontier to test himself against it, conquer it, and then move on in his restless and sometimes neurotic quest for identity confirmation—despite the fact that his essential identity remains hidden.

The maintenance of his romantically fictional qualities often prevents the homosexual from achieving significant—or lasting—relationships which usually require commitment and trust through his self-revelation. Personally isolated, heroically engaged in conquering his sexual frontier, the homosexual is also logically freed from the formal and informal constraints of heterosexual or homosexual social mores.

The entire cluster of Western myth and motif permeates the American male consciousness. The danger and excitement of its historical tradition and its personally enlarging symbolic appeal, offer most males relief from the bland redundancy of contemporary standardized life. For the homosexual male, its attraction springs from the melodramatic persona which offers him impeccable style, physical success and a heightened sense of self-earned personal worth. The romantic alien offers coherence to the homosexual's dilemma about how he relates to a hostile or closed heterosexual society.

Calder notes that the mythical hero—the archetypal outsider—conveys the themes of loneliness and shared danger. Men who share these conditions are frequently emotionally vulnerable to each other. Loneliness and danger creates an intimacy which is similar to that of love.[5] The personal threats and deprivations which men sense in isolation, dramatically increase the importance of comradeship forms. Recognizing their similarities, these aliens together develop creative survival techniques, because frontier confrontation (or heterosexual society for the homosexual) demands the very best personal qualities and skills from aliens.

Unfortunately, "civilized" society offers few, if any, outlets for these aliens' unique characteristics. Thus, the homosexual as outsider confronts heterosexual mores and finds no viable entrance in society for his unique erotic orientation.

To the Western hero, the civilized East is ultimately irrelevant to him. Its entrenched social order will not allow the outsider to prove himself superior, according to his own terms. In the cult of the Western hero, his proportions are shaped and measured by his terrain, but are not dominated by it. Even as the frontier offers a challenge, it also provides him with an escape. Conversely, the established community represents civic responsibility and a social structure which attempt to tame or confine him. As settlements occur within the Western motif, appearances of respectability become paramount. The element of hypocrisy occurs in many of the heroic alienation stories.

Within the contemporary homosexual milieu, the Western motif lends additional political-symbolic parallels as homosexuals attempt to "civilize" each other. In homophile movements, gay liberation forces and gay community social groups, ideologies are shaped and policies become structured. With such homosexual "settlements" come figurative and literal fencing of behavior, rustling of people and ideas, and even range wars.

The politics of western stories, as well as homosexual concerns, indicate that control of territory often results in control of people. Rival homosexual outlaw leaders utilize their charisma to control their gangs. In the western tradition, the use of the gun as a sexual symbol of virility and social power, is transposed into penile displays used by homosexuals as reference points for their claims to power.

Additionally, as in westerns, women (even lesbians) remain ornamental or intrinsically unimportant to male homosexual themes and interests. Despite postures of equality offered by homosexual males to lesbians, such men have no real emotional or political investments in the concerns of women. Women remain serviceable, but vestigial—similar to women's real value in the heterosexual system.

The archetypal outsider as a mythical hero generally tested the community, established his identity by what he did (perhaps even exposing his real persona), and was then free to travel on. Against this pattern, the aging hero contradicted his earlier values of transient freedom by searching for personal or social commitment. He attempted to settle into a society for which he was not prepared, and in which he was offered few opportunities for success by the more dramatic and romantic standards.

Within this dilemma, the homosexual also shares one critical source of alienation, both from heterosexual society, as well as his homosexual peers. The imaginary myth of non-conformity in a modern society, confronts the equally celebrated value for safety in uniform behavior. The homosexual's image as outlaw must be camouflaged as responsible citizen; the paradox provides chronic alienation. Commitment to one or the other alternatives, is difficult for the maturing homosexual to achieve. Often, his preparation for one persona, makes the other ambiguous to him.

While there is a personal need, even benefit, for cultural heroes, the traditional archetypal outsider is too dangerous for contemporary life. He is safely lionized in artistic productions, or he is cosmetically duplicated in the rigors of *group* endeavor: social task forces, hiking groups or romantic world cruises now provide contemporary heroic adventures. The romance of the homosexual alone, however, soon grows stale. So, the homosexual desperately trades in his "gun" for credit cards, health plans, property investments and gourmet cooking classes. The male homosexual is no different from his heterosexual counterpart— the single swinger—who wears himself out traversing the sexual frontier.

For both, contemporary heroics are merely tied to brief encounters and erotic flings which relieve one from the routine requirements to be an "upstanding" citizen. In modern American society, our conveniently sanitized environment makes few demands. Its institutions refine and domesticate its spiritual rebels. Thus, to test one's identity as an independent man, requires frequent rebellions against rigidly interlocking social systems. Such a task appears overwhelming, as well as antithetical to the popular urge to cooperate in any task accomplishment—sports, business, government or inter-personal endeavors. Weekend rebels, or cosmetic dissenters, amuse rather than move social institutions.

Additionally, the homosexual always rebels as a villain, rather than a patriotically romantic figure. There is no general social admiration for his imaginative goals, heroic exploits or sense of style. Presently, the homosexual thus seems consumed with metamorphosing his threatening outlaw image into the pleasantries of its being just another personal option. He fails to recognize that such apologetics cannot dispel heterosexual myths of his criminal deviance, or dangerous role modeling for children. He threatens the essential morality of society much less than he challenges the sexual politics of male heterosexuality.

John Rechy views this homosexual antagonism against heterosexual male power as a form of sexual warfare. In *The Sexual Outlaw,* Rechy considers the archetypal outsider as a survival symbol for homosexuality. He ritualizes homosexuality as a personally rigorous, lonely existence, lived in total commitment to outlaw sex. Each time the sexual outlaw engages in his hunt for public sexual contact, he uses other homosexual outlaws as a united front which helps him politically defy heterosexual oppression. While many homosexuals who pass as heterosexual disdain Rechy's often exploitative metaphor—as well as outlaw practice—R. O. D. Benson notices that any homosexual leaves order and authority behind once he confronts his own anti-heroic identity:

> He must not ignore the fact that the adverse judgments of society may affect him. He is an outcast; he is a criminal who has not yet been caught.[6]

While Rechy chooses a range war concept to embrace the homosexual's ethical confrontation with the "eastern" heterosexual establishment, he tends to allow his sexual outlaws to be dominated by their terrain. The romantic cruelty and unrealistic beauty which Rechy lauds as endemic to his anonymous sexual encounters tend to involve his heroes in an endless life hunt without hope, in parks, alleys and toilets.

In Rechy's perpetual warfare, the homosexual is never fulfilled, but rather will be sexually annihilated by his own comrades through the passing of time. Indirectly, Rechy elevates sexual suicide as the culmination of a series of heroic acts. The penis is his weaponry, the orgasm his ammunition; yet he keeps his declared war against heterosexuals essentially secret. Rechy's homosexual warriors need only fulfill their genital technique as symbolic anarchy. Any emotional fulfillment they may gain perhaps accrues from Rechy's eulogy that, at least, his heroes' passing will be mourned with honor.

In Rechy's apocalyptic vision of a televised sexual orgy of homosexual confronting heterosexual—his sexual Dachau for heterosexuals to view, and join—he expresses a sentiment of war, if not a realistic version of it. He calls the homosexual to continue the sexual battle, heroically and totally. One recalls the Kamikaze pilots who launched themselves completely and finally, in romantic affiliations with themselves as their own heroic death instrument. Exhilaration follows extremes.

Within his vision, however, Rechy does offer the dynamic of a heroic self turning from the personal confinement of the mechanically civilized, to the demanding challenges of an erotic frontier. Here, the homosexual has access to a masculine tradition in which he can frame his own definition and expression of himself. As he fulfills his tradition, only his skill and circumstance will save him from the social consequences of his passion.

In confinement, either socially or circumstantially, the controls of social convention often conflict with personal human capacities for affection or erotic desire, between men. These rebel urges supercede formal aspects of social convention. Thus, emotional involvements occur between males, as natural relief to various social constrictions imposed on them over time, or by great stress. Usually, such shared anxiety, danger or deprivation metamorphoses into expressions of love or erotic exchange.

James Kirkwood focuses on the ambivalence within these homoerotic exchanges. In his novels, such male relationships can later be denied, rationalized or even confirmed. Whatever their meaning, erotic liaisons do occur. In *Some Kind of Hero,* the narrator is confined with another American POW in a small cell in a North Vietnamese prison camp. The two men's extreme circumstances and physical proximity help to create a framework for friendship and mutual regard. During a bombing attack, the narrator and his companion unite violence with sexualized love; external stress pushes them to a sexual extreme . . . for relief:

The bombing continued, sometimes at a distance, sometimes dangerously close, as we kept up our physical taking and forcing and giving-up and taking and wrestling until we had each come through two massive orgasms. And we lay on the floor awash in sweat and semen and blood, too.[7]

Later, the narrator's friend dies in the camp. He is left suspended with a new sexual dimension to his identity with which he must deal.

In *P.S. Your Cat Is Dead,* Kirkwood creates an unemployed actor who traps a gay burglar in his apartment. While the thief is unconscious, the narrator describes carrying him to the kitchen to tie him up:

> Holding someone in my arms—a phrase of closeness, affection even. None of this, of course, but there was a certain intimacy that was, well, eerie.[8]

Despite the narrator's ingenuous dismissal of his feelings' meaning, the book concludes with both men leaving for Mexico together, forsaking the "unreality" of social convention, former female lovers, etc. While Kirkwood attaches an ambivalent quality to homosexual love—as though affection is somehow integral to two men's mutual battle against adversity—imprisoned men do seem capable of achieving great depths of emotional commitment and erotic candor about their feelings.

Alexander Berkman, writing in *Prison Memoirs of an Anarchist,* describes a married heterosexual friend who desired someone to love while confined in a male prison:

> I did not realize it at the time . . . but I know now that I was simply in love with the boy; wildly, madly in love. It came very gradually. For two years I loved him without the least taint of sex desire. . . . But by degrees the psychic stage began to manifest all the expressions of love between the opposite sexes. I remember the first time he kissed me.[9]

Edward E. Loftin records more violent aspects of prison sexuality, in which sexual force is often used by heterosexual males to humiliate and control others. Writing to members of JOIN HANDS (a gay prisoner support group), Loftin remarks that handsome or physically powerless men are forced to submit to sexual assault by stronger males, or male packs. The exceptionally strong or older males are exempt from attack. Homosexual males are not preyed upon if they willingly take sexual partners, or request to be segregated in gay prison units. Either alternative does not necessarily alleviate emotional brutality.

Prison guards often exhibit attitudes similar to the general heterosexual male population's; they hypocritically traffic in the homosexual behavior they claim to despise. While guards prohibit homosexuality, some unofficially condone or engage in it themselves. If male inmates establish loving relationships, guards use these sexual alliances to manipulate potential prisoner solidarity with threats or rumors of impending transfer.[10] Any emotional unity that men might achieve together despite the stress of isolation, is effectively rendered as impotent. The parallel to male relationships in open society being fragile and subject to dissolution, is obvious.

Also, Bettelheim's study of Jewish concentration camp prisoners' fears over loss of personal competence and personality integration, were directly linked to their fear of impotency. Therefore, Jewish prisoners frequently masturbated, or indulged in some homosexual behavior, in order to retain their masculine potency, rather than to experience erotic pleasure.[11]

The stress of confinement in harsh isolation creates the social context for men to turn erotically towards each other, regardless of psychological motives. So, the stress from social invalidation of homosexual love prevents viable long term relationships between male partners in general society. As in concentration camps where Jewish friendships were quite tenuous, so homosexuals learn to tolerate superficial and randomly erotic companionships—thus avoiding the strain of emotional involvement which can be severed by discovery and/or punishment.

Jewish prisoners developed work companions. These were similar to homosexual friendships which share the freight of danger, misery or luck of their sexually dominated social tasks intrinsic to the homosexual milieu. Then, like most men within confinement contexts, these homosexual "prisoners" of heterosexual prejudice, as well as homosexual mores, do not overly tax their male relationships.

Obviously, deep emotional attachments are not encouraged when social experiences are framed in frustration, fear, suspicion or guilt. Homosexuals may thus learn to prefer surfaces, rather than deal with a full comprehension of what they do to each other, and themselves. In this manner, homosexuals—as the Jews with the Nazis—disregard the possibility of resisting what heterosexuals do to them.

Treatment in extreme is noted by Bettelheim's report of Nazi "scientists' " early efforts to achieve racial purification. Experiments in sexual alteration were conducted to improve society by selectively exterminating those who carried "undesirable" genes. Homosexuals and other "sexual offenders" were among the first prisoners to be sterilized.[12]

There exists a similar attitude, and often treatment, towards homosexuality in America. This sexual orientation is viewed as a disease within a healthy (heterosexual) society. American institutions cheerfully advocate sterilization of homosexuals, using the medical euphemism of "behavior modification therapy."

Psychologist Mark Freedman states that such "therapy" depends on creating high anxiety in one area of sexuality (homosexual desire), while diminishing it in another area (heterosexual desire).[13] The logic here is that homosexual "patients" (either voluntary or involuntary) must be reinforced to become more heterosexual and less homosexual. To achieve this goal of eradicating homosexuality, various laboratory experiences are devised, which are separated from real life contexts freely available to all men. George Weinberg believes these aversive techniques of psychological behavior modification now used on homosexuals, are possibly part of a general plan to subordinate *all* individuals for the "good" of society.[14]

Behavior modification therapy varies, but each technique attempts to "purify" the homosexual's identity. Each technique is merely an experiment in social conformity. Each represents a favorite instrument and bias of the heterosexual social engineer who administers any one of the following alternatives: *systematic desensitization* (patient learns to gradually relax sexual anxieties), *moral persuasion* (propaganda often accompanied with drug therapy), *masturbation* (with pictures of nude women), *emetic persuasion* (vomiting), *brain surgery,* and *Homosexuals Anonymous.* Here, science assumes the posture of humanistic altruism, as a motive for inducing homosexuals into psychic conformity.

Weinberg cites one patient's pattern of behavior as a model for the heroic requirements within the homosexual condition. His patient needed to believe in a dream, in the possibility of an erotic love relationship with another male homosexual. He needed to sense that a community existed where he would be well received once he accepted himself.

His discovery of the homosexual ghetto institutions did help to prevent him from feeling like an isolated outcast. His reasonable fantasy received tangible confirmation in other homosexuals, as his self-esteem also enlarged. Weinberg astutely generalizes his patient's need as a form of heroism—the highest assertion of one's sense of individuality:

> A guiding fiction in one form or another is the fuel each of us needs to exist alone. Without this fiction—our own idiosyncratic sense of what a hero is and what we must do to become one—our motive force is depleted. Who can say how much of our everyday life is touched by such dreams![15]

In Bettelheim's discussion of the Jewish hero in concentration camps, he emphasizes the Nazis' maneuvers to make each prisoner feel merely a part of the mass. Individuality was suppressed. What the individual suffered, others would watch with emotional detachment since such horrors "didn't really happen"—personally to them. Thus, prisoners were essentially psychically detached from themselves—as well as each other—even as they were physically welded together in mass attitude and behavior.

Yet, when a prisoner lost all hope for personal survival in such close confinement, this strangely freed him to act heroically for others. The SS tried to prevent the development of martyrs or heroes. Individual actions were blocked or were converted into group responsibility for individual infractions. The independent actor was punished, or the group was; thus the collective acted as sanction against any dangerous individual heroics.

So, the dynamic between the confined self and a restrictive society seems to be sparked by a dream element in heroic self-conception. The individual passionately calls forth his identity from the radical mythology of the alien, the stranger or the outsider. From this, he has his emotional confrontation with sexual politics. Thus, the homosexual manifests his identity in aspects of escapism, in reaction to heterosexual tyrannies of conformity and confinement.

Ted Clark views a similar submission-dominance pattern in the attempted containment of adolescents by adults. In *The Oppression of Youth,* Clark discusses the value investments which adults have in maintaining their traditionally formal perspectives of social reality. Basic social forms and content must remain stable, or at least appear to, in order to regulate the social hierarchy. No actual change is allowed, but only the illusions of change.[16]

As youth periodically rebel in favor of their own dreams, they also tend to convert the various yearnings of their erotic identity into a romantic cycle, a series of ecstatic adventures to be concluded in tacit imitations of adulthood. Generally, young people pretend and hide, in order to avoid the responsibility for their minor extremes by which they challenge adult expectations. Ultimately, the techniques of adult hegemony carry tempting rewards, as well as deprivations, as youth forfeit their romantic visions:

> Youth cling to the invisibility conformity allows them. Terrified of being exposed as different, as outsiders to be ridiculed or condemned, young people often stop thinking and stop feeling. They simply go along. With blank faces, imitation life styles, a nice, pleasant personality, few complaints and always of a vague nature, young people by and large trade individuality, their own needs and desires, creativity, and insightfulness for safety in numbers.[17]

These reactions by youth to adult constrictions is similar to those of homosexuals who cooperatively assimilate into heterosexual society, or imitate images prepared for them by heterosexuals and homosexuals alike.

It seems that oppressed people learn to be manipulative in self-serving roles which offer them the most profitable security. Collectively identified and contained, adolescents are unable to extricate themselves from meaningless "teen" rituals or infantile traditions which deflect their individual potency. They do not develop clear ideologies about themselves, in order to understand or combat pervasive strategies of oppression altruistically conceived by adults to manage them.

Such was the pattern of Jewish prisoners and their Nazi monitors. Theirs was also an essentially child-parent relationship. So, the homosexual confronts (hetero)sexual politics with his potentially radical mythology. In numberless ways, he submits to the vague pleasantries of conformity to his monitors' wishes. He engages in numbing escapism. He is an erotic coward.

Rechy resents this homosexual capitulation to the heterosexual "enemy." He attempts to elevate homosexual *promiscuity* as some sort of harbinger to a sexual revolution. He claims street sex to be a radical political statement. Yet, Rechy's sexual "rhetoric" remains merely a whisper of conspiracy. This is because the mechanical techniques of heterosexual society always allow the archetypal outsider access to his symbolic tradition, but only through the radical mythologies of appearance, rather than actual accomplishment.

The social machine permits the romance of challenge to authority, because it profits from these forms of creative stimulation and psychic energy which are then thrust into the socio-economic system. Mere simulations of rebellion, with their focus on style rather than substance, carry few threats to the patriarchal structure of formalized sexual politics.

Kate Millett analyzes this American political structure and finds that all institutions within it are rooted in authoritative masculine values. All are similarly constructed by role divisions into dominant and subordinant; they are energized by competition and reward. These social, economic and political roles are primarily designed from sexual delineations. Gender attachments reinforce role distinctions artificially; technical specialties related to task performances, are ranked by erotic potency. Primary performance is usually masculine and secondary performance is regarded as feminine.

Thus, any revolutionary challenge to such patriarchically controlled social structures, ultimately appears as sexual anarchy. Any rebellious re-examination of the social machine, disturbs the equilibrium of a technical society bent on abstracting humanity. Sexual anarchy threatens to diffuse the role-task dichotomy. It unharnesses the individual from the current technical control of his erotic impulse.

Sexual anarchy against the heterosexual male power ethic results in accelerated paternalistic confinement of subordinates, i.e., the psychic castration of threatening males. Thus, Louis Wirth comments in *The Ghetto* that, traditionally an imagined threat, "The Jew has been in a class with women. . . ."[18] And Bettelheim remarks that Jewish prisoners were mistreated similarly to what ". . . a cruel and domineering father might use against helpless children."[19]

Homosexual males also share the child-woman subordination role in heterosexual male politics. Homosexuals predominantly disavow their status reduction, either by conforming to images of sexual aberration, sexual outlawry, or "domesticated" heterosexuality. Unfortunately, any such reaction to their oppression contains elements of fantasy with very real psychological repercussions for the individual homosexual.

Because homosexuals present a sexual threat to male heterosexual power structures, heterosexuals find advantage in allowing homosexuals to play out their part in the radical mythology of the male frontier hero. Even children eventually exhaust themselves in their harmless games. So, homosexuals who elevate the heroic role engage in forms of alienation through fantasy. Left in the imagination, this fantasy contributes little to reality.

While fantasy is a valid method of relating to one's world, it can also split a man from the reality of himself—or from others. R. D. Laing remarks in *The Politics of Experience* that "For most of our social lives, we largely gloss over this underlying fantasy level of our relationship."[20] Fantasy as escape allows the homosexual the safety of conformity to heterosexual expectations. Fantasy as heroics, the acting out of individual visions of the self freely on one's environment, remains largely unfocused in most homosexuals' consciousness.

However, heterosexual males, too, have an investment in conformity to fantasy patterns; they provide them with illusions of personal power and freedom, which so many heterosexuals feel they lack. These socially shared and valued fantasy forms represent techniques of social engineering—people control—used by powerful men to dominate men in general. As Jack Nichols mentions in *Men's Liberation,* most fantasy patterns are linked to erotic potency and skill. "Masculinist values provide many of the aggressive, success-oriented, sex-conqueror fantasies that fill thousands of so-called erotic books crowding today's market."[21]

Male fantasy constructions primarily depend upon technique—the displays of success. Thus, most men engage in living as though life is a romantic cycle, an ecstatic series of adventures always prized by some heroic figure-as-pattern. Then, as Wilson Bryan Key believes, such ecstasy is linked with each man's preoccupation with discovery of meaningful *images,* rather than persons.[22] Real persons are merely used to momentarily satisfy a restless glutting of one's sensations—minus the complications of durable involvement. This forms the basis for Key's term of "tit culture," in which the American male's quest for adventure is limited to erotic surrogates.

In America, sexuality between people is a primary threat to personal freedom, because it requires a wider range of intimacy for fulfillment than the highly touted orgasm is now able to provide. Intimacy threatens the current cult of "individualism," i.e., "do your own thing," even if it includes doing someone else's. Intimacy jeopardizes highly stylized forms of fantasy alienation—the remote cool of machismo. Thus men are socially encouraged to consume synthetic value substitutes, to use people as commodities, and to avoid sexual maturity by sexually repressing themselves through their limited fantasy outlets.

Ultimately, pornography, salacious humor and equations of sexuality with conquest, voyeurism, exhibitionism and narcissism compound to blend male sexuality into an innocuous erotic passivism. Against this blend, the American male dresses, drives and drinks into the Playboy mirage of virile success—if he can afford to pay for it. Most male subscribers to this manufactured sexuality, need such stimulation to rouse them from the torpor of their sexual repression.

Interestingly, the intrusion of homosexuality into the heterosexual heroic scheme, helps to betray the strongest form of sexual repression used by heterosexual males. In his study of the American male, Alfred Kinsey displayed photographs, drawing and paintings of nude males to over four thousand men used in his investigation of male sexual behaviors. Over one half of the males he interviewed were erotically aroused by viewing male nudes. Kinsey concluded that a strong homosexual *fantasy*, probably involves every American male to some degree.[23]

Despite the close proximity of "tit culture" to "gay world," the homosexual still serves as the object on which the heterosexual male projects his "inner enemy," his repressed homosexual interests. Heroes require their villains who threateningly plot against the general welfare. Villains supply reasonable substitutes for real or sensed failures to achieve personal satisfactions. So, the Nazis created an international conspiracy of Jewish intellectuals and plutocrats which threatened the vigor, purity and destiny of Germany. This fantasy justified the victimizers' punishment of their victims:

> Projection is the result of an inner conflict. Desires that are unsuccessfully repressed and have to be projected are an "inner enemy" of the personality. For this the Jew was much better suited than any external enemy. He was the enemy living inside the structure of a society where he was not fully integrated.[24]

Likewise, the homosexual lives within the structure of the American male "tit culture." He is created into a fantasy form, a projection of an unresolved inner conflict which the heterosexual male must deny. And yet, even homosexual males often share this conflict concerning their own erotic identities, in addition to their suffering as heterosexuals' "reasons" for general economic, social, moral or political problems. The "gay world," then, exists on the grand scale in the imagination of many heterosexuals. Homosexuals recognize its limitations.

In David Noebel's homophobic book, *The Homosexual Revolution,* its bias captures the essential hysteria of heterosexual suspicions that—unlike the Jew—the homosexual is too well integrated into society:

> . . . The "Homosexual International" . . . a worldwide conspiracy that has spread all over the globe; has penetrated all classes, operates in armies and in prisons; has infiltrated the press, the movies and the cabinets; and it all but dominates the arts, literature, theater, music and TV. . . . Members of one conspiracy are prone to join another conspiracy. This is one reason why so many homosexuals, already enemies of society in general, become enemies of capitalism in particular. Without being necessarily Marxist, they serve the end of the Communist International *in the name of their rebellion against the prejudices, standards, and ideal of the 'bourgeois world. . . .*[25] [emphasis in original]

In other minds, fear projection broadens to even greater proportions; the homosexual criminal is everywhere—his crime is sexual rebellion against the heterosexual male political structure which passes for capitalism, liberty, freedom, rightness, *ad nauseum.* Thus, French photographer Patrice Calmettes believes that ". . . Everything now is homosexual, that's a fact. Everything you touch is homosexual . . . I think the whole world is directed by homosexuals and you can't do anything about it."[26]

Sexuality as a political threat consumes the imaginations of the more liberal and intellectual caste; again, homosexuality emerges as a fantasy form to support the logical rationale for social ills. In an article written for *Harper's,* Norman Podhoretz, editor of the Jewish magazine *Commentary,* champions patriarchal politics as representative of heterosexual heroism. Podhoretz criticizes the rise of pacificism in post-Vietnam America in "The Culture of Appeasement." He parallels this current sociopolitical mood with England's indifference to the Nazi preparation for World War II. He cited homosexuality as a primary influence for "antidemocratic pacifism of the anti-war ethos."

Podhoretz claims that homosexuals hold "a generalized contempt for middle-class or indeed any kind of heterosexual adult life." He thinks homosexuals are bored with heterosexuality.

Thus, homosexuals lack interest in patriotism which he equates with "fatherhood and all that fatherhood entailed: responsibility for a family and therefore an inescapable implication in the destiny of society as a whole."[27] Again, the archetypal family pattern is called forth to justify heterosexual male political interests.

Podhoretz defines homosexuality as anti-cultural, as an asocial force with pacifistic overtones directly responsible for America's failures to match a Soviet arms build-up. To Podhoretz, homosexuality is treasonable because it does not appear to ratify patriarchal principles of power—as social control.

These principles are modeled on the family institution, the nucleus of heterosexual male vigor in politics and economics. Thus, apparent antipaternalism is antidemocratic. Perhaps Podhoretz' misrepresentation of homosexual indifference to the social welfare is a projection of his own impotency of sentiment. Homosexual "indifference" might possibly reveal Podhoretz' frustrated cynicism towards powerful social forces which he feels powerless to change.

General social indifference is an amorphous opponent. Homosexual "indifference" is a convenient target group to fault; a sympathetic audience already exists for Podhoretz' facile logic, much as Germany was ready for its Hitler. Yet, Podhoretz fails to consider the rise of homosexual social activism during the counterculture upheavals of the 1960's. Despite Podhoretz' intellectual posture, contemporary American homosexuals' "pacifism" has nothing to do with foreign cultural attitudes of a pre-World War II England.

In contrast, over-stimulation was the major dynamic within the social techniques of the 1960's counter culture activities. This dynamic developed as a humanistic reaction to the ruling technocrats of social formalism. The American social complexion was actually one of foment: the Vietnam war, domestic racial unrest, student protest, political corruption and ecological pollution activated domestic concern.

Protest became a life-style. Social disconnection helped communicate people's feelings of powerlessness, even as hippies sought to construct an erotic festival from life itself. The subsequent surfeiting of values, the exhaustion from participation, even the perpetual staging of personal commitments to a cause, deteriorated into what Vance Packard calls the malaise following social upheaval.[28]

The 1960's thus provided a social context for radical mythology and sexual politics to converge within the shared ethos of "do your own thing." The paradox is obvious. However, quasi-movements emerged as collective protest, human liberation and counter culture. Jonathan Eisen claims that the violent individualism within these collective movements helped to shape an "outlaw cult."

In *Altamont: Death of Innocence in the Woodstock Nation,* Eisen considers that this period spawned an egotistical self-image by which Americans glorified themselves in the ideology of being unique, of being morally superior to corrupt social institutions or leaders.[29] Illusions of superiority fused with heroic narcissism. From this social matrix developed the *neo-homosexual,* the gay male who demonstrates his right to love men, in parades, task forces or to the neighbors next door. He, too, engages in the romantic vanity of the archetypal outsider who searches for his heroic orgasm. The excitement of his very persona is achieved each time he displays himself to heterosexual view and receives an erotically charged response.

The very erotic passion intrinsic to radical mythology and sexual politics converges as a "cultural phenomenon" for Theodore Roszak. In *The Making of a Counter Culture,* he separates youthful disenchantment with American society from the realm of a merely political movement. Instead, he romanticizes the social protest efforts of the alienated young as a force moving America towards some utopian destiny. Roszak claims that youth share an invisible sense of moral imperative. They replace an intellectual ideology with an experiential consciousness transformation. Intuition, rather than fallacious logic, makes one a more sensitive human. A radical sense of self and other are the only worthy subjects of social transcendence.

Unfortunately, Roszak's counter cultural transformations seem limited to white, middle class endeavors. He even speculates that other minority groups will have to wait for this elite vanguard to establish social patterns for them to imitate. In Roszak's logic, one must first achieve middle class status, in order to experience proper disenchantment—in order to revolt.

In contrast to Roszak's romantically mythical quality ascribed to the energy of the "youth culture," Michael Lerner claims that such elitist philosophers advocate superficial forms of self-centeredness. Lerner takes exception to those who say that social revolution is impossible unless the self is successfully transformed into "higher" states of awareness. He believes this contention ignores the majority population, by aristocratically isolating a few spokespersons within the framework of a uniquely "superior" cause.

Lerner believes any such "mythical we"[30] within any counter movement merely creates status ranking. Any alleged youth "culture" does not include all youth. An apparently altruistic elite posing as social revolutionaries, arouse public reaction through orgiastic rhetoric. As charismatically heroic figures, they stimulate themselves before their audiences to achieve the erotic agitation they so deeply crave. Then perhaps the real heroic cultural strategists are those adult observers (like Roszak) who convert youth's erotic self-indulgences into curious phenomena of social criticism, patriotic energy and honest aspiration—and then term it all as the idealism of the innocent.

Carroll Quigley cleaves through such adult sentimentality by claiming that youth's social idols are actually a series of anti-heroes who rise to cheat or thwart the system with style,[31] and then are replaced by others whose outlaw techniques are more romantically outrageous. These alienated heroes are models for youth to imitate, pretending that their militant acts strike against the symbols of established social evil. In their imitation of anti-heroics, youth claim to strive for idealistic selflessness, social reform, brotherly love or truth. However, their efforts are often theatrical techniques thinly passing for revolutionary substance.

This alien stance eventually isolates social group from social group. It inevitably confines each individual within an expediently assumed persona. Such revolutionary forms merely maintain the technical aspects of the very social machine which dissident groups (youth, blacks, women or homosexuals) seek to disavow. Thus, Lerner notices that while youth revolted against the production ethic of America's rigidly controlled bureaucratic and economic system, young people did not revolt against its parallel consumption ethic.

Youth continued to endorse the very system it also fought against—by changing the subjects of the social sales pitch. Readily available sex, drugs, alcohol and other commodities were at first freely exchanged, "in love." Then they were bargained for, and sold. Profits grew. The "hip" entrepreneurship was reborn. The "scene" determined role affectations; flowers, love-ins, be-ins, sit-ins and erotic music "laid back" any theoretical resolve to the youth "movement." The propaganda was "do your own thing." The "revolution" sold out—or bought in—to the formal structures of capitalism. However, the larger social context continually prepares to manufacture additional opportunities to arouse the romantic alien to celebrate the sensed need to liberate the self from cyclical erotic suppression.

Unfortunately, this rhythm of action and reaction often dissolves any potentially realistic confrontation between social issues. Erotic energy is controlled by what Roszak terms "repressive desublimation."[32] Any ideological or actual attempts to liberate confined people from economic, political, personal or sexual oppression, are initially met by resistance from the power majority.

Simultaneously, as Roszak notes, the Playboy images of total erotic permissiveness are provided as erotic but high-priced accoutrements of the "swinging life." Anything less than total capitulation to achievement of these commercially designed and produced insignias of success (and there is an increasing array from which to choose), create the sense of personal failure, even a publicly visible indictment. Any erotic liberation is effectively "desublimated" by converting private passion into public displays of self-chosen goods, services and attitudes which imitate the image of erotic liberation.

At this point, Lewis Yablonsky believes that the hippie movement's posture of total rejection of American society, is only a "reaction formation" responding to a romanticized feeling of alienation.[33] It also satisfies the general society's need for the perpetuation of its own radical mythology. Society provides avenues for most social challenges to receive partial empathy, but always absorption into the entire cultural dynamic. Traits of the alien stimulate the social order. In *The Hippie Trip,* Yablonsky notes that parts of society appear to validate the hippies' belief system as well as their illusions of being an alienated elite community:

> The "straight" community's almost positive response to this deviant pattern may be partially accounted for by a traditional American worship of aggressive, adventuresome, sexually free heroes who "go it alone" ("do their own thing") unencumbered by social restraints or standard moral conscience.[34]

Along with Yablonsky, Philip Slater cites the importance of

media in escalating the romantically dissident images and attitudes of American protest groups. Slater believes the social reformation attempts of radical groups in the 1960's were exaggerated. The media monitored the thrust, structure, uniformity and eventual demise of counter culture affirmations and denials. Slater claims that more people currently hold counter cultural values than they did in the 1960's. He believes that media personnel have missed this increase, because it is too slow a social change. The faddist "revolution" was short-lived because it died of over-exposure. The media lost interest in sustaining its theatrical coverage; instead, media over-focused on other social issues and monitored social attention.[35]

Additionally, Slater points out another internal deterrant to social change, based on the conflict between immediate gratification and gradual achievement of social aims. There is a division between radicals who wish to reform social institutions nihilistically, and those who desire more gradual changes in personal motives or values.

Slater believes that American social critics must incorporate both emphases which currently exist as contradictions to effective change. He calls for a shift in focus from social criticism, to that of individual responsibility for inner renewal:

> Radicals must learn to live with such contradictions. They can't afford the luxuries of intellectuals, who are much too fond of playing out a romantic fantasy in which they, as lonely heroes, battle bravely against a crass multitude and/or a totalitarian social structure. We are no more likely than anyone else to recognize the ways in which our own behavior creates the forces that plague us from outside; in all private myths the hero is an injured innocent.[36]

In contrast to the romantic hedonism of the erotic warfare for social freedom in the 1960's, American attitudes in the 1970's are framed in moral cliches of moderation. Formal and informal mores of the multiple patriarchal institutions continue to offer dissidents security, predictability and boredom. The action of the social machine attempts an increased regulation of behavior, value and desire by attaching rewards for "turning one's self in" as a ward of the pleasure state.

Any quest for the heroic orgasm now concentrates on "new" technical outlets for erotic energy. People attempt to regulate their "bio-rhythms" in harmony with external circumstances, in order to achieve better "self-production." Badges of success remain cosmetic; they pass as health, fitness, insight, cooperation and accumulation. If they hurt, strain or cost more, people enjoy their "adjustments" better. Even psychological, religious and quasi-spiritual "movements" now systematize opportunities for people to savor multiple orgasms in company with each other. These pass as union with God, Other or the Self. Inadvertently, Slater's call for inner renewal has become a collective fascination with selfhood, in which one has spiritual ecstasies from contemplating the answerable mysteries of the phallic ambulatory male. The territory is interior. The "hero's" enemy is self-ignorance. The issue is to display, or watch others display. And yet, as Alan Watts remarks, what now passes for self-understanding, cannot instantly transform one into a model of virtue.[37]

Antagonists to the self-hypnosis of such inner renewal argue that heterosexual male politics continue to oppress any real challenges to paternalistic social institutions. At this point in time, the archetypal outsider appears to be vaginal. The current critics of masculine technical systems now emerge from feminist efforts for social reform. Abortion disputes, divorce laws, parenting disputes and ultimately female and male homosexuals' demands for "gay liberation" are the hottest social issues. Social alienation—or romantic outlawry—now focuses on basically sexual challenges to heterosexual male domination and regulation of erotic identities.

While many women now espouse vaginal prerogatives as being equal to traditionally phallic ones, a majority of women continue to gain their security by allowing their vagina to be used as penile ratification for masculine politics, economics and personality. They remain "vaginal machines." Their primary function is to facilitate the formal and informal structure for domination-subordination by sex, and the appropriate erotic rhythms for exercise of phallic techniques. As technicians of their own vaginal machines, these women maintain equilibrium and impetus for those institutionalized male systems of biology, labor, production and religion. Vaginal techniques—obedience, hygiene and fulfillment—provide romantic props necessary to masculine operations.

However, feminists and pro-abortionists currently insert the "Lysistrata-factor" of sexual rebellion into such phallic logic, simultaneously disrupting the safe rhythms of vaginal techniques. The radical mythology of the feminist movement creates a spectre of sexual parity with heterosexual males. And so gay liberation appears even as a more radical challenge, because it appears to circumvent vaginal ratification for masculinity in a manner difficult for heterosexual men to dispute.

After the initial social shock of feminist and homosexual confrontation with American social institutions, both are being absorbed into the all-encompassing "rhythm" of concern over social technique. Within the gay movement, there is as much a definitional, ethical and strategical division between various homosexuals, as now exists between radical feminists and women of the traditional vaginal machine. At one point, homosexuals confronted heterosexual forms of negative confinement and regulation, with their own social visions and personal expressions. Now, homosexuals evidence repressive tendencies to desublimate themselves into those very heterosexual forms offered as accommodation to their social deviance.

In effect, the gay radicalism of the 1960's has been replaced with homosexual imitations of "heterosexual citizenship." Homosexual social confrontations have stylistically altered to become production and consumption strategies of reasonable behavior. More than ever before, the homosexual now experiences a wide media coverage and general social awareness. Transvestites have invaded the soap operas and elementary school children know "gay" means more than happy.

Yet, such publicity merely confines the homosexual identity in as rigid, but now more familiar, constraints of social tolerance, concern for therapeutic reform and appeals to remain silent or hidden for the sake of social decorum. Additionally, such publicity also escalates the threatened heterosexual to wider violence against the "growing" homosexual problem. As with the western outlaw, the homosexual identity—with time—is experiencing the visible effects of various "civilizing" heterosexual techniques. It has been made less profitable, even uncomfortable, for the homosexual to refuse available modes of heterosexual citizenship. If he retains his outlaw status, he is mistreated accordingly. If he gives it up for heterosexual citizenship, he could very well relinquish some of the better features of his minority sexual identity.

Much has been written to clarify and distort the growing social consciousness of homosexuality, from both heterosexual and homosexual sources. Yet, it was the offshoot of the radical activism of the 1960s, that pushed types of homosexual militancy, information and a vociferous search for a homosexual identity into the open. These opposed the social conspiracy to keep "homosexual history" a secret.

Tim Denesha chronicles the historical social threads of homosexuality in *Gay Source*. He claims that radical love defines radical subculture; therefore, such subcultures are always *anti-cultural*.[38] Denesha believes that the success of "gay liberation" depends on this special sub-culture becoming aware of itself through traditions contained in a cosmic framework.

Thus, the publication of the *Kinsey Report* on American males' sexual behavior (1948), and the Stonewall Inn gay bar riots against police harrassment (1969) were epochal reference points in homosexual consciousness. Denesha believes that Stonewall marked the epiphanal moment of gay social transformation. There, gays became "one" and gay liberation marked the birth of "a major American social, political, cultural entity. . . ."[39] Unfortunately, much of Denesha's enthusiasm seems based on the radical element of same-sex love being in "natural" affiliation with radical political philosophy. The rhetoric of social "oneness" is as misleading as a belief that gay liberation is a major social entity.

Dennis Altman enlarges Denesha's social vision by convincingly attaching this entity of gay liberation to the counter culture's quest for spiritual values. Altman cites homosexuality as both cause and effect of the broader social movements of the 1960's. He focuses on the male heterosexual establishment's hegemony over the American Dream, to which minority groups had no accessible paths for its achievement. He believes that the hippie movement, the Pill, orgiastic rock music, shatteringly violent film themes, experimental art forms, draft resistance, the search for deeper consciousness through gurus or psychedelic drugs, and a softening of sex role dichotomy through modification of male apparel, interests and behaviors, made reinterpretations of the Dream more immediately available to all.

These examples, along with a general relaxation of sexual conventions, are Altman's new models of minority challenges to society's conformist structures and its materialistically consumptive techniques. God help us.

Such models represent less substantive human freedoms than they purvey cosmetic statements about desired freedoms. Society is able to tolerate and absorb diversity—but it is also able to ameliorate it.

Thus, after the idealistic turmoil of the 1960's, the oppressive structures of technological progress and human management continue as before. The repressive desublimations of homosexual consciousness paradoxically exist quite nicely with the litany of homosexual heroes and social analysts whose exploits and pronouncements have been canonized in fictional and nonfictional publications. Such exchanges between writers on homosexuality now arise from the foment of the 1960's—as a homosexual manifesto—a paper erection for readers to examine and believe that all is well (or shall be) in the gay world.

Here, Altman emerges as one of the more articulate, yet sometimes ambivalent historian-philosophers of homosexual nostalgia. In *Homosexual: Oppression and Liberation,* Altman curiously undercuts himself in a dialectic of contention and self-rebuttal. On the one hand, he lauds a growing consciousness of homosexual political unity, and on the other hand he cites homosexual division into straight underground and square gayworld. While he claims the gay world is the most tolerant of racial integration, he also includes the probability that white homosexual males are as racist as their heterosexual counterparts. In his focus on the relationship of the feminist movement to that of gays, he subdivides essential differences between homosexual males and lesbians. Gay men are allegedly a sexual category, while lesbian women form a sexual *role* category; the difference is unclear. However, Altman concludes that homosexual males probably share similar degrees of chauvinistic attitudes towards all women, which heterosexual males also generate and maintain.

Altman's dialectical discussion ends on the implication that the gay movement (regardless of its diverse "specialties") is agreed on the need for massive social revisions. He admits that it is no longer clear what barriers must be conquered to achieve this utopian change. Perhaps this is one of his more lucid illustrations of the current status of homosexual "liberation."

Robert McQueen also analyzes diverse homosexual "specialties," but considers them more as a political liability. Writing "The Great Gay Movement Gayme" for the *Advocate,* McQueen states that "Unity is still an illusive dream for the gay community."[40] With a potential 20 million homosexuals in America, he estimates that perhaps only 100,000 are directly involved in movement organizations or efforts. Such apparent apathy makes homosexual politics a spectator sport. Citing factionalism and competition for leadership and media attention as reasons why so few major changes have been made for homosexual equality in law, employment or general social treatment, McQueen could be speaking for any minority group's political endeavor.

Obviously, the majority of dissident youth or blacks in the 1960's and 1970's did not converge on Altamont, Woodstock or Selma, Alabama. A majority of housewives does not wish to trade its "contractual prostitution" for the heady options of personal freedom championed by Betty Friedan, Kate Millett or Gloria Steinem. Any choice involving personal risk is usually frightening. So, the closet syndrome bewailed by McQueen is a convenient withdrawal from the homosexual's commitment to the rigors of self-actualization—or revelation. Most minority members learn to be content with their social assignment: society rewards their cooperation.

Along this line, McQueen says that society does recognize "gay economic clout." This translates into the larger social structures as power forms of money and votes. So industry now aims at a gay market and gay voters, much as capitalistic sensitivities were expressed towards youth's buying power and women's "needs." Perhaps these new modes which now appear to incorporate the homosexual into general society, represent a type of civic detente. Given the historicity of heterosexual male power ethics, such detente with homosexuality will most likely assume pleasant forms of psychological or social detention, which do not threaten either heterosexuals or homosexuals too severely.

Gradually, the homosexual who wishes to avoid the risks but receive the rewards of heterosexual citizenship could become disaffiliated from other repressed minority groups. Then he would lose access to a broader base of civic appeal for social change. Unwittingly, the homosexual who grasps for visible power displays, could redefine himself as a "professional homosexual."

If he believes he will receive rewards for imitation of heterosexual goals, values and strategies, the temptation is to pretend that one is not as reprehensibly "homosexual" as those who cannot or will not adjust to the appearance factor required by detente. Thus, he imprisons his latent personal alternatives within specialized forms of political expression. Additionally, the appeal of erotic detente could also escalate rank and status divisions between homosexuals. Even now, homosexual factionalism is primarily inspired by embarrassment over the assimilation failure of radically appearing homosexuals into heterosexual society.

Assimilation success by homosexual leaders is often heralded—and rationalized—as a type of vanguard epic, often typical of social movement rhetoric. A movement's leaders logically universalize the benefits of their sweeping social vision, in order to convince the opposition to capitulate, as well as their own constituency to believe and follow suit. Accordingly, Altman presents the merits of homosexuality for heterosexuals, as though this minority behavior contains the ultimate chance for heterosexuals' own social liberation.

He even broadens his arguments to epic proportions, concluding that all people are gay and that all people are straight. He prophesies that any identity distinction now based only on sexual terms, will eventually dissolve into a more positive "indistinct humanity."[41]

Unfortunately, identity without distinctions—even definition without distinction—is a romantically utopian ideal. Many gay liberation proponents employ the jingo "gay is good"—for everybody, but the logic is fallacious. Currently, much of what passes for gay is not even good for homosexuals. Despite Altman's claims that homosexuals are more sexually aware than heterosexuals (dubious), this "heightened consciousness" does little more than obscure other available dimensions of interest or commitment.

Homosexual promiscuity and superficial obsession with sexuality cannot be explained away as faults of a general social pressure against same-sex behavior. This sexual license can be rationalized as an advantage of "human" liberation, much as heterosexuals justify their ambient sexual permissiveness as the pursuit of personal freedom. For both male groups, the search for the heroic orgasm relies less on an object choice, than it requires a submergence of self in the process of erotic adventure.

Yet, the archetypal outsider is nervous. Originally, gay liberation members espoused erotic free play in order to protect their gay "ideology" from the grim puritanism of the more formal society. From the "revolution is fun" premise, gay liberation now seems to minimize blatant public displays of openly excessive sexual behaviors, in favor of imitations of heterosexual respectability and avenues to power. The Jerry Rubin philosophy for being a radical Yippie—as an excuse to rebel—has changed to careful moderation of image and demeanor for the homosexual—despite Gay Pride Week parades or tricycle races.

Ironically, as white homosexual males gain access to white

heterosexual male power structures, they tend to emulate those against whom they grieve. Concomitantly, Slater notices that pursuit of civil redress through "legitimate" pathways often erodes the initial radical intention in the process.[42] Homosexual leaders now claim that contemporary forms of homosexuality offer "good" to both straight and gay.

However, Slater's thesis that people must presently live out the desired goals of political changes—even before they are achieved—contains the most reasonable and viable proof for any homosexual political philosophy. Any projection of new political possibilities can only be compared against current realities, rather than utopian fantasies. Despite the homosexual trend towards "good behavior," homosexual ghetto realities have not progressed beyond parallel heterosexual ethics, values and goals— all of which are concerned with exploitation, acquisition and sexual superficiality.

The onus is on the homosexual minority to devise its own ethical discipline in practice, as well as ideology. Sharing the mutually uplifting diversities available to homosexuals is one mode for achieving a future share in full citizenship, as well as human potential. Homosexuals have developed awareness, sensitivities and skills apart from mere erotic techniques, which contain a vitality of benefit to all. But, the significant danger in such sharing—as well as in retaining their distinct separation—is that the larger social context to which homosexuals must make their civil appeal is not sufficiently agitated to sympathy.

Individuals form collectives, and collectives often form coalitions because they are agitated towards each other in sympathetic social vision. Unfortunately, homosexual minority appeals usually succeed only if the entire social context is in foment; such dynamic for collective actions sometimes operates sympathetically. For homosexuals, it operates briefly.

Social foment provides the realignment of formal and informal traditions and techniques, before society again grows more rigid. These dynamic contexts are usually in association with economic or military conflict, or uniquely dramatic social phenomena such as student militancy, labor distress, ecological threats, racial oppression or religious discrimination.

At present, there is little dynamic context for homosexual minority issues to blend into the larger society's sense of distress. One group's grief is not always felt as grievous to many. Thus, homosexuals lack a general social focal point to which they can attach their cause. Social mores are now fairly rigid. The social context lacks a sympathetic dynamic. Americans are not now moved by radical psychology.

Slater examines the American myth of individualism as a fantasy of being "special." The heroic estimation of the self assumes a pseudo-radical pose. As each "does his own thing," while others watch, then one expects that a special superiority will be granted or at least acknowledged by others. Yet, Slater argues that this mythical specialness is actually unneeded in a technological and bureaucratic social system. Collective uniformity is the most desirable response which the social machine requires of people.

To guarantee this, pseudo-radical psychology is allowed to exist, is even encouraged, to provide a social conversion technique. One's narcissistic dreams of an exceptional self are translated into forms of personal aggrandizement. By such dreams, economies profit. Concentration on a group's or individual's "uniqueness" easily converts into short-range task consciousness.

Leaders define issues and mobilize people into various task accomplishments; individuals are seemingly released to pursue their self-actualization (on a short-range basis). Leaders formulate an occasional long-range vision for their constituencies; individuals assume this vision as definitive of their own individual dreams of the disenfranchised—but exceptional—self. They busy themselves at task accomplishment to make the dream come true, as a form of heroic effort.

Invariably, many political activists—and homosexuals are no exception—train themselves to exchange long-range thinking for short-range preoccupation. Long-range social strategies tend to diffuse through too gradual a social change. It is tempting to opt for immediate gratification as a goal, and thereby reinforce people's short-range desires. Thus, the possibility for dramatic social change in favor of homosexuals often converts to radical parodies of social gains. Professional homosexuals hold several seats on municipal boards and legislative bodies, more homosexual themes are aired in films and talk shows, and both heterosexual and homosexual alike consider real social progress is transcending traditional homophobia.

The professional homosexual, as with other frustrated radicals, remains eager to exchange his frustration, his erotic rebelliousness for emotional security. He wants to convert his alienating stigma to social respectability.

What such transcendent radicals really seek is a new order of social stability and simplicity for the complex sense of their own humanity which disturbs them. Paradoxically, the "establishment" yearns for more novelty and chronic change to punctuate the humdrum rhythms of technological advancement.

Transcendent radicals often value past traditions, a sense of community, and depth of relationships. Conversely, the establishment values futuristic promises of a technologically refined society that are chronically invalidated by the social instability intrinsic to rapid technological change.

Such polarized values and visions of transcendent radicalism and the establishment are both caught in the leveling effect of technology. The tension of diversity is necessary and good for any social order; by this diversity, democracy refines itself as a human system for self-transcendence.

Continuing conflicts of interest, diversity, and the challenge of group against group and individual against individual, generally prevents democracy from becoming a technique which levels all human variation into final agreement with social forms.

However, those social changes advocated for the homosexual's benefit, now serve to distract him from the various aspects of his alienated miseries. Inadvertently, the democratic form is now looked to as the ideal form which unfortunately camouflages the oppressive reality of the technological form. Despite anti-homosexual laws, religious tradition and general social attitude, democracy does not misuse the homosexual. It merely provides the avenue to a more subtle abuse.

In effect, the contemporary homosexual is urged to assimilate into the heterosexually dominated social machine through the democratic techniques of integration—into social conformity. Believing he trades his alienation for transcendent "freedom," he will merely become another element within a massive collective energized by competition, manufactured individuality and slogans of "brotherhood."

Erich Fromm warns that only negative results can follow such human incorporation into our technologically inspired social machine. He believes the rhythm of the machine hypnotizes people to function in illusions of being—an individual. Perhaps his warning applies to the nebulous ideology of homosexuals now seeking full civil rights within a basically technical social system.

Perhaps heterosexual citizenship implies an erotic impotency. Then the homosexual identity as sexual outlaw retains a uniquely eroticized individuality which will disappear should he successfully imitate heterosexual values and behaviors. Already, the homosexual is choosing, or is being offered, access to these uniform socialization models. Fortunately, his same-sex orientation prevents an "authentic" imitation, because heterosexual males still cannot emotionally afford to remove their invalidating stigma from homosexual alienation.

Dotson Rader claims in his article "Gay Liberation—All the Sad Young Men," that gay liberationists who lose their outlaw status may also lose their creative and regenerative consciousness.[43] Rechy worries that should homosexual males win their battle with heterosexual males, they will end the unique existence of the homosexual identity.[44] And Fromm implies that perhaps moral disobedience must now be considered virtuous, in order morally to combat the narcosis of obedience to social systems, rather than the self:

> The "organization man" is not aware that he obeys; he believes that he only conforms with what is rational and practical. Indeed, disobedience has become almost extinct in the society of organization men, regardless of their ideology. Yet one must remember that the capacity for disobedience is as great a virtue as the capacity for obedience.[45]

Thus, the "new human" which Altman praises gay liberation for helping to *undefine*—even as it defines—also carries the potential to eradicate the homosexual as we now know him. Jacques Ellul speaks of such eradication as a social technique at work to abstract Man, the Human Race, or You.

Ellul considers our social system as a machine which functions independently of human value, behavior and aspiration. Its operational totalitarianism attempts to converge all political, social and human systems in order to achieve productive efficiency. Society's technicians (capitalists, politicians, militarists or religionists) do not design this convergence; it happens as a spontaneously evolutionary result of plural techniques within the social machine. Uniform efficiency is the chilling goal of this "evolution." Ellul adds that "Our human techniques must therefore result in the complete conditioning of human behavior. They must assimilate man into the complex 'man-machine,' the formula of the future."[46]

The pseudo-spontaneity within this methodical evolutionary technique, could perhaps entirely overwhelm any erotic spontaneity in the human character, imagination and spirit. The "new human" could very well become a mere collection of automatic responses with few personalized capacities. Any creative powers would deteriorate to rewarded imitations of impersonal technical accomplishments within available technical systems. Even now, spectatorship is a growing trend in American society complete with its toggery, faddism and mechanical repetitiousness.

If we examine our use of leisure time, we find it filled with technical mechanisms which compensate for creativity, even as it integrates strangers in ritualized skill performances. Vacations are spent learning how to be human; they are often frantic extravaganzas of working to have fun. As in work, the man at leisure is generally programmed to disassociate mental activity from physical involvements; expressions of feeling are also regulated.

Thus, many people learn to believe in their relative importance, if they function with style and skill within available forms. They become instrumental to the social operation they enter; they exist as a means to the accomplishment of some distant end which is rarely achieved. Consequently, work and leisure blandly blend together as limiting opportunities for a person to experience risk, challenge, growth or insight—in other words, a person need only adjust to impersonality in order to assimilate into the rhythms of the social machine.

As in leisure and work, even contemporary art forms reveal the "artist" as a social seismographer who charts human fluctuations within the various social systems. While much of American art reflects technique, some of our art forms do direct attention to interior madness—which appears to be a rational refuge from the absurdity of mechanical technology.

And yet, advertising may best popularize the psychology of technique because it attaches progressive ideals to life-styles, and then teaches men the need to imitate them. Thus, advertising creates a type of psychological collectivism, a reality vacuum in which men feel empty, incomplete or alienated unless they willingly enter the technical frameworks manufactured for their enclosure and participation. Ellul remarks that "Advertising offers us the ideal we have always wanted (and that ideal is certainly not a heroic way of life)."[47]

The pseudo-idealism which activates many social institutions can appear in multiple forms. Ecstatic phenomena, pornography, revolutionary movements, religion, war and sexual experimenta-

tion are all permitted—even desired—by the technically organized social machine. Each form accelerates the tempo of
social progress. However, human characteristics of guilt, fear,
habit or esteem often provide a lag to this progressive tempo.
Then, pseudo-idealism serves to check, punish or hold various
expressions of erotic ecstasy; social tensions result which alter
with time, custom and redistribution of personally erotic expressions.

Thus, restriction and ecstasy promote energetic social tensions
which technique ultimately resolves by integrating apparent
anarchies into the social whole. Inevitably, the goal of ecstasy is
that of power and domination. One's personal ecstatic energies
deploy into the social group in various manners; these energies
diffuse and are incorporated for collective gain.

It is apparent that homosexuals carry unique forms of ecstatic
energy. The social tension between heterosexual and homosexual
males contributes to the states of restriction and ecstasy which
alternate between both male groups. This tension activates the
tempo of social progress. Socialization characteristics of American males currently make homosexual and heterosexual goals
antithetical to each other.

Yet, the movement towards rapproachement, a kind of civic
detente in which homosexuals seem to be achieving more social
understanding and recognition of their identity as salvageable—if
not normal—is merely a heterosexual (even a schizoid homosexual) technique to solve the "homosexual problem."

Obviously, our socio-technical systems allow many individuals
to express their ecstasy in seemingly new ways. Criticism of
society, revolutionary activity, publication of "deviant" material, or even sensuous behavioral experiments flood so many
personal expressions into our culture that people cannot avoid
giving them often equivalent (and diluted) value. The best, the
most dangerous, even the most uniquely personal ideas and
behaviors are integrated into, and then controlled by, the social
machine. Unfortuantely, humans are subsequently integrated as
well:

> This does not mean that ideas have no worthwhile effect on the public
> at all. They have a great effect, but not the effect their creators
> intended. Henry Miller's erotic petard . . . finds a reader whose
> sexual life is thwarted, who is upset by the conditions of his work, his
> lodgings, his political life. This has created in him a thirst for revolt.

The pornographic element unfetters his imagination and plunges him into an erotic delirium that can satisfy his contracted needs. But Miller's book, far from pushing a man to revolt, vicariously satisfies the potential revolutionary, just as the sexual act itself stills sexual desire. . . .

Seeing his discontent expressed far better than he could express it himself, he is satisfied vicariously with an official revolt and ceases to criticize . . . at least for a while—but by then he will have received the next issue.[48]

In summary, the homosexual's attempt to organize his sexuality into a social movement to achieve equality with heterosexuals, is perhaps an honest but futile effort to achieve public endorsement of his own erotic ecstasy. The homosexual's overtures momentarily excite the heterosexual into confrontation, personal speculation or even commitment to homosexual political interests. But typically, the homosexual's discontent must match the heterosexual's discontent with idealistic justice. Even most homosexuals cannot sustain their interest in their "official revolt."

Ellul believes that basic human impulses are too *unpredictable* in their complex social consequences. It is necessary, therefore, that all social ecstatic movements, that all erotic energies be absorbed into the technical milieu of managed behaviors. While the homosexual's traditionally *laissez-faire* sexuality provides one necessary impulse to social progress, because it is useful to heterosexual male identity, i.e., virility, such erotic energy must also be rendered predictable.

At present, the homosexual impulse does less to intimidate, than it does to excite the white heterosexual male who is intent on achieving his own heroic orgasm, his own quest for being somehow erotically "special." Within any man's erotic impulse, are those possible energies asserted through a man's imagination, spirituality, emotion, and life design. By adolescence, most men's individual assertions of their erotic impulses have been aggressively confined by social technique; they are localized, rationalized and regimented into reflexively uniform acts, emotions and beliefs.

Most American males enter their masculinity socialization through the heterosexual model: its emphasis is erotic technique via the Playboy mystique. This model regulates most men's creativity, intention and emotional engagement with others.

Frequency and duration, efficiency in self-expression, desire for pleasurable pseudo-variety, and a preoccupation with the "gadgetry" of erotic paraphernalia, all indicate a permeation of the technical element in men's erotic consciousness.

Caught in the wet dream of manufactured imagination, such men feel liberated only within the patterned regularity of their erotic (often sexual) rituals. The various media help to make heterosexual male erotic models quite predictable, stylized and publicized for men to view and compete against. Minor variations of the "heroic orgasm" are thus manufactured for mass consumption. Yet, the theme of radical chic adventures in erotic virility remains similar, in whatever form it appears. It inspires fears of social impotency in men who can't keep (it) up. These fears translate into task preoccupations with making the "gun" go off, the "switch" providing the necessary power, the "charts" registering cumulative success.

Within radical chic adventures, individualism is often presented as a standard model—of collective "humanism." Each man can choose from a variety of packaged adventures into those infinite possibilities of self-awareness or more meaningful encounters with others. Weekend endurance seminars, group psyche-rubs in hot tub contemplation or merely the massive rush to the tennis and hand ball courts, now codify, encompass and soothe away potential self-radicalism.

Homosexual males also participate in the heterosexual male model. Currently, homosexuals, because of their erotic alien role, carry an atmosphere of radical chic. Yet, the homosexual wants his participation in society to be legitimized by heterosexual males. In actuality, he partially asks for self-eroticism to be exchanged for group titillation. The result will be that many male homosexuals' erotic energy will be dissipated by collective requirements to reveal everything to everyone. They wish their eroticism to be monitored and, in effect, to abide by social rules demanding equal participation.

Homosexuals want to learn the corporate method for inflating egos rendered already flaccid by overemphasis on technique. Yet, the homosexual will not achieve a less disenfranchising or repressive social identity for himself through corporate efforts of political movements or gay liberation. He will offer his erotically radical identity to the dominant male group's varying need to intensify its chronically flagging erotic vitality.

Thus, gay liberation, the sexual revolution, Third World coalitions, strikes, sit-ins and similar vigorous demonstrations are tolerated as *elan vital* in our society of technique. Linking causes, duplicating strategies, winning or losing changes in law, business, government, religion, education or the military are not the most important issues in the homosexual's concern about his low social status. His acceptance, understanding, ostracism or punishment by heterosexual male dominated social institutions will continue to wax and wane, according to the intensity of conflict between restriction and ecstasy needed by such institutions.

Social institutions are merely those superficial structures of beliefs, values and practices which satisfy the apparent complexion of social harmony. They are reflections of a deeper structure of hidden totalitarianism which is intrinsic to social machines. Human environments or social systems presently exist as corollary shadows to more pervasive technical systems.

However, the very amorphousness of this deeper totalitarian structure also allows the individual to believe in whatever philosophy, ideology or endeavor which he might select as supreme. He can even cherish the myth that the individual exists solely for himself.

Thus, any of the individual's allegedly radical beliefs, constructions, or social movements (whether gay or straight) vitally help to increase the tempo of the social machine through these periodic confrontations of personal interest groups. Ironically, prejudice, as much as love, can provide a social impetus. Thus, the ecstasy of hatred which homophobic heterosexuals feel, is as orgiastic as the ecstasy of belief that homosexuals experience in promoting sexual equality as a *cause celebre*.

When any human "specialty" or "condition" (race, Jewishness, poverty, sexuality, etc.) is elevated to a metaphorical level, as required by *cause celebre,* such a specialty swallows the unique personality into a metaphorical representation of himself. Jewishness, blackness, feminism or homosexuality imply an attitude, a quality or a purpose which pass as a likeness to persons. And when a metaphorical designation of persons is then transposed into a social cause—either by its proponents or opponents—the metaphor generates a collective social constraint. Any metaphorical "specialty" in a *cause celebre* then limits the individual, even as it promises erotic relief through group cohesiveness. It implies that potential benefits or liabilities could accrue only through collective action.

Whether one is for or against a *cause celebre,* both sides engage in an attempted resolution of their frustrations. Frustration breeds action. Action is erotic. Action is also task oriented. The task for homosexuals appears to be the achievement of social equality. The task for heterosexual opponents is to thwart this aim to varying degrees. Thus, erotic ecstasy faces institutional restriction (which is also erotically ecstatic).

Yet, not all homosexuals completely embrace or deny the metaphorical intention in gay liberation; accordingly, they act or do not act freely. All self-identifying homosexuals are nevertheless psychologically affected; some identify completely with their social cause, others withdraw even more into secret isolation and many vacillate between extreme alternatives.

However, beneath the apparent task of opposing erotic impulses (homosexual desire for equality and heterosexual reaction to this desire), exists the eventual resolution of their social disagreement. The effective regulation of the homosexual's currently alien identity—now monitored by both straights and gays—will absorb him into social harmony with the patriarchal machine. Heterosexual opponents of the homosexual metaphor of liberation will continue to resist and then adapt to it, as they gradually and profitably absorb it into their sociotechnical structures. Already, significant trends outline a future for the male homosexual, which he unwittingly supplements himself.

Traditions still have impact on current masculine affairs. In the male competition for masculinity verification, heterosexual males still enhance their own feelings of virility in relation to legal, moral and social treatment of homosexual invalidators of the general masculinity profile. Violence is one technique used in this male competition; parody, social reconstruction, collective sharing and sexual incorporation are other broad technical categories for resolving competition.

However, more humanistic males acting as utopian speculators, would cancel such technically competitive realities. Altman does so when he claims that our society is now progressing towards a "greater acceptance of human sexuality . . . a decrease in the stigma attached to unorthodox sex and a corresponding increase in overt bisexuality."[49] Perhaps Altman represents the current ambivalence recorded in heterosexual and homosexual attempts to comprehend and deal with their complex meanings to each other. Even Altman seems lost in the myriad of prevalent public statements and overt reactions of both male groups, which he attempts logically to reconcile.

He concludes that heterosexual tolerance of homosexuality will increase the number of hidden homosexuals angry enough to emerge and identify with "gay liberation." The question still remains as to why the homosexual would be angered at a growing social acceptance of more equitable sexual expressions?

Perhaps any gains or losses to be achieved by homosexuals collected within the current metaphor of their sexual "specialty" or "condition," can best be predicated on the technological state of our future society. These future visions might make Hitler's techniques for achieving his idealistic Third Reich pale by comparison. What lies ahead of all of us can only be surmised from clues offered to us by those male social engineers now busy with their blueprints.

One clue appeared in L'Express of Paris, which published a series of textual extracts outlining American and Russian scientists' contemplations of a utopian society in the year 2000: "The visions of these gentlemen put science fiction in the shade."[50] Though merely hinted, perhaps the future of society is modeled after the perfect machine, in which the homosexual will also participate.

After all, this interim period before the "golden age" of technology must also include gay liberation and other social movement phenomena. It seems probable that concern about internecine conflict, social inequality, legal and economic reform or even moral re-armament are necessary preludes to the technical obviation of all human friction.

Already, well-intentioned men argue hopefully for human universalism as a remedy for current human fractionalism (the New Man in a New World favored by Fromm). All men will be saved by techniques of conversion; the dissident, the independently creative, the alien and the dreamer will be harmonized into perfectible "lovers of mankind," unwarped by "tribal loyalties."

If and when the homosexual learns how to relinquish his sexual "deviance," "perversion" and "threat" to male heterosexual norms, his erotic domestication will be complete. He will be absorbed into a socially leveling harmony with a larger social vision than his own. As an archetypal outsider, his once special human definition will become obsolete—he will be demythologized.

Even heroes require enemies. Yet, fabricated heroics are only momentarily necessary to a society moving towards eventual amelioration of major social differences. Then, erotic individuality remains the final heroic stance in an approaching age which attempts to systematize everything—including sexuality.

The homosexual who refuses the civilizing effects of psychological study and treatment, legal confinement, religious understanding and social acceptance, now exists as an anarchist of the affections, in the unregulated autonomy of the heart. Homosexuality *per se* does not guarantee this, any more than does a heterosexual orientation. Only the erotic individualism of the constant rebel can violate those arbitrary behavioral categories which are constructed to regulate and contain the freedom of the self. This freedom is maintained, says Norman O. Brown, by one's violation of common sense.[51]

Brown believes that our consciousness of the self-as-symbolic marks the real transformation of each man's world. Ultimately, the homosexual as symbolic social alien then carries qualities of magic and madness which critically illuminate the deadening effects of "logical" social formula and technique. Then, how one conceives himself offers the chance to escape from socially passive experiences into creative freedom. Already, within homosexual groups the deadening technique of collectivism reveals a growing loss of personal experimentation in living.

Consequently, to prevent his disappearance by such pseudo-assimilation, the homosexual must keep his fantasy to himself. To remain personally intact, he also seems to need to preserve a rebel nature with its degrees of dangerous challenge to the status quo.

Inevitably, these private visions become the homosexual's anarchical engagements of his creative self with others. They clash with public visions.

Public visions include attempts to integrate overt behaviors into well regulated task accomplishments. To achieve this, rewards are attached to behaviors. Thus, the more covert elements of the human personality—those most difficult for others to reach or control—are often voluntarily offered for integration into collective visions.

At this point, heterosexual males allow homosexual groups politically to emerge and grow. This helps to construct a common sense of identity among homosexuals which can be more conveniently controlled and absorbed into the social system.

Corporately, homosexuals commit themselves to ideals, rituals or shared systems of values, and aid their own social integration. For minority members, the group seems to offer access to feelings of greater self-worth, a reduction of alienation and relief from loneliness. Minority members are as vulnerable to the rhetoric of being special as they are to implicit promises of social acceptance if they only cooperate.

The homosexual's receptivity to the ideal of social equality broadens to include techniques which convert to conditioned reflexes, which in turn are reinforced by his collective participation. From camp behavior to studied imitation of machismo, or from cruising to serving as guest speakers for heterosexual groups, the homosexual is conditioned to be gay.

Neutralized individualism anesthetizes the neo-homosexual. Caught in structures of repetitious activity which accentuate often passionless self-indulgence, the homosexual is numbed by both homosexual and heterosexual demands to conform to social expectations not always his own.

Curiously, his self-consciousness is escalated rather than soothed by various tasks manufactured to suit a popular taste for heroics. Then allegiances, ideals, identities and social goals homogenize into comfortable safety for the homosexual too confused, timid or without resources to exist independently. It is much easier to be what someone tells us to be.

To relinquish one's passions is the beginning of eventual forfeiture of freedom. George Orwell speaks of synthetic passions in *Brave New World*. These "Violent Passion Surrogates" are causes, manifestoes, techniques and programs which link men together in well orchestrated pantomimes of feeling. Ellul also agrees that we will arrive at the point where social manipulation of our internal senses will ". . . produce a conviction or an impression of happiness without any real basis for it."[52] Then even injustice, despair, anxiety and impotency can be flattened into technical equations with sacrifice, patience, awareness and utilitarianism.

Obviously, passion surrogates will not guarantee the homosexual his erotic independence, his spiritual or ethical initiative, or even his self-contained identity. Now, too many neo-homosexuals wish to assimilate conveniently into the malaise of massification. There is safety in hiding within the appearances of good behavior. Any prisoner soon recognizes the rewards his captors offer for simulation of their expectations.

Looking to the future, we see most men serving themselves as technicians of their own fate. Each man concentrates on modifying his techniques to permit smoother functioning and more rapid, predictable results. The stimulation in each man's hunger for social change, is merely the pleasure of uniform repetition moving each man through the sensation of change. Then men feel the exhilaration of the competition with each other to become the same—first.

The neo-homosexual now enters this ecstasy of motion, this tempo of the social machine, as little different from his heterosexual counterpart. His homosexual orientation, imagination or mystery will be studied in those mechanics' manuals of psychosexual technique. His intangible spirit will transmute into the accessible tangibles of style, goods and social efficiency. His social rhythms will operate apart from personal will or desire. The neo-homosexual will become a clownish stunt rider on his tiny motorcycle of opportunity. He will lead his small parade into the political circle of human understanding and acceptance. And he will be charmed by any applause.

Even Altman claims that gay liberation rejects violence for erotic play. Such liberation, he claims, will bring us our every desire, because we shall see "a new perception of the world that is remarkably radicalizing."[53] And yet Altman's "heavenly" vision is given a more hellish prospect for the neo-homosexual by Ellul, who sees something deadlier in social politics than blithe playfulness.

Bent on radical assimilation into a benign society, the archetypal outsider wishes to be free from the myth of his erotic alienation. His romance with himself is ending. He now urges his own domesticated imprisonment. And once he gains his uniform facelessness of social integration, he will again learn to love whatever he is told to be:

> With the final integration of the instinctive and the spiritual by means of these human techniques, the ediface of the technical society will be completed. It will not be a universal concentration camp, for it will be guilty of no atrocity. It will not seem insane, for everything will be ordered, and the stains of human passion will be lost amid the chromium gleam. We shall have nothing more to lose, and nothing to win. Our deepest instincts and our most secret passions will be analyzed, published, and exploited. We shall be rewarded with everything our hearts ever desired. And the supreme luxury of the society of technical necessity will be to grant the bonus of useless revolt and of an acquiescent smile.[54]

10/DIALOGUE: Letter to a Former Lover

> I love this chastity, which is the pause of peace of
> our fucking, between us now like a snowdrop of
> forked white fire.[1]
> —D. H. Lawrence, *Lady Chatterley's Lover*

Dear M——:

I write to you now one final time, not to disrupt your present life or to antagonize your feelings; my departure from the emotional impasse we had reached nearly five years ago caused quite enough distress for both of us.

I only want to tell you who I have become, because you figured so prominently in all my thoughts and choices, as well as the general drift of my life. I've compared the many times I've had with other men against the memory of my experiences with you. And I discovered differences which were not so vast in quality or kind. I only had to assign them meaning, to enjoy or hate—or at least tolerate—why I chose to do what I did.

I heard from J—— that you're married now. I'm glad you've found someone to share your life with. I understand that you're still continuing with your art design. I hope you'll reconsider, and experiment with fine art—I always believed you had more inner vision than just to interpret planes and angles for advertisements.

I hear so little else about you. You're safe. I won't intrude into the new existence you've created with her, not even "accidentally." I couldn't tolerate the careful politeness, the tense silence or the too-animated attempts we might make to appear voluble. Your wife would never understand our former relationship. It would only cause awkwardness all around. Too many unan-

297

swered questions hang starkly between people who try to withhold or pretend. I remember they did with us, then.

I practice avoiding pretense, M———. It makes my life a little
easier, a bit more authentic. The last week I was with you, when
you told me you were having an affair with Mrs. ———, I was
shocked. I had to pretend I wasn't hurt. I tried so hard, perhaps
you didn't understand that my not revealing any feeling was
because I was afraid that if I responded, I would feel too much. I
said nothing. It was best to let you explain, so I could absorb and
understand, even while I hated you with such exquisite depth. Yet
I never really understood what happened; I'm not sure you
did—then.

I felt inadequate for you. I thought I hadn't loved you correctly,
as if there were some formula I hadn't discovered. I finally read
some books on homosexuality and learned that your transition
from me to women was a fairly common occurrence among
homosexual men. I'm one of the less privileged "four percent"; I
have to content myself exclusively with men. I thought you were
the same.

I listened to your speech. I appreciate your agony now; I didn't
then. After I left you, I made the mistake of agreeing to an
immediate love affair with another man who was also dealing with
the loss of his lover. We talked about both of you incessantly. It
seemed to help, consoling each other by reminiscing, weighing
each detail, convincing each other we had both been badly used.
We decided to live together. I see now that we both pretended that
I was his ex-lover J———, and R——— was you. I wore his former
lover's bathrobe and slippers and sat in "his chair," reading
novels. R——— watched me a lot, brooding about things he would
never articulate. We both drank heavily. We stopped talking very
much to each other after the first month, except for perfunctory
items to help pass the time agreeably. We had little in common
except grief. Philosophically, he wanted to cover his life with a
veneer of elegance—handmade furniture, original art, antiques,
theater tickets, and wealthy, handsome homosexuals. I was an
ornament.

In bed, we never met. We carefully aimed ourselves in each
other's direction, but somehow we missed our mark. He kissed
me like he had memorized the motion. He held me as if I were
something he had just polished and didn't want to smudge me by
touching. He considered sex to be a right we both had, because we
shared an agreement to live together as lovers. He offered me my

"right," like someone would politely pass dessert to a dinner guest. We nibbled at each other to prevent emotional starvation, I suppose; I always felt tenuous, somehow out of place. One night, he turned towards me half asleep and began to pull me into him, catching my hair in his fingers as he covered my face with his mouth whispering the other man's name. We laughed about the error. I carefully rehearsed his name as we undressed to have sex. I was afraid I would name you, and hurt his feelings. We never loved each other; we had sex with memories.

I caught him kissing a man in the bathroom, at a party. He apologized for being so carelessly drunk. He began to come home quite late from recitals or dinner engagements. A mutual friend told me he was seeing a wide variety of other men. R—— confessed; he asked if we could have an open relationship. He cruised parks; he had sex in his office during the day. I think he somehow hated himself, rather than me. I never learned why. I left him.

I lived alone for several years. When you and I separated, I told you that you were forcing me out on the streets again. What else could I do? I tried to stop myself, but I picked up men in bars, hitchhiking, in parks, and at parties—I even tried a steam bath, but I felt trapped by men wandering in those hot, damp, shadowy rooms, wrapped in their towels and smiling those glittering, suggestive smiles of invitation. I led a profligate life. I fucked anyone, anywhere—everywhere. I began the process with someone, so it would end quickly. I didn't really care. I had nothing to lose but time.

Others felt the same. In the dark, I undressed—as though my body were someone else's, and I was merely attending to it. I pulled men onto me like someone would lower a window shade—and I tried to shut out what I did. Sometimes successfully, usually not. I knew if I performed well enough, my partner would never notice that I wasn't really there with him. I'd withdraw way back into my mind, so I could function as though I were watching two other people have sex together, abstractly, with as much disinterest as reading a magazine in a dentist's office.

Most of all, I remember the hands—so many hands grabbing, rubbing, gouging, pulling. I rarely felt a light touch of tenderness. Only hurried desire. And the weight of lust. There is no heavier load than a man bent under his own intentions, preoccupied with analyzing the private pressures of his own orgasm. When they finished, they would remain on my back or stomach, squirming a little, sweating a little, recovering their breath before they'd ask if I'd like to clean up. What a laugh! As though what we had done together was somehow messy or embarrassingly inconvenient.

I met D——in a gay bar. He asked if he could borrow a cigarette. I had noticed that he had been watching me for about an hour. I was charmed that young men still used old lines so innocently. I gave him a ride home. He invited me into his house for tea. He made no advances beyond leaning across the couch to kiss me. I was impressed. I went back each night for a week—for tea, conversation about art, music, men, life, and then the kiss. Each time we talked, I didn't realize he was drawing me into a dramatic production; he directed while I rehearsed my im-promptu lines. We upstaged each other constantly, but each performance was intensely beautiful, and in the beginning he forgave me my natural abilities.

One night, D—— built a fire and piled cushions on the floor beside it. We drank wine and silence. He laid there beside me, watching the firelight, his smooth skin burning. The flame reflected in the eye which watched me, as though something deep inside of me was being ignited by thoughts he had never spoken, of ideas which made me afraid to speak. And I desired him, because he seemed caught in the absence of desire. I moved closer to his face and touched it with my cheek. I wanted to press my eye against his and force him to see only me.

I moved into his house a week later. Together, we created a dissipated nostalgia, an atmosphere of the 1920's woven into the romantic anguish of Ludwig of Bavaria (we had both read *The Dream King*). And our life together began to resemble a dream, as though we walked and talked together in fog, without past or future, but only the roseate glow of firelight and candles, per-fumed tea and Billie Holliday records. He hung crystals in windows. The broken brilliance would refract colors onto the walls, the furniture and us. We sat together in late afternoons, spellbound, watching each other's faces splashed with reds and blues and oranges. The antique clock would chime, and we would sit still, waiting for something magical to occur between us that would blot out the practical necessities of two men living together—shopping, cooking, cleaning and existing from day to day without a plan.

The lack of concrete plans disturbed me. I forced him to say he loved me. He would comply when he drank too much, which was almost daily. I could depend on the alcohol to help him phrase the truth that he really didn't love me at all. We only acted out love together, like a plot—dramatically. In bed, we would lie beside each other, he forcing me to wait for some small movement which indicated he wanted me, as I wanted him. I would yield and reach for his fingers at rest by his side. I would hold his hand, waiting for some slight pressure in return, hinting that perhaps he wanted me, or would condescend to allow me to turn towards him in the dark. To begin love required an act of will, a deliberate decision that sex could be included in our dreams, in small amounts.

Beneath the painting his former mistress had designed for him before she returned to the East, he'd pull me, slowly against his chest, pinning me there as though we were diving deeply into ourselves together, holding out until the final moment when we felt as if our lungs would burst and we rushed to meet the air and release in each other. How reticent he was in sex. He imaginatively designed a sexual setting, sadly, like a domestic tragedy. He choreographed a small repertoire of dramatic conventions which we always observed together during the daytime. But at night, in bed together, he suffered some kind of stage fright. I whispered his lines and he repeated them, woodenly.

I knew he didn't love me the first time he pushed me against a bureau knob during a drunken argument; I cut my scalp and bled a lot. He begged me to help him be a better person, to open himself emotionally, to learn what he needed to do to love a man. But I think he could never really love anyone. He only needed to be adored. He was too controlled, too conscious of himself as an actor. He could never relax between takes, because he was always on—for himself. He drank more, retreated into somber moods and became increasingly violent—verbally and physically. Abuse seemed to give him nervous release and a sense of dramatic outrage. We decided to separate. I kept the house. I kept everything as it had been when we lived together. I became curator of a museum, where I allowed no one to visit.

During the next several months, I lived there alone. I wanted to believe that some night he would come back to me, knock on the door; I would let him in, and we would both repair the damage we had caused each other. I developed compulsive patterns. After work, I would go home immediately to wait for the end of our separation. Hour after hour, I'd half-heartedly busy myself with inane projects until dark. Then I would light the candles, play the old phonograph records, pour a drink and walk from room to room remembering where he had sat, when he had turned to speak to me, the wry laugh, the mysteriously coiled hair, the tapered fingers toying with a cigarette. I watched from the windows, staring at the street, starting at sounds that I thought might be D——tapping at the door. He never returned.

I began to cry constantly. I invented dialogues that we would have when we met again—full of promises and happiness. I became obsessive in my thoughts of him. I was caught in the dream.

I remembered long quiet, summer nights with a dog barking across the fields; the leisurely dinners we would prepare, the walks across the beach—never together—but each of us alone, looking for shells as though we were children without care in the moonlight, until the week-end concluded, forcing us to pack and return to the city. While he slept in the car, I would watch his face illuminated by passing headlights. At those moments, while he was asleep, I felt as though he were truly mine, without defense, without guile, just there—simply with me. I walked from room to room, talking to us—for us—drinking myself into an emotional paralysis. I called my former psychiatrist, the one I had told you I'd never have to return to see. One more small defeat was nothing compared to the hellish existence I had maintained by staying in the house we had shared.

I saw Dr.——and told him I thought I was psychologically breaking down. I told him everything about myself this time, and about your, R——'s and D——'s behavior. He concluded that I chose men who had a need to depend on me. I wanted them for this reason—to feel I was worthwhile. When I couldn't discern what they particularly needed, I selected a clue and tried to supply what I thought they wanted from me. I didn't become me—rather, I became an imitation of what each man expected me to be. Perhaps I did this with you, too; or you with me—I still can't be sure. I always wondered if our age difference placed me in the role of surrogate father for you. I never wanted to play that part; I just happened to have had some of the experiences and feelings you were going through, as I was growing up. You seemed to ask for advice, so I gave it as best I could. I wanted to help you, but now I wonder if so much helping of one by the other, places the helped at a disadvantage. I didn't believe we were competing. Sometimes I felt you were, but attributed it to your testing yourself against me, in order to develop yourself.

We were both so different that I thought our own interests complemented and stimulated, rather than created ideological or emotional friction. You always had such fine abilities. I was so very proud of you, even when you told me you failed in some minor event. Perhaps I didn't praise you enough, M——, to comfort your trust in my deep care for you. I can't delve too much into what might have been: each of our choices, statements or moods could have been modified to better suit us in a thousand different variations. We chose what we did, and were, for the moment—without being stalled by careful maneuvers or regrets. How else could we live?

Dr. —— suggested that I attempt to establish more egalitarian relationships with men. To get D—— off of my mind, I gave up the house and moved from one apartment to another. I didn't decorate, I didn't entertain, I didn't care. I merely stored myself—wherever I happened to be.

To manage an "egalitarian" love—even a friendship—I practiced withholding my thoughts and feelings each time I met some new man. I selected safe topics to cover myself. I thought that if part of me (the part that could be hurt) remained inaccessibly mysterious, the man would be intrigued and reveal more of himself to get to know me more thoroughly. Also, I hoped to curb my ferocious tendency to want always to know why people do what they do, or say what they say. Motives—concerning me— make me suspicious. I decided egalitarianism didn't mean that I had to spread out my soul for someone to explore the first time they met me. A slow unfolding would be best—like a poker game—I wouldn't tip my hand first.

I went out to public places again—usually bars. What fun! I think I expected I would meet someone like myself—a little lonely, a little lost, nursing emotional wounds over a slow drink in the brisk noise of a crowded room. Men approached me with wonderful openers. "May I talk with you?" "Sure." We would both smile. "What do you do?" (I never knew if they meant employment-wise or sexually. I was cautious—egalitarianism, you know.) "What do *you* do?" (I countered.) "You seem really different from the rest of these guys." (I would graciously return their compliment and wonder what in the hell they meant.) The conversation usually ended: "I have a very strong sex drive, and I'd like to make it with you." Or, "I'd really like to get better acquainted with you, but not here. Why don't we spend some time at my place?"

Sometimes I would—I was curious to see if something less adolescent would occur. Sometimes I just felt an excessive fatigue, worn out by the same tired line. I wanted to go home, sit in the tub, scrub the night from my skin and fall asleep alone—without the regrets I flashed forward to as the usual aftermath of what would be just another pick-up for an amusing toss in bed.

I was no longer amused by my ability to prove that I was still desirable to strangers. I think I had lost my self-confidence, because I couldn't retain a man for more than several months (sometimes a day). I know, with you it was five years, but I didn't meet you in a gay bar; I didn't go with you to bars after we lived together. We managed a balanced life in the "straight" world.

By now, I was living a double life: one at night, on the sex hunt; the other, passing my day at work with people who never knew what I did alone. They would ask if I had an enjoyable weekend, etc. I became very adept at changing pronouns, inventing beautiful blonde dates and appearing to be the single swinger. I hated the deception.

I decided to merge my daytime and nighttime personas into one me, about a month after I met—and left—B———. I met him in a bar. He sat at a table with a friend, night after night. He watched me off and on for several weeks. Finally, he sent his friend to where I was standing to invite me to their table. B———was considerably younger than I, somewhat naive, but with an open, friendly manner. He seemed happy. I wanted to be. We talked. I saw him frequently after that, but always in the bar.

One night, he invited me home with him. I tried to explain that I didn't want to have sex, because I was trying to sort out some rather confused concepts about myself being a homosexual. He listened and sympathized. He felt similar problems with his own identity. He hadn't been "out" very long, and wasn't used to the sexually charged atmosphere of the "gay life."

He asked if we could have sex, because he thought I expected him to ask. I refused. Over the weeks of seeing him, we continued to develop an emotional rapport, of sorts. I think I grew to like him. I walked into his apartment one night, closed the door, took off my clothes and told him I thought it was time we quit teasing one another with inevitabilities. He laughed.

Perhaps his youth, his inexperience, his lack of being stereotypically "gay," helped B—— to retain a tenderness, even a lighthearted and humorous attitude towards sex. We lighted candles in the bathroom and watched leaf-like shadows dance on the walls, wind-caught. Together in the water, quiet like a pond, we contemplated each other's eyes watching for one of us to begin. Limbs wound against limbs, we moved through a liquid passion, without embarrassment or rules. I saw the candlelight coat his wet body like a marble sculpture, bleeding like melting ice from the insistent heat of what was my need finally to love someone. And I couldn't. We had nothing in common between us but the water and our desire for sex rising like geysers each time we crushed against each other.

In bed, before we fell asleep, his hand would stretch across the sheet, touching me alive until I thought I would never want to sleep again. I would turn to watch him slowly move towards me, rising from the mattress to dance slowly around me like a monument charmed into mobility. His face would descend to find mine, waiting, for the beginning which I thought would never end. I wondered if I could ever love a young man, like a god, who took such little notice of himself, or me, because he never listened to what I'd say. He would press his mouth against mine, pushing me into a silence, making me hold the question back, so he wouldn't have to say he didn't love me.

He watched old movies on television, smoked grass and liked to cook. I thought he should finish college. He drew me naked, in pastels, for his art class which he rarely attended. I was more embarrassed taking off my clothes for that, than for our erotic voyages in the bathtub. He left me for someone younger than I, shortly after he finished the drawing. I saw it, once, when he told me he had reconsidered our relationship and thought he wasn't quite ready for something permanent.

I didn't cry. I didn't return to Dr.———. I didn't even resent what I felt had been a misrepresentation of feelings, camouflaged by a lot of intense sexuality and a jolly attitude.

I became militant. I decided that if I were a homosexual, I had better find out what that meant. The first time I went to a bookstore to buy books on homosexuality, I wore sunglasses and hoped to God the clerk would act nonchalant. I read avidly, and returned to buy everything I could find on the topic. I tried to get the same clerk.

I joined homophile organizations and subscribed to gay periodicals. I went to gay bars, gay moviehouses, developed gay friendship groups (the ones who knew my address and telephone number), swam at gay beaches, shopped in gay stores, attended a gay church and got involved in gay politics. I became professionally gay. Then I began to "come out" to colleagues at work.

Broaching the homosexual topic was sometimes difficult, and

sometimes amazingly easy. I selected people for whom I had developed fondness and trust; I chose the right moment to unleash my secret. Some already knew; some didn't care. I felt I had to confess what I was, in order to "be honest" about who I was. I wanted them to know *me*. Women accepted my self revelation better than men. People didn't seem to alter their opinion of me, even though I pushed gayness to an extreme.

I used every psychological argument, every anthropological study, all of the logic I could muster from my readings, to explain why my sexual orientation was merely a historical, sociological and biological minority phenomenon. Religion and social mores—based on heterosexual male uneasiness with their own sexuality—made me the social pariah because I was a homosexual. They listened. Politely. But I don't think they always really understood too much beyond the fact that what I said incensed me to loquaciousness. Try explaining what blue looks like to a blind man, M——, and you'll know how I felt. Despite all, they knew me as a person with whom they worked; they watched my skills and learned to trust me as an equal. I guess this helped them also accept my sexual orientation.

I didn't march in gay parades. I did stuff envelopes for homosexual civil rights groups and served on educational liaison committees in touch with heterosexual institutions. I met a lot of homosexual people who seemed concerned about much more than sex.

Or so I first thought. In my gay church, I recognized that to withdraw from heterosexual religious groups in order to worship freely as gay people, was a pathetic attempt to reconstruct a past from which these people had been expelled or made to feel sinfully uncomfortable because of heterosexual Christian beliefs that homosexuals are immoral. I didn't notice any deep Christian commitment or strong ethical values emerging from these gay churches. I noticed imitative religious forms permeated with a gay bar mentality of sexual awareness for people in the church. I decided to withdraw from gay churches, and any church for that matter. I don't need the American protestant brands of scriptural interpretation to condemn *or* justify my homosexuality. Pallid rituals, social fellowship, and the clubby atmosphere of church do not make me feel better about myself as a spiritually, intellectually and morally growing person. I don't need sympathy sharing from gays, in the guise of religiously inspired love and charity— covering up our shared defeat.

Gay political groups also seemed to attract homosexuals who valued their public visibility as gays crusading for a legitimate civil grievance. "Them" vs. "Us" attitudes seemed to divide me from heterosexuals, as well as the less militant homosexuals. I read campaign literature, studied political issues, argued movement strategy, and agreed that homosexuals don't have full civil rights because their sexual orientation is a minority behavior. Yet, I have never been discriminated against because of what I am. I know much of what is presented about us in the media is distorted and libelous. Yet, I don't think politics will change heterosexuals' feelings or ideas about homosexuality. I think public education will—in media, in schools, and in other social institutions which provide an instructional avenue, especially for the young. Homosexual civil rights efforts are necessary, but they reinforce one set of stereotypes about gay people, even as they attempt to attack more damaging stereotypes. The exchange is subtle.

As I patronized gay stores, restaurants, beaches and bars, I noticed that they are *all* a context for sexual opportunity. Sure, I enjoyed the relaxation of casual contact with people of my own sexual persuasion, but I always felt like a sexual target, someone who was probably available merely because I was where gay people congregated. I had difficulty meeting men on multiple levels of social exchange. The common denominator to most of my encounters was the sexual potential. It really became fatiguing.

The gay movie houses were boring. I saw poorly produced films with similarly trite plots; I've experienced the meeting and seduction with more imagination, flair and range. Old men masturbating under their hats or raincoats, while they tried to entice me from watching the movie, seemed pathetic. Gay periodicals usually concerned crotch commentaries; content was limited to fantasy arousal by pictures of men whom I rarely see in real life. Feature articles on problem-solving the gay life, the philosophical depths of sexual technique, health problems and artistic biographies were just as slick and innocuous as heterosexual publications which emphasize glamor, sex and emotional adventure.

I cancelled my subscriptions, withdrew my membership from gay groups, and limited my selection of gay friends to those whom I thought would contribute to a wider range for my life, than those men who redundantly concentrated on who slept with whom, which couple just broke up, who bought what, who traveled to which trendy spa, who did what in bed with their latest trick ("What a hunk—kinky, too!"), as well as other important gay gossip.

I recognized that the visible gay life is a ghetto. A trap that walls us in psychologically, socially and sexually like a slow moving spiral turning us in on ourselves. The men who travel the rounds of such gay haunts are usually the same people, trading loss for loss. The majority of homosexual men are blended into the general heterosexual society. They live their lives in a more constructive way than in the habitual sex hunt, the coquettish display, the watching for the effect of being watched.

I need to avoid gay haunts. I need to blend socially, and trust that I'll meet valuable men, under less pressured, less ritualized and less personally restricting social circumstances. I won't find "Mr. Right" sitting on a bar stool or slipping down a steam bath hallway to peer at group sex in the shower room. Or else I'll find him back there again after we've broken up, waiting and watching for someone like me—a little lonely, a little trusting, and not yet entirely jaded by sexual experiences with men who disappear.

I want to pursue a variety of constructive experiences for my life now, M——. I am not gay. I am a homosexual person with an infinite number of talents and possibilities which I now recognize I should begin to actualize.

I don't want to wind up spending my money on another trip around the world, or another man intent on the trip for himself. I can't visualize myself raising poodles, buying young men, or counting my blue chips when I'm 75. Much of what I've chosen has involved errors in judgment; a lot of it, self-indulgence in my erotic fantasies. Most of it resulted in my placing too much faith in sex, to the exclusion of also living undefined exclusively by homosexuality.

I plan to return to the university and major in another field of interest than my first one. I want to explore ideas and broaden my intellectual capacities. I want to explore people, places and projects which I've avoided until now. I want to live fully, without the exclusiveness of feeling sorry for myself because I haven't succeeded in acquiring a lover. I need to include many men in my life (whether heterosexual or homosexual), and learn how each one is special, how each contributes to a more mature and broadened combination of my personal capacities. I also need to include women, my parents, my sister and the young, the old, the sick, the crippled—the whole variety of human experience in my experience of life.

I have finished compartmentalizing my life. I am through with narrow restrictions. Gay closets, as well as straight closets both lead to solitary confinement.

And so, M——, I've offered you what insight I can about my experiences and contemplations which were forced upon me when we separated. Some I chose, some were accidental events to which I could only adapt my often faltering, but always growing philosophy of what life could mean to me as a homosexual male.

I think you were my catalyst. I can say that now, where before, I believed that I couldn't continue to live without you. I had established you as my reason for being alive. My only reason. You did what you had to do, because you changed while with me—as we all do through time. I would never have wanted you to be a static person for my convenience—or even my pleasure. To have served each other in that manner would have worn out both of us.

I do appreciate loving you. I do remember. And in recollection, I preserve what you meant to me then, even as I alter the meaning within the self I anticipate I will become. And you will go with me, always, M———, as I hope I do with you. And yet, separation is only attached to time and place—and these change on us. So you are here, with me now, even as I write and remember. As I trust you do me—occasionally—and without regret.

G——

Notes

Preface: Advance Payments for Single-Room Occupancy

1. James Baldwin, *Giovanni's Room* (1956; New York: Dell Publishing Co., Inc., 1971), p. 191.
2. Ben Shahn, *The Shape of Content* (1957; Cambridge, Mass.: Harvard University Press, 1963), p. 122.
3. Kate Millett, *Sexual Politics* (1969; New York: Avon Books, 1971), p. 46.
4. Baldwin, *Giovanni's Room,* p. 223.

Chapter 1: Homo Erectus Awakens to Vaginal Consciousness

1. Edward T. Hall, *The Hidden Dimension* (1966; Garden City, New York: Anchor Books, 1969), p. 138.
2. Geza Roheim, *The Gates of the Dream* (New York: International Universities Press, 1973), pp. 434, 435.
3. John Steinbeck, *The Grapes of Wrath* (1939, New York: Bantam Books, 1972), pp. 37, 38.
4. James Dickey, *Deliverance* (1970; New York: Dell Publishing Co., 1973), pp. 150, 151.
5. Norman O. Brown, *Love's Body* (New York: Vintage Books, 1966), p. 50.
6. Vern L. Bullough, *The Subordinate Sex* (1973; Chicago: University of Illinois Press, 1974), pp. 16, 17.
7. *Ibid.,* pp. 61, 62.
8. *Ibid.,* p. 96.
9. Donald Webster Cory, *Homosexuality: A Cross Cultural Approach* (New York: The Julian Press, 1956), p. 137.
10. *Ibid.,* p. 101.
11. *Ibid.,* p. 106.
12. *Ibid.,* p. 126.
13. *Ibid.,* p. 127.
14. *Ibid.,* pp. 122, 123.
15. C. A. Tripp, *The Homosexual Matrix* (1975; New York: Signet, New American Library, 1976), pp. 68, 69.
16. Warren Farrell, *The Liberated Man* (New York: Bantam Books, 1975), pp. 79, 80.
17. David Riesman, *The Lonely Crowd* (1950; New Haven: Yale University Press, 1960), p. 154.
18. Robert Ardrey, *The Territorial Imperative* (1966; New York: Dell Publishing Co., 1971), p. 313.

19. *Ibid.*, p. 312.
20. *Ibid.*, p. 314.
21. Gordon W. Allport, *The Nature of Prejudice* (Reading, Mass.: Addison-Wesley Publishing Co., 1954), p. 361.
22. Herb Goldberg, *The Hazards of Being Male* (1976; New York: Signet, New American Library, 1977), p. 39.
23. Allport, *The Nature of Prejudice,* p. 375.
24. *Ibid.*, p. 375.
25. *Ibid.*, p. 33.
26. George Orwell, *1984* (1949; New York: The New American Library, 1961), p. 205.
27. John Hartland-Swann, *An Analysis of Morals* (London: Ruskin House, George Allen & Unwin Ltd., 1960) p. 73.
28. S. I. Hayakawa, *The Use and Misuse of Language* (1943; Greenwich, Connecticut: Fawcett Publications, 1966), p. 228.
29. Patricia N. Dutcher, "The Meaning of Whiteness," in *Straight/White/Male,* ed. Glenn R. Bucher (Philadelphia: Fortress Press, 1976), p. 89.
30. Ardrey, *The Territorial Imperative,* p. 51.
31. Millett, *Sexual Politics,* p. 312.
32. *Ibid.*, p. 327.

Chapter 2: Homo Chronic Slips Deeper into Vaginal Confinement

1. Sigmund Freud, *The Future of an Illusion,* trans. W. D. Robson-Scott (Garden City, New York: Doubleday Anchor Books, 1953), p. 53.
2. Ralph Ellison, *Invisible Man* (1947; New York: The New American Library, Inc., 1964), p. 7.
3. Lawrence K. Frank, *The Conduct of Sex* (New York: Grove Press, Inc., 1963), pp. 113, 115.
4. Society of Medical Psychoanalysts, *Homosexuality* (New York: Random House, 1962), p. 309.
5. Marc Feigen Fasteau, *The Male Machine* (1975; New York: Dell Publishing Company, 1976), p. 203.
6. *Ibid.*, p. 205.
7. Desmond Morris, *The Human Zoo* (New York: Dell Publishing Co., Inc., 1969), p. 95.
8. Warren Farrell, *The Liberated Man* (New York: Bantam Books, 1975), p. 227.
9. *Webster's Seventh New Collegiate Dictionary* (Springfield, Mass.: G. & C. Merriam Company, c. 1963), p. 264.
10. Peter Fisher, *The Gay Mystique* (1972; New York: Stein and Day, 1973), p. 35.
11. Edmund Bergler, *Homosexuality: Disease or Way of Life?* (New York: Collier Books, 1967), pp. 42, 43.
12. Thomas S. Szasz, *The Manufacture of Madness,* (New York: Harper & Row, Publishers, Inc., 1970), pp. 279, 280.
13. Alan P. Bell and Martin S. Weinberg, *Homosexualities: A Study of Diversity Among Men and Women* (New York: Simon and Schuster, 1978), p. 218.
14. William H. Masters and Virginia E. Johnson, *Homosexuality in Perspective* (Boston: Little, Brown and Company, 1979), p. 394.
15. *Ibid.*, p. 407.
16. *Ibid.*
17. *Ibid.*, p. 408.

18. Julius Fast and Hal Wells, *Bisexual Living* (New York: Pocket Books, 1975), pp. 231, 232.
19. Donald Webster Cory and John P. LeRoy, *The Homosexual and His Society* (New York: Citadel Press, 1963), p. 63.
20. *Ibid.,* pp. 63, 64.
21. Cynthia Proulx, "Sex as Athletics in the Singles Complex," *Saturday Review of the Society,* 1 May 1973, p. 65.
22. Eugene C. Kennedy, *The New Sexuality: Myths, Fables, and Hang-Ups* (1972, Garden City, New York: Image Books, 1973), p. 67.
23. Society of Medical Psychoanalysts, *Homosexuality,* p. 239.
24. C. Kerenyi, *The Religion of the Greeks and Romans* (New York: E. P. Dutton & Co., Inc., 1962), p. 195.
25. *Ibid.,* p. 64.
26. Willard Beecher and Marguerite Beecher, *Beyond Success and Failure* (1966; New York: Pocket Books, 1972), p. 85.
27. Price M. Cobbs and William H. Grier, *Black Rage* (New York: Basic Books, Inc., 1968), p. 125.
28. *Ibid.*
29. *Ibid.*
30. Mart Crowley, *The Boys in the Band* (1968; New York: Dell Publishing Company, 1969), pp. 41, 42.
31. *Ibid.,* pp. 77, 78.
32. Walter C. Alvarez, *Homosexuality: And Other Forms of Sexual Deviance VS. Sue March, Gay Liberation* (New York: Pyramid Books, 1974), p. 60.
33. Mark Thompson, "Sissies," *The Advocate,* No. 229 (30 Nov. 1977), p. 23.
34. *Ibid.*
35. "The Lavender Panthers," *Time,* 8 Oct. 1973, p. 73.
36. Laud Humphreys, *Out of the Closets* (Englewood Cliffs, New Jersey: Prentice-Hall, Inc., 1972), p. 73.
37. Dennis Altman, *Homosexual: Oppression and Liberation* (New York: Avon Books, 1973), p. 127.
38. Andrew Kopkind, "Mixed Singles," *New Times,* 1 Oct. 1976, p. 44.
39. *Ibid.*

Chapter 3: Dialogues: The First Series

1. Bruno Bettelheim, *The Informed Heart* (New York: Avon Books, 1971), p. 74.

Chapter 4: Voiding the Disadvantages of Early Toilet Training

1. Dennis Altman, *Homosexual: Oppression and Liberation,* p. 24.
2. Jean Genet, *Our Lady of the Flowers,* trans. Bernard Frechtman (1963; New York: Panther Books, 1969), p. 241.
3. Gordon W. Allport, *The Nature of Prejudice,* p. 385.
4. Havelock Ellis, *Psychology of Sex* (New York: Emerson Books, Inc., 1944), p. 139.
5. Lester A. Kirkendall and Robert N. Whitehurst, *The New Sexual Revolution* (New York: Donald W. Brown, Inc., 1971), p. 2.
6. Rollo May, *Love and Will* (New York: W. W. Norton & Company, 1969), p. 39.

7. Kate Millett, *Sexual Politics*, p. 307.
8. *Ibid.*, p. 309.
9. *Ibid.*
10. *Ibid.*, p. 313.
11. May, *Love and Will*, p. 46.
12. Lawrence K. Frank, *The Conduct of Sex*, p. 112.
13. Desmond Morris, *The Human Zoo*, p. 88.
14. Myron Brenton, *Friendship* (New York: Stein and Day, 1974), p. 43.
15. *Ibid.*
16. James Dickey, *Deliverance*, p. 90.
17. Francesco Scavullo, *Scavullo on Men* (New York: Random House, 1977), p. 100.
18. *Ibid.*, p. 26.
19. John Howard Griffin, *Black Like Me* (New York: Signet Books, 1960), pp. 85, 88.
20. Eldridge Cleaver, *Soul on Ice* (New York: Dell Publishing Co., Inc., 1970), p. 164.
21. *Ibid.*, p. 167.
22. *Ibid.*
23. *Ibid.*, p. 85.
24. "Gay Abandon," *People*, 28 Nov. 1977, p. 124.
25. *Ibid.*
26. Gail J. Putney and Snell Putney, *The Adjusted American* (New York: Harper Colophon, 1966), p. 128.
27. *Ibid.*, p. 129.
28. Warren Farrell, *The Liberated Man*, p. 234.
29. *Ibid.*, pp. 234, 235.
30. Lionel Tiger, *Men in Groups* (New York: Random House, 1969), p. 112.
31. *Ibid.*, p. 216.
32. Scavullo, *Scavullo on Men*, p. 108.
33. "The Heterosexual Solution: A Dilemma for Gay Mormons," *The Advocate*, No. 235 (22 Feb. 1978), p. 13.
34. Diagram Group, *Man's Body: An Owner's Manual*, ed. David Heidenstam (1976; New York: Paddington Press, Ltd.), p. F01-04.
35. Myron Brenton, *The American Male* (New York: Fawcett Publications, Inc., 1975), p. 163.
36. Dennis Sanders, *Gay Source: A Catalog for Men* (New York: Coward, McCann & Geoghegan, Inc., 1977), p. 210.
37. Allport, *The Nature of Prejudice*, p. 156.
38. John Rechy, *Numbers* (New York: Grove Press, 1967), p. 66.
39. *Ibid.*, p. 67.
40. Brenton, *The American Male*, p. 161.
41. Rechy, *Numbers*, p. 67.
42. Glendon Swarthout, *Bless the Beasts and Children* (1970; New York: Pocket Books, 1974), p. 24.
43. Jim Bouton, *Ball Four* (1970; New York: Dell Publishing Co., 1971), pp. 231, 232.
44. Brenton, *The American Male*, p. 162.
45. Sigmund Freud, *Totem and Taboo*, trans. A. A. Brill (1918; New York: Vintage Books, 1946), p. 160.
46. Lance Rentzel, *When All the Laughter Died in Sorrow* (1972; New York: Bantam Books, 1973), p. 109.
47. *Ibid.*
48. Karl Menninger, *The Crime of Punishment* (1966; New York: The Viking Press, 1970), p. 183.

49. "Dispatch," *The Advocate*, No. 231 (28 Dec. 1977), 11.

50. Allport, *The Nature of Prejudice*, pp. 142, 143.

Chapter 5: Evacuating the Self from the Habit of Incontinence

1. Oscar Wilde, *The Picture of Dorian Gray* (New York: The New American Library of World Literature, Inc., 1962), p. 143.

2. Robert H. Rimmer, *The Harrad Experiment* (New York: Bantam Books, 1966), pp. 170, 171.

3. Yukio Mishima, *Forbidden Colors*, trans. Alfred H. Marks (New York: Berkley Medallion Books, 1974), p. 59-61.

4. Lionel Tiger, *Men in Groups*, p. 136.

5. Kate Millett, *Sexual Politics*, p. 298.

6. *Ibid.*, p. 299.

7. J. Herbert Fill, *The Mental Breakdown of a Nation* (New York: Franklin Watts, Inc., 1974), p. 23.

8. *Ibid.*, pp. 66, 68.

9. Erich Fromm, *Marx's Concept of Man* (New York: Frederick Ungar Publishing Co., 1970), p. 10.

10. *Ibid.*, p. 26.

11. Erich Fromm, *Man for Himself* (Greenwich, Connecticut: Fawcett Premier Books, 1947), p. 64.

12. Desmond Morris, *The Human Zoo*, p. 95.

13. Erich Fromm, *Escape From Freedom* (New York: Holt, Rinehart & Winston, Inc., 1941), p. 148.

14. Everett L. Shostrom, *Man, the Manipulator* (New York: Bantam Books, 1968), p. 25.

15. Darwin Porter, *Butterflies in Heat* (New York: Manor Books, Inc., 1976), pp. 66, 67.

16. Jacques Ellul, *The Technological Society*, trans. John Wilkinson (1964; New York: Vintage Books, 1967), p. 325.

17. Shostrum, *Man, the Manipulator*, p. 17.

18. *Ibid.*, p. 161.

19. *Ibid.*, p. 159.

20. Thomas A. Harris, *I'm OK–You're OK* (1967; New York: Harper & Row, Publishers, 1969), p. 53.

21. *Ibid.*, p. 5.

22. C. A. Tripp, *The Homosexual Matrix*, pp. 90, 91.

23. Maxwell Maltz, *Psycho-Cybernetics* (1960; New York: Pocket Books, 1966), p. 18.

24. Eric Berne, *Games People Play* (1964; New York: Grove Press, Inc., 1967), p. 15.

25. *Ibid.*

26. *Ibid.*, p. 14.

27. David Riesman, *The Lonely Crowd*, p. 152.

28. *Ibid.*, p. 154.

29. Fromm, *Escape from Freedom*, p. 180.

30. Gordon Merrick, *The Lord Won't Mind* (1970; New York: Avon Books, 1971), p. 42.

31. Rimmer, *The Harrad Experiment*, pp. 227, 228.

32. *Ibid.*, p. 233.

33. Charles Silverstein and Edmund White, *The Joy of Gay Sex* (New York: Crown Publishers, Inc., 1977), p. 183.

34. *The Joy of Sex: A Gourmet Guide to Love Making*, ed. Alex Comfort (New York: Simon and Schuster, 1972), p. 13.

35. Millett, *Sexual Politics*, p. 312.
36. *Ibid.*, p. 328.
37. *Ibid.*, p. 329.
38. Norman O. Brown, *Love's Body* (New York: Vintage Books, 1966), p. 174.
39. Geza Roheim, *The Gates of the Dream*, p. 372.
40. James George Frazer, *The Golden Bough* (1922; New York: The Macmillan Company, 1951), p. 596.
41. William Golding, *Lord of the Flies* (New York: Capricorn Books, 1954), p. 68.
42. Tiger, *Men in Groups*, p. 153.
43. Sigmund Freud, *Totem and Taboo*, trans. A. A. Brill (New York: Vintage Books, 1946), p. 44.
44. *Ibid.*
45. *Ibid.*, p. 45.
46. *Ibid.*, p. 41.
47. Tiger, *Men in Groups*, p. 187.
48. Robert M. Brake, "Not in Our Schools," *Skeptic*, No. 22 (Nov./Dec. 1977), 36.
49. Freud, *Totem and Taboo*, p. 38.
50. *Ibid.*, p. 183.
51. *Ibid.*, p. 174.
52. Thomas S. Szasz, *The Manufacture of Madness*, p. 286.
53. *Ibid.*, p. 287.
54. *Ibid.*, p. 288.
55. *Ibid.*
56. Millett, *Sexual Politics*, p. 307.
57. Brown, *Love's Body*, p. 174.
58. Plato, *The Symposium*, trans. W. Hamilton (1951; Baltimore, Maryland: Penguin Books, 1965), p. 86.
59. Brown, *Love's Body*, p. 171.
60. Herb Goldberg, *The Hazards of Being Male*, p. 181.
61. Michael Schofield, *Sociological Aspects of Homosexuality* (London: Longmans, Green & Company Ltd., 1965), p. 189.
62. Goldberg, *The Hazards of Being Male*, pp. 181, 182.
63. *Ibid.*, p. 137.
64. *Ibid.*, p. 136.
65. Yukio Mishima, *Sun and Steel*, trans. John Bester (New York: Grove Press, Inc., 1970), pp. 41, 42.
66. *Ibid.*, pp. 54, 55.
67. *Ibid.*, p. 87.
68. Gene D. Phillips, "The Boys on the Bandwagon," *Take One*, 2, No. 8, in *Sexuality in the Movies*, ed. Thomas R. Atkins (Bloomington & London: Indiana University Press, 1975), p. 170.
69. *Ibid.*
70. *Ibid.*
71. John Rickman, ed., *A General Selection from the Works of Sigmund Freud* (New York: Doubleday & Company, 1957), p. 133.
72. Ernst Breisach, *Introduction to Modern Existentialism* (New York: Grove Press, 1962), p. 193.
73. *Ibid.*, p. 195.
74. *Ibid.*, p. 196.
75. Gail J. Putney and Snell Putney, *The Adjusted American*, p. 8.

76. James Hillman, *Suicide and the Soul* (New York: Harper Colophon Books, 1973), p. 40.
77. Fromm, *Escape from Freedom*, pp. 208, 209.
78. Hillman, *Suicide and the Soul*, p. 64.

Chapter 6: Dialogues: The Second Series

1. Yukio Mishima, *Thirst for Love*, trans. Alfred H. Marks (1969; New York: Berkley Medallion Books, 1971), p. 165.

Chapter 7: The Homosexual Ghetto: Dachau Becomes a State of Mind

1. Kate Millett, *Sexual Politics*, p. 341.
2. Rainer Maria Rilke, *"Ueber Kunst,"* (pp. 41–49) *Verse und Prosa aus dem Nachlass*. Leipzig: Gesell der Freunde der Deutschen Bücherer, 1929. *Letters to a Young Poet*, trans. M. D. Herter (New York: W. W. Norton & Co., c. 1934), cited in Norman O. Brown, *Life Against Death: The Psychoanalytical Meaning of History* (Middletown, Conn.: Wesleyan University Press, 1959), p. 66.
3. Thomas S. Szasz, *The Manufacture of Madness* pp. 242, 243.
4. *Ibid.*, p. 244.
5. *Record* (New York: Newsletter of Evangelicals Concerned, Inc., Winter 1978), p. 2.
6. Mark Freedman, *Homosexuality and Psychological Functioning* (Belmont, California: Brooks/Cole Publishing Company, 1971), pp. 3, 4.
7. *Ibid.*
8. George Weinberg, *Society and the Healthy Homosexual* (1972; Garden City, New York: Anchor Books; Anchor Press/Doubleday), 1973), p. 135.
9. Bruno Bettelheim, *The Informed Heart*, p. 120.
10. Viktor E. Frankl, *Man's Search for Meaning* (1959; New York: Pocket Books, 1975), p. 12.
11. Howard Brown, *Familiar Faces, Hidden Lives* (New York: Harcourt Brace Jovanovich, 1976), p. 39.
12. Wardell B. Pomeroy, *Dr. Kinsey and the Institute for Sex Research* (New York: Harper & Row, Publishers, 1972), p. 273.
13. *Ibid.*
14. John Reid, *The Best Little Boy in the World* (1977; New York: Ballantine Books), p. 30.
15. *Ibid.*, pp. 30, 31.
16. Wilhelm Reich, *The Sexual Revolution*, trans. Therese Pol (1945; New York: Farrar, Straus and Giroux, 1974), p. 108.
17. Erik Erickson, *Identity: Youth and Crisis*, p. 297.
18. Frankl, *Man's Search for Meaning*, p. 24.
19. Howard Brown, *Familiar Faces, Hidden Lives*, p. 41.
20. Frankl, *Man's Search for Meaning*, p. 48.
21. Bettelheim, *The Informed Heart*, p. 286.
22. Freedman, *Homosexuality and Psychological Functioning*, p. 97.
23. *Ibid.*, p. 100.
24. *Ibid.*

25. Hugh Dalziel Duncan, *Symbols in Society* (New York: Oxford University Press, 1968), p. 217.
26. *Ibid.,* p. 209.
27. Millett, *Sexual Politics,* p. 342.
28. Duncan, *Symbols in Society,* p. 166.
29. Bettelheim, *The Informed Heart,* p. 131.
30. Reid, *The Best Little Boy in the World,* p. 63.
31. Duncan, *Symbols in Society,* p. 109.
32. *Ibid.*
33. *Ibid.*
34. Frankl, *Man's Search for Meaning,* pp. 79, 80.
35. R. O. D. Benson, *In Defense of Homosexuality: Male and Female* (New York: The Julian Press, Inc., 1965), p. 224.
36. Gordon W. Allport, *The Nature of Prejudice,* p. 45.
37. Erich Fromm, *Beyond the Chains of Illusion* (New York: Simon and Schuster, Inc., 1962), p. 14.
38. *Ibid.,* 30.
39. Carol A. B. Warren, *Identity and Community in the Gay World* (New York: John Wiley & Sons, 1974), p. 118.
40. Laud Humphreys, *Out of the Closets* (Englewood Cliffs, New Jersey: Prentice-Hall, Inc., 1972), pp. 74, 75.
41. Calvin Hall and Gardner Lindzey, *Theories of Personality* (1957; New York: Wiley Publishers, 1966), p. 270.
42. Bettelheim, *The Informed Heart,* p. 89.
43. *Ibid.,* p. 98.
44. Melvin DeFleur and Sandra Ball-Rokeach, *Theories of Mass Communications* (New York: David McKay & Co., 1975), p. 146.
45. C. G. Jung, *The Undiscovered Self,* trans. R. F. C. Hull (New York: Mentor Books, 1959), p. 115.
46. Lance Morrow, "Blacks on TV: A Disturbing Image," *Time,* 27 March 1978, pp. 101, 102.
47. Harry F. Waters, Martin Kasindorf and Betsy Carter, "Sex and TV," *Newsweek,* 20 Feb. 1978, p. 59.
48. David Stein, ed., "True Crime News," National Gay Task Force *Action Report,* March 1978, p. 2.
49. Edmund Bergler, *Homosexuality: Disease or Way of Life?* p. 27.
50. Fromm, *Beyond the Chains of Illusion,* p. 119.
51. *Ibid.,* p. 121.
52. Erickson, *Identity: Youth and Crisis,* p. 313.
53. *Ibid.,* p. 317.
54. Wilson Bryan Key, *Media Sexploitation* (1976; New York: Signet Books, 1977), p. 282.
55. Erickson, *Identity: Youth and Crisis,* p. 282.
56. *Ibid.,* p. 299.
57. *Ibid.,* 298.
58. *Ibid.,* p. 264.
59. Marshall McLuhan and Quentin Fiore, *The Medium Is the Massage* (New York: Bantam Books, 1967), p. 63.
60. *Ibid.,* 26.
61. *Ibid.*

62. *Ibid.*, p. 61.
63. Wilson Bryan Key, *Subliminal Seduction* (New York: The New American Library, 1974), p. 11.
64. *Ibid.*, p. 72.
65. *Ibid.*, p. 66.
66. *Ibid.*, p. 61.
67. *Ibid.*, p. 65.
68. Howard Brown, *Familiar Faces, Hidden Lives*, p. 41.
69. Humphreys, *Out of the Closets*, p. 14.
70. Benson, *In Defense of Homosexuality*, p. 225.
71. Fromm, *Beyond the Chains of Illusion*, p. 150.
72. Bettelheim, *The Informed Heart*, pp. 156, 157.
73. Carl Wittman, "Refugees from Amerika: A Gay Manifesto," San Francisco *Free Press* (December 22–January 7, 1970), cited in *Out of the Closets: The Sociology of Homosexual Liberation*, by Laud Humphreys, pp. 13, 14.

Chapter 8: The Homosexual Ghetto: The Haute Rigor of Small-Group Survival

1. Louis Wirth, *The Ghetto* (1928; Chicago: Phoenix Books, The University of Chicago Press, 1962), p. 290.
2. Robert M. Pirsig, *Zen and the Art of Motorcycle Maintenance* (New York: William Morrow and Company, Inc., 1974), p. 297.
3. Jacques Ellul, *The Technological Society*, p. 6.
4. *Ibid.*, p. 131.
5. *Ibid.*
6. Bruno Bettelheim, *The Informed Heart*, p. 209.
7. Wirth, *The Ghetto*, p. 110.
8. Gail J. Putney and Snell Putney, *The Adjusted American*, p. 27.
9. Philip Slater, *The Pursuit of Loneliness* (Boston: Beacon Press, 1970), p. 15.
10. Suzanne Gordon, *Lonely in America* (New York: Simon and Schuster, 1976), p. 29.
11. R. D. Laing, *The Politics of Experience* (1967; New York: Ballantine Books, 1975), p. 95.
12. Thomas S. Szasz, *The Manufacture of Madness*, p. 244.
13. Martin Duberman, "The Anita Bryant Brigade," *Skeptic*, No. 22 (Nov./Dec. 1977), 28.
14. Erich Fromm, *Beyond the Chains of Illusion*, p. 19.
15. David Riesman, *Individualism Reconsidered* (1954; New York: The Free Press, 1965), pp. 59, 60.
16. *Ibid.*, p. 59.
17. *Ibid.*
18. Dennis Altman, *Homosexual: Oppression and Liberation*, p. 142.
19. Abraham Myerson, "The 'Nervousness' of the Jew," *Mental Hygiene*, IV, 69, as cited in *The Ghetto*, by Louis Wirth (1928 Chicago: Phoenix Books, The University of Chicago Press, 1962), p. 69.
20. Howard James, *Children in Trouble* (1969; New York: David McKay Company, Inc., 1971), p. 118.
21. Kathyryn Burkhart, *Women in Prison* (Garden City, New York: Doubleday & Company, Inc., 1973), pp. 365, 366.

22. Martin Hoffman, *The Gay World: Male Homosexuality and the Social Creation of Evil* (New York: Basic Books, Inc., 1968), p. 178.
23. Bettelheim, *The Informed Heart*, pp. 160, 161.
24. Martin S. Weinberg and Colin J. Williams, *Male Homosexuals: Their Problems and Adaptations* (1974; New York: Penguin Books, 1975), p. 296.
25. Carol A. B. Warren, *Identity and Community in the Gay World* (New York: John Wiley & Sons, 1974), p. 69.
26. Bettelheim, *The Informed Heart*, p. 187.
27. *Ibid.*, p. 184.
28. Warren, *Identity and Community in the Gay World*, p. 37.
29. *Ibid.*, p. 39.
30. *Ibid.*, p. 32.
31. Gilbert Cantor, "The Need for Homosexual Law Reform," in *The Same Sex: An Appraisal of Homosexuality*, ed. Ralph W. Weltge (Philadelphia: Pilgrim Press, 1969), pp. 90, 91.
32. Laud Humphreys, *Out of the Closets: The Sociology of Homosexual Liberation*, p. 82.

Chapter 9: The Archetypal Outsider

1. Herbert Marcuse, *An Essay on Liberation* (Boston: Beacon Press, 1972), p. 64.
2. Budd Schulberg, *What Makes Sammy Run?* (1941; New York: Bantam Books, 1961), p. 247.
3. Ayn Rand, *The Virtue of Selfishness* (New York: Signet Books, 1964), p. 22.
4. Jenni Calder, *There Must Be a Lone Ranger* (1974; New York: Taplinger Publishing Co., 1975), pp. 18, 19.
5. *Ibid.*, p. 3.
6. R. O. D. Benson, *In Defense of Homosexuality: Male and Female*, p. 225.
7. James Kirkwood, *Some Kind of Hero* (New York: The New American Library, Inc., 1976), p. 73.
8. James Kirkwood, *P.S. Your Cat Is Dead* (1972; New York: Warner Books, Inc., 1972), p. 76.
9. Alexander Berkman, *Prison Memoirs of an Anarchist* (New York: Schocken Books, 1970) cited by Karel Weiss, *The Prison Experience: Under the Mask—An Anthology About Prejudice in America* (New York: Delacorte, 1976), pp. 156, 157.
10. Karla Jay and Allen Young, *After You're Out* (New York: Links Books, 1975), pp. 141, 142.
11. Bruno Bettelheim, *The Informed Heart*, p. 196.
12. *Ibid.*, p. 234.
13. Mark Freedman, *Homosexuality and Psychological Functioning*, pp. 8, 9.
14. George Weinberg, *Society and the Healthy Homosexual*, p. 59.
15. *Ibid.*, p. 67.
16. Ted Clark, *The Oppression of Youth* (New York: Harper Colophon, 1975), p. 156.
17. *Ibid.*, p. 165.
18. Louis Wirth, *The Ghetto*, p. 268.
19. Bettelheim, *The Informed Heart*, p. 131.
20. R. D. Laing, *The Politics of Experience* p. 31.
21. Jack Nichols, *Men's Liberation* (New York: Penguin Books Inc., 1975), p. 200.
22. Wilson Bryan Key, *Media Sexploitation*, p. 17.

23. *Ibid.,* pp. 31, 31.
24. Bettelheim, *The Informed Heart,* p. 222.
25. David A. Noebel, *The Homosexual Revolution* (1977; Tulsa, Oklahoma: American Christian College Press, 1978), pp. 109, 110.
26. Francesco Scavullo, *Scavullo on Men,* p. 52.
27. Norman Podhoretz, "The Culture of Appeasement," *Harper's,* Oct. 1977, p. 31.
28. Vance Packard, *A Nation of Strangers* (New York: David McKay Company, Inc., 1972), p. 228.
29. Jonathan Eisen, *Altamont: Death of Innocence in the Woodstock Nation* (New York: Avon Books, 1970), p. 18.
30. Michael Lerner, "Youth Culture and Social Revolution," in *Counterculture and Revolution,* ed. David Horowitz, Michael Lerner and Craig Pyes (New York: Random House, 1972), p. 188.
31. Carroll Quigley, "Youth's Heroes Have No Haloes," *Today's Education,* 60, No. 2 (Feb. 1971), p. 29.
32. Theodore Roszak, *The Making of a Counter Culture: Reflections on the Technical Society and its Youthful Opposition* (Garden City, New York: Doubleday, 1969), p. 14.
33. Lewis Yablonsky, *The Hippie Trip* (1968, Baltimore, Maryland: Penguin Books, Inc., 1973), p. 314.
34. *Ibid.,* p. 328.
35. Philip Slater, *The Pursuit of Loneliness,* p. 106.
36. *Ibid.,* pp. 136, 137.
37. Alan Watts, *The Book: On the Taboo Against Knowing Who You Are* (1966; New York: Collier Books, 1971), p. 122.
38. Tim Denesha, "The History You Didn't Hear About," in *Gay Source: A Catalog for Men,* ed. Dennis Sanders (New York: Coward, McCann & Geoghegan, Inc., 1977), p. 98.
39. *Ibid.,* 103.
40. Robert I. McQueen, "The Great Gay Movement Gayme," *The Advocate,* No. 233 (25 Jan. 1978), p. 19.
41. Dennis Altman, *Homosexual: Oppression and Liberation,* p. 237.
42. Slater, *The Pursuit of Loneliness,* p. 125.
43. Dotson Rader, "Gay Liberation—All the Sad Young Men," *Evergreen,* No. 84 (Nov. 1970), pp. 18, 20, 74-75, 78-79.
44. John Rechy, *The Sexual Outlaw* (1977; New York: Dell Publishing Co., 1978), p. 301.
45. Erich Fromm, *Beyond the Chains of Illusion,* p. 166.
46. Jacques Ellul, *The Technological Society,* p. 395.
47. *Ibid.,* p. 407.
48. *Ibid.,* p. 425.
49. Altman, *Homosexual: Oppression and Liberation,* p. 236.
50. Ellul, *The Technological Society,* p. 432.
51. Norman O. Brown, *Life Against Death* (1959; Middletown, Connecticut: Wesleyan University Press, 1972), p. 254.
52. Ellul, *The Technological Society,* p. 436.
53. Altman, *Homosexual: Oppression and Liberation,* p. 236.
54. Ellul, *The Technological Society,* pp. 426, 427.

Chapter 10: Dialogue: Letter to a Former Lover

1. D. H. Lawrence, *Lady Chatterley's Lover* (1957; New York: Grove Press, Inc., 1977), p. 374.

Bibliography

Allport, Gordon W. *The Nature of Prejudice*. Reading, Mass.: Addison-Wesley Publishing Company, 1954.

Altman, Dennis. *Homosexual: Oppression and Liberation*. New York: Avon Books, 1973.

Alvarez, Walter C. *Homosexuality: And Other Forms of Sexual Deviance VS* (Sue March, *Gay Liberation*). New York: Pyramid Books, 1974.

Atkins, Thomas R., (Ed.), *Sexuality in the Movies*. Bloomington and London: Indiana University Press, 1975.

Ardrey, Robert. *The Territorial Imperative*. 1966 New York: Dell Publishing Co., 1971.

Baldwin, James. *Giovanni's Room*. 1956. New York: Dell Publishing Co., Inc., 1971.

Beecher, Willard and Beecher, Marguerite. *Beyond Success and Failure*. 1966. New York: Pocket Books, 1972.

Bell, Alan P. and Weinberg, Martin S. *Homosexualities: A Study of Diversity Among Men and Women*. New York: Simon and Schuster, 1978.

Benson, R. O. D. *In Defense of Homosexuality: Male and Female*. New York: The Julian Press, Inc., 1965.

Bergler, Edmund. *Homosexuality: Disease or Way of Life?* New York: Collier Books, 1967.

Berne, Eric. *Games People Play*. 1964. New York: Grove Press, Inc., 1967.

Bettelheim, Bruno. *The Informed Heart*. 1960. New York: Avon Books, 1971.

Bouton, Jim. *Ball Four*. 1970. New York: Dell Publishing Co., 1971.

Brake, Robert M. "Not In Our Schools." SKEPTIC, No. 22, Nov./Dec. 1977.

Breisach, Ernst. *Introduction to Modern Existentialism*. New York: Grove Press, 1962.

Brenton, Myron. *The American Male*. New York: Fawcett Publications, Inc., 1975.

Brenton, Myron. *Friendship*. New York: Stein and Day, 1974.

Brown, Howard. *Familiar Faces, Hidden Lives*. New York: Harcourt Brace Jovanovich, 1976.

Brown, Norman O. *Life Against Death*. Middletown, Conn.: Wesleyan University Press, 1959.

Brown, Norman O. *Love's Body*. New York: Vintage Books, 1966.

Bucher, Glenn R. (Ed.), *Straight/White/Male*. Philadelphia: Fortress Press, 1976.

Bullough, Vern L. *The Subordinate Sex*. 1973. Chicago: University of Illinois Press, 1974.

Burkhart, Kathyryn. *Women in Prison*. Garden City, New York: Doubleday & Company, Inc., 1973.

Calder, Jenni. *There Must Be a Lone Ranger*. 1974. New York: Taplinger Publishing Co., 1975.

Clark, Ted. *The Oppression of Youth*. New York: Harper Colophon, 1975.

Cleaver, Eldridge. *Soul on Ice*. 1969. New York: Dell Publishing Co., 1970.

Cobbs, Price M. and Grier, William H. *Black Rage*. New York: Basic Books, Inc., 1968.

Comfort, Alex, (Ed.). *The Joy of Sex: A Gourmet Guide to Love Making*. New York: Simon and Schuster, 1972.

Cory, Donald Webster. *Homosexuality: A Cross Cultural Approach*. New York: The Julian Press, Inc., 1956.

Cory, Donald Webster and LeRoy, John P. *The Homosexual and His Society*. New York: Citadel Press, 1963.

Crowley, Mart. *The Boys in the Band*. 1968. New York: Dell Publishing Company, 1969.

DeFleur, Melvin and Ball-Rokeach, Sandra. *Theories of Mass Communications*. New York: David McKay & Co., 1975.

Diagram Group. *Man's Body: An Owner's Manual*. Heidenstam, David, (Ed.). 1976. New York: Paddington Press, 1977.

Dickey, James. *Deliverance*. 1970. New York: Dell Publishing Co., 1973.

"Dispatch." THE ADVOCATE. Los Angeles: No. 231. 28 Dec. 1977.

Duberman, Martin. "The Anita Bryant Brigade." *Skeptic,* No. 22, Nov./Dec. 1977.

Duncan, Hugh Dalziel. *Symbols in Society*. New York: Oxford University Press, 1968.

Eisen, Jonathan. *Altamont: Death of Innocence in the Woodstock Nation.* New York: Avon Books, 1970.

Ellis, Havelock. *Psychology of Sex.* New York: Emerson Books, Inc., 1944.

Ellison, Ralph. *Invisible Man.* 1947. New York: The New American Library, Inc., 1964.

Ellul, Jacques. *The Technological Society.* 1964. Translated by John Wilkinson. New York: Vintage Books, 1967.

Erickson, Erik. *Identity: Youth and Crisis.* New York: W. W. Norton, 1968.

Farrell, Warren. *The Liberated Man.* New York: Bantam Books, 1975.

Fast, Julius and Wells, Hal. *Bisexual Living.* New York: Pocket Books, 1975.

Fasteau, Marc Feigen. *The Male Machine.* 1975. New York: Dell Publishing Company, 1976.

Fill, J. Herbert. *The Mental Breakdown of a Nation.* New York: Franklin Watts, Inc., 1974.

Fisher, Peter. *The Gay Mystique.* 1972. New York: Stein and Day, 1973.

Frank, Lawrence K. *The Conduct of Sex.* New York: Grove Press, Inc., 1963.

Frankl, Viktor E. *Man's Search for Meaning.* 1959. New York: Pocket Books, 1975.

Frazer, James George. *The Golden Bough.* 1922. New York: The Macmillan Company, 1951.

Freedman, Mark. *Homosexuality and Psychological Functioning.* Belmont, California: Brooks/Cole Publishing Company, 1971.

Freud, Sigmund. *The Future of an Illusion.* 1927. Translated by W. D. Robson-Scott. Garden City, New York: Doubleday Anchor Books, 1953.

Freud, Sigmund. *Totem and Taboo.* 1918. Translated by A. A. Brill. New York: Vintage Books, 1946.

Fromm, Erich. *Beyond the Chains of Illusion.* New York: Simon and Schuster, Inc., 1962.

Fromm, Erich. *Escape from Freedom.* New York: Holt, Rinehart & Winston, Inc., 1941.

Fromm, Erich. *Man for Himself.* 1947. Greenwich, Connecticut: Fawcett Premier Books, 1965.

Fromm, Erich. *Marx's Concept of Man.* New York: Frederick Ungar Publishing Co., 1970.

"Gay Abandon." PEOPLE, 28 Nov. 1977.

Genet, Jean. *Our Lady of the Flowers*. 1963. Translated by Bernard Frechtman. New York: Panther Books, 1969.

Goldberg, Herb. *The Hazards of Being Male*. 1976. New York: Signet Books, 1977.

Golding, William. *Lord of the Flies*. New York: Capricorn Books, 1954.

Gordon, Suzanne. *Lonely in America*. New York: Simon and Schuster, 1976.

Griffin, John Howard. *Black Like Me*. New York: Signet Books, 1960.

Hall, Calvin and Lindzey, Gardner. 1957. *Theories of Personality*. New York: Wiley Publishers, 1966.

Hall, Edward T. *The Hidden Dimension*. 1966. Garden City, New York: Anchor Books, 1969.

Harris, Thomas A. *I'm OK–You're OK*. 1967. New York: Harper & Row, Publishers, 1969.

Hartland-Swann, John. *An Analysis of Morals*. London: Ruskin House, George Allen & Unwin Ltd., 1960.

Hayakawa, S. I. *The Use and Misuse of Language*. 1943. Greenwich, Conn.: Fawcett Publications, Inc., 1966.

"The Heterosexual Solution: A Dilemma for Gay Mormons." THE ADVOCATE. Los Angeles: No. 235, 22 Feb. 1978.

Hillman, James. *Suicide and the Soul*. New York: Harper Colophon Books, 1973.

Hoffman, Martin. *The Gay World: Male Homosexuality and the Social Creation of Evil*. New York: Basic Books, Inc., 1968.

Humphreys, Laud. *Out of the Closets: The Sociology of Homosexual Liberation*. Englewood Cliffs, New Jersey: Prentice-Hall, Inc., 1972.

James, Howard. *Children in Trouble*. 1969. New York: David McKay, Inc., 1971.

Jay, Karla and Young, Allen, (Ed.). *After You're Out*. New York: Links Books, 1975.

Jung, C. G. *The Undiscovered Self*. Translated by R.F.C. Hull. New York: Mentor Books, 1959.

Kennedy, Eugene C. *The New Sexuality: Myths, Fables, and Hang-Ups*. 1972. Garden City, New York: Image Books, 1973.

Kerenyi, C. *The Religion of the Greeks and Romans*. New York: E.P. Dutton & Co., Inc., 1962.

Key, Wilson Bryan. *Media Sexploitation*. 1976. New York: Signet Books, 1977.

Key, Wilson Bryan. *Subliminal Seduction*. New York: The New American Library, 1974.

Kirkendall, Lester A. and Whitehurst, Robert N. *The New Sexual Revolution*. New York: Donald W. Brown, Inc., 1971.

Kirkwood, James. *P.S. Your Cat Is Dead*. New York: Warner Books, Inc., 1972.

Kirkwood, James. *Some Kind of Hero*. New York: The New American Library, Inc., 1976.

Kopkind, Andrew. "Mixed Singles." NEW TIMES, 1 Oct. 1976.

Laing, R.D. *The Politics of Experience*. 1967. New York: Ballantine Books, 1975.

"The Lavender Panthers." TIME, 8 Oct. 1973.

Lawrence, D. H., *Lady Chatterley's Lover*. 1956. New York: Grove Press, Inc., 1977.

Horowitz, David, Lerner, Michael and Pyes, Craig, (Ed.), *Countercul-ture and Revolution*. New York: Random House, 1972.

Lorenz, Konrad. *On Aggression*. Translated by Marjorie Kerr Wilson. New York: Bantam Books, 1970.

Maltz, Maxwell. *Psycho-Cybernetics*. 1960. New York: Pocket Books, 1966.

Marcuse, Herbert. *An Essay on Liberation*. Boston: Beacon Press, 1972.

Masters, William H. and Johnson, Virginia E. *Homosexuality in Perspective*. Boston: Little, Brown and Company, 1979.

May, Rollo. *Love and Will*. New York: W.W. Norton & Company, 1969.

McLuhan, Marshall and Fiore, Quentin. *The Medium Is the Massage*. New York: Bantam Books, 1967.

McQueen, Robert I. "The Great Gay Movement Gayme." THE ADVOCATE, No. 233, 25 Jan. 1978.

Menninger, Karl. *The Crime of Punishment*. 1966. New York: Viking Press, 1970.

Merrick, Gordon. *The Lord Won't Mind*. 1970. New York: Avon Books, 1971.

Millett, Kate. *Sexual Politics*. 1969. New York: Avon Books, 1971.

Mishima, Yukio. *Forbidden Colors*. Translated by Alfred H. Marks. New York: Berkley Medallion Books, 1974.

Mishima, Yukio. *Sun and Steel*. Translated by John Bester. New York: Grove Press, Inc., 1970.

Mishima, Yukio. *Thirst for Love*. 1969. Translated by Alfred H. Marks. New York: Berkley Medallion Books, 1971.

Morris, Desmond. *The Human Zoo*. New York: Dell Publishing Co., 1969.

Morrow, Lance. "Blacks on TV: A Disturbing Image." TIME, 27 March 1978.

Nichols, Jack. *Men's Liberation*. New York: Penguin Books, Inc., 1975.

Noebel, David A. *The Homosexual Revolution*. 1977. Tulsa, Oklahoma: American Christian College Press, 1978.

Orwell, George. *1984*. 1949. New York: The New American Library, Inc., 1961.

Packard, Vance. *A Nation of Strangers*. New York: David McKay Company, Inc., 1972.

Pirsig, Robert M. *Zen and the Art of Motorcycle Maintenance*. New York: William Morrow and Company, Inc., 1974.

Plato. *The Symposium*. Translated by W. Hamilton. 1951. Baltimore, Maryland: Penguin Books, 1965.

Podhoretz, Norman. "The Culture of Appeasement." HARPER'S, Oct. 1977.

Pomeroy, Wardell B. *Dr. Kinsey and the Institute for Sex Research*. New York: Harper & Row, 1972.

Porter, Darwin. *Butterflies in Heat*. New York: Manor Books, Inc., 1976.

Proulx, Cynthia. "Sex as Athletics in the Singles Complex." SATURDAY REVIEW OF THE SOCIETY, 1, May 1973.

Putney, Gail J. and Putney, Snell. *The Adjusted American*. New York: Harper Colophon, 1966.

Quigley, Carroll. "Youth's Heroes Have No Haloes." TODAY'S EDUCATION, Feb. 1971.

Rader, Dotson. "Gay Liberation—All the Sad Young Men." EVERGREEN, No. 84, Nov. 1970.

Rand, Ayn. *The Virtue of Selfishness*. New York: Signet Books, 1964.

Rechy, John. *Numbers*. New York: Grove Press, 1967.

Rechy, John. *The Sexual Outlaw*. 1977. New York: Dell Publishing Co., 1978.

RECORD. p. 2. New York: Newsletter of Evangelicals Concerned, Inc., (Winter) 1978.

Reich, Wilhelm. *The Sexual Revolution*, 1945. Translated by Therese Pol. New York: Farrar, Straus and Giroux, 1974.

Reid, John. *The Best Little Boy in the World*, 1976. New York: Ballantine Books, 1977.

Rentzel, Lance. *When All the Laughter Died in Sorrow*, 1972. New York: Bantam Books, 1973.

Rickman, John, (Ed.), *A General Selection from the Works of Sigmund Freud*. New York: Doubleday & Company, 1957.

Riesman, David. *Individualism Reconsidered,* 1950. New Haven: Yale University Press, 1960.

Rilke, Rainer Maria. *"Ueber Kunst," Verse und Prosa aus dem Nachlass.* Leipzig: Gesell der Freunde der Deutschen Bucherer, 1929. In *Letters to a Young Poet.* Translated by M. D. Herter. New York: W. W. Norton & Co., 1934.

Rimmer, Robert H. *The Harrad Experiment.* New York: Bantam Books, 1966.

Roheim, Geza. *The Gates of the Dream.* New York: International Universities Press, Inc., 1973.

Roszak, Theodore. *The Making of a Counter Culture: Reflections on the Technical Society and its Youthful Opposition.* Garden City, N. Y.: Doubleday, 1969.

Sanders, Dennis. (Ed.), *Gay Source: A Catalog for Men.* New York: Coward, McCann & Geoghegan, Inc., 1977.

Scavullo, Francesco. *Scavullo on Men.* New York: Random House, 1977.

Schofield, Michael. *Sociological Aspects of Homosexuality.* London: Longmans, Green & Company Ltd., 1965.

Schulberg, Budd. *What Makes Sammy Run?* 1941, New York: Bantam Books, 1961.

Shahn, Ben. *The Shape of Content,* 1957. Cambridge, Mass. Harvard University Press, 1963.

Shostrom, Everett L. *Man, the Manipulator.* New York: Bantam Books, 1968.

Silverstein, Charles and White, Edmund. *The Joy of Gay Sex.* New York: Crown Publishers, Inc., 1977.

Slater, Philip. *The Pursuit of Loneliness.* Boston: Beacon Press, 1970.

Society of Medical Psychoanalysts, *Homosexuality.* New York: Random House, 1962.

Stein, David. (Ed.), "True Crime News." National Gay Task Force ACTION REPORT, March 1978.

Steinbeck, John. *The Grapes of Wrath,* 1939. New York: Bantam Books, 1972.

Swarthout, Glendon. *Bless the Beasts and Children.* 1970. New York: Pocket Books, 1974.

Szasz, Thomas S. *The Manufacture of Madness.* New York: Harper & Row, 1970.

Thompson, Mark. "Sissies," THE ADVOCATE, No. 229, 30 Nov. 1977.

Tiger, Lionel. *Men in Groups.* New York: Random House, 1969.

Tripp, C. A. *The Homosexual Matrix.* 1975. New York: New American Library, 1976.

Warren, Carol A. B. *Identity and Community in the Gay World.* New York: John Wiley & Sons, 1974.

Waters, Harry F., Kasindorf, Martin and Carter, Betsy. "Sex and TV," NEWSWEEK, 20 Feb. 1978.

Watts, Alan. *The Book: On the Taboo Against Knowing Who You Are.* 1966. New York: Collier Books, 1971.

Webster's Seventh New Collegiate Dictionary. Springfield, Mass. G & C Merriam Company, 1963.

Weinberg, George. *Society and the Healthy Homosexual.* 1972. Garden City, New York: Anchor Press/Doubleday, 1973.

Weinberg, Martin S. and Williams, Colin J. *Male Homosexuals: Their Problems and Adaptations.* New York: Penguin Books, 1975.

Weltge, Ralph W. (Ed.), *The Same Sex: An Appraisal of Homosexuality.* Philadelphia: Pilgrim Press, 1969.

Weiss, Karel (Ed.), *The Prison Experience: Under the Mask—An Anthology about Prejudice in America.* New York: Delacorte Press, 1976.

Wilde, Oscar. *The Picture of Dorian Gray.* New York: New American Library, 1962.

Wirth, Louis. *The Ghetto.* 1928. Chicago: Phoenix Books, The University of Chicago Press, 1962.

Yablonsky, Lewis. *The Hippie Trip.* 1968. Baltimore, Maryland: Penguin Books, Inc., 1973.